POPE URBAN II'S COUNCIL OF PIACENZA

Pope Urban II's Council of Piacenza

March 1–7, 1095

ROBERT SOMERVILLE

Great Clarendon Street, Oxford OX2 6DP

Oxford University Press is a department of the University of Oxford.
It furthers the University's objective of excellence in research, scholarship,
and education by publishing worldwide in

Oxford New York

Auckland Cape Town Dar es Salaam Hong Kong Karachi
Kuala Lumpur Madrid Melbourne Mexico City Nairobi
New Delhi Shanghai Taipei Toronto

With offices in

Argentina Austria Brazil Chile Czech Republic France Greece
Guatemala Hungary Italy Japan Poland Portugal Singapore
South Korea Switzerland Thailand Turkey Ukraine Vietnam

Oxford is a registered trade mark of Oxford University Press
in the UK and in certain other countries

Published in the United States
by Oxford University Press Inc., New York

© Robert Somerville 2011

The moral rights of the author have been asserted
Database right Oxford University Press (maker)

First published 2011

All rights reserved. No part of this publication may be reproduced,
stored in a retrieval system, or transmitted, in any form or by any means,
without the prior permission in writing of Oxford University Press,
or as expressly permitted by law, or under terms agreed with the appropriate
reprographics rights organization. Enquiries concerning reproduction
outside the scope of the above should be sent to the Rights Department,
Oxford University Press, at the address above

You must not circulate this book in any other binding or cover
and you must impose the same condition on any acquirer

British Library Cataloguing in Publication Data

Data available

Library of Congress Cataloging in Publication Data

Data available

Typeset by SPI Publisher Services, Pondicherry, India
Printed in Great Britain
on acid-free paper by
MPG Books Group, Bodmin and King's Lynn

ISBN 978–0–19–925859–8

1 3 5 7 9 10 8 6 4 2

Contents

Preface	vii
List of Abbreviations	viii
1. Pope Urban II's Council of Piacenza: Introduction	1
Background	1
Civitas Placentina/Concilium Placentinum	5
Dates – Location of Sessions – Liturgical Order	6
Attendance	8
Conciliar Cases	11
Piacenza and the First Crusade	15
2. Enactment, Circulation, and Survival of the Canons of Piacenza	17
Enactment and Circulation	17
Introduction	17
Gesta Romanae aecclesiae contra Hildebrandum	18
Bernold of Constance	24
Summary	28
Survival	29
Introduction	29
Polycarpus Supplement (Φ): preamble + fifteen canons + concluding notice on tenth preface for the mass	30
Lists of Canons in Medieval Manuscripts beyond Φ	32
JL 5694 (IP 5.248–49, no. 14) – c. 8, and c. 9 partim	43
Canon Law Collections	44
Narrative Sources	50
Conclusion	51
Appendix I: English Translation of Bernold of Constance's Description of the Council of Piacenza	54
Appendix II: Vagrant Canons	58
3. The Historiography of the Canons of Piacenza	60
4. The Transmission of the Canons of Piacenza (with an Edition)	71
Introduction	71
The *Polycarpus* Supplement (Φ), JL 5694 [IP 5.248–49, no. 14], and the *Gesta Romanae aecclesiae*	72
Transmission beyond Φ and the *Gesta*	75
Canon Law Collections	81
Annalista Saxo and Gerhoch of Reichersberg	84
Edition and Translation	85
Edition	89
Translation	99

5. **Commentary on the Canons**	102
Introduction	102
Commentary	103
6. **Legislation from the Councils of Urban II between Piacenza and Rome (April 1099)**	116
Introduction	116
Council of Tours, March 1096	118
Council of Nîmes, July 1096	121
Lateran Council, 1097	123
Council of Bari, October 1098	125
Council at St. Peter's, Rome, April 1099	127
Postscript	134
Bibliography	137
Indices	143

Preface

The place of the Council of Piacenza within Urban II's pontificate will be discussed below, in the first chapter and in the *Postscript*. This synod can easily get lost in modern historiography because of the Council of Clermont eight months later where the First Crusade was proclaimed. Yet Piacenza, with an extensive corpus of legislation, is a landmark not only for Pope Urban's reign but also for developments in the High Medieval Church generally. The assembly merits a detailed study even though the surviving evidence, apart from multiple and widely circulated renditions of the canons, is not plentiful. Various stories emerge in the pages that follow but the most important by far is about the content and survival of the *decreta Placentina*.

I have collected information about Piacenza over a number of years and in the process incurred many debts. Throughout the notes my gratitude is recorded to numerous friends and colleagues who answered questions and provided details about texts and manuscripts (and with apologies for any oversights in this regard). Special thanks are due to the librarians whose manuscripts are described in subsequent chapters and who offered information about their treasures. Several people also deserve special mention. Consuelo Dutschke, Columbia University's Rare Book and Manuscript Librarian, cheerfully answered countless questions about manuscript hands, provenance, and dating. Robert Scott, head of Columbia's Digital Humanities Center, not only made electronic resources available but has endured with erudite good humor a historian's love affair with what might be considered retrograde word-processing technology. Several editors in Oxford have been very patient while waiting for this book's completion, and my current editors, Stephanie Ireland and Emma Barber, facilitated the volume's production in several special ways. *Piacenza* is decidedly better because Martin Brett read an earlier draft and made thoughtful suggestions for improvements. His learning and his willingness to share it is well known, and an investigator of late eleventh-century Church councils could ask for no better reader. It goes without saying, of course, that only I bear responsibility for mistakes in what follows.

Piacenza was in the final stages of production when I learned of the death on August 11 of Professor Alfons Becker. Although we never met in person, over many years we corresponded about Urban II. The long-awaited third volume of Professor Becker's monumental work on Pope Urban (MGH, Schriften 19.3), is slated to appear by the end of this year, a book anticipated by many but by no one more than the present writer. *Requiescat in pace*.

Columbia University
Feast of St. Gregory the Great, 2011

List of Abbreviations

The following abbreviations will be used throughout. For details see the bibliography.

AHC	*Annuarium historiae conciliorum*
BAV	Biblioteca apostolica Vaticana
BEC	*Bibliothèque de l'École de chartes*
BL	British Library
BMCL	*Bulletin of Medieval Canon Law,* New Series
BNF	Bibliothèque nationale de France
COD	*Conciliorum oecumenicorum decreta*
DA	*Deutsches Archiv*
GP	*Germania pontificia*
GaP	*Gallia pontificia*
IP	*Italia pontificia*
JL	see Jaffé, *Regesta*
Lib. de lite	*Libelli de lite*
MGH	Monumenta Germaniae historica
MGHSS	MGH Scriptores
PL	*Patrologiae,* Series Latina
ZRG, Kan. Abt.	*Zeitschrift der Savigny-Stiftung für Rechtsgeschichte,* Kanonistische Abteilung

1

Pope Urban II's Council of Piacenza: Introduction

BACKGROUND

> By the favor of God and St. Peter, the lord pope now prevailed almost everywhere, and in central Lombardy, in the city of Piacenza, among those schismatic and against them, he arranged for a general synod... around the middle of Lent.[1]

So wrote Bernold of Constance (+1100) in his *Chronicon*, providing a contemporary witness to Pope Urban's plan to assemble an important council early in the year 1095. The idea of convening a 'general synod', or 'general council', probably had been in the pope's mind for some time.[2] Regulating clerical orders generated by the Wibertine Schism, and doing so in what he termed a general synod, was a major concern in the widely circulated letter dispatched to Bishop Pibo of Toul between late 1089 and Piacenza.[3]

The papal schism that was the backdrop for much that happened throughout Urban II's pontificate erupted formally in early 1080 between Gregory VII and Archbishop Wibert of Ravenna. Wibert owed his appointment to the German ruler Henry IV, and styled himself Pope Clement III. The early 1080s were increasingly difficult years for Pope Gregory and his supporters, as Wibertine sympathizers appeared beyond Henrician circles and even among former Gregorian cardinals.[4]

---

[1] Bernold, *Chronicon*, ed. Pertz 461 / ed. Robinson 518: *Domnus papa, Deo et sancto Petro prosperante, iam pene ubique praevaluit et in media Longobardia, in civitate Placentia, inter ipsos scismaticos et contra ipsos, generalem sinodum condixit....circa mediam quadragesimam.* Cf. JL 5670 (IP 5.248, no.14), ed. Heinrich Hagenmeyer, *Epistulae et chartae ad historiam primi belli sacri spectantes* (Insbruck 1901) 137, no. iii, issued on September 19, 1096: *Bonitati uestrae gratias agimus, quod inter schismaticos et haereticos constituti, quidam semper in fide catholica permansistis.*

[2] The words *synodus* and *concilium* are synonyms at the end of the eleventh century. Both terms occur within five lines of one another in the synodal preamble accompanying the legislation of Piacenza (see the edition in Chapter 4). The adjective *generalis/-e* does not appear there, but cf. JL 5694 (discussed in Chapter 2, under *Survival*, Section iv.). For this terminology in general see Somerville–Kuttner, *Pope Urban* 181–85, with literature cited, and especially the perceptive analysis by Horst Fuhrmann, 'Das Ökumenische Konzil und seine historischen Grundlagen', *Geschichte in Wissenschaft und Unterricht* 12 (1961) 676 (repr., without footnotes, but with a bibliographical supplement, in id., *Einladung ins Mittelalter*, 3rd ed. [Munich 1988]).

[3] JL 5409: written after the Council of Melfi in September, 1089; see, inter al., the discussion in Somerville–Kuttner, *Pope Urban* 182–86.

[4] The history of this schism and the concomitant upheavals thoughout western Christendom are well known and need not be discussed here. Two works of the last dozen years that offer excellent perspectives on Pope Gregory and his times are Cowdrey, *Pope Gregory*, and Blumenthal, *Gregor VII*.

The future of the Gregorian papacy was at that point uncertain. Gregory's situation at Rome became untenable, and he was rescued from the besieged Eternal City by his Norman allies in 1084. The pontiff moved south with the Normans, dying in what he considered exile at Salerno in May 1085, and his memory as a great reformer depended on supporters mainly based in southern Italy.

After a hiatus that lasted almost exactly a year, the venerable Abbot Desiderius of Montecassino emerged on May 24, 1086, as Gregory's successor, taking the name Pope Victor III. But Victor passed away only sixteen months later, and following another significant interval, on March 12, 1088, Gregorian cardinals meeting at Terracina chose as pope Cardinal-bishop Odo of Ostia, who took the name Urban II. A former Cluniac monk and prior and a disciple of Abbot Hugh, Odo was also a savvy church diplomat who had been a cardinal since 1079.[5] As pope he immediately embraced the Gregorian legacy, proclaiming that he desired to follow totally in the footsteps of Pope Gregory.[6] Despite occasional forays as far north as Rome, however, Urban spent his early years in southern Italy, awaiting the outcome of military events in the north that would in great part determine his future. In the meantime, he visited churches, worked to solidify political relationships, and strove to fold into the Roman obedience the Latin-Greek usages and hierarchy found in this world of mixed languages and cultures.[7]

More than any pope since Leo IX (1049–54), Urban II moved around throughout western Europe. The main steps and basic chronolology of this activity are well established, and can be outlined in five stages:[8]

1. At Rome in late 1088 and the first half of 1089, then mainly in southern Italy until his return to Rome in November 1093.

2. To northern Italy in late summer 1094, remaining there until summer 1095.

For two more recent, specialized studies, both dealing with local activity but with different perspectives on the reforms of the eleventh-century Church, see Bruce Brasington, 'A Note on Selected Glosses to the Collection in V Books (Vat. lat. 1339)', BMCL 25 (2002–2003) 9–14; and Maureen C. Miller, 'Masculinity, Reform, and Clerical Culture: Narratives of Episcopal Holiness in the Gregorian Era', *Church History* 72 (2003) 25–52.

[5] For the details of Odo-Urban's life and career, see in Becker, *Papst Urban* 1. See also Robert Somerville, 'Urban II, Pope', *Dictionary of the Middle Ages* 12 (1988) 302–4, id., 'Urban II (1088–99)', in Frank Coppa (ed.), *The Great Popes through History: An Encyclopedia* (Westport CT 2002) 107–12. Ivan Gobry, *Deux papes Champenois, Urbain II & Urbain IV* (Troyes 1994), offers a popular treatment of these two Urbanic pontificates. For an interpretation of Pope Urban's pontificate see Giuseppe Fornasari, 'Tra assestamento disciplina e consolidamento istituzionale: un'interpretazione del pontifcato di Urbano II', in Lothar Kolmer and Peter Segl (eds.), *Regensburg, Bayern und Europa: Festschrift für Kurt Reindel* (Regensburg 1995) 213–28.

[6] See Somerville-Kuttner, *Pope Urban* 41–2 (CB 1–2).

[7] See, e.g., ibid. 178 ff.

[8] See the basic chronology in JL; Becker, 'Voyage' 136–39, id., *Papst Urban* 2. 435–58, specifically for the sojourn in France in 1095–96, and Somerville, 'Pseudo-Council' 18–22, provide additional information. Ziese, *Wibert* passim, chronicles the parallel activity of Urban's papal rival, Clement III/ Wibert of Ravenna.

3. Across the Alps in August 1095, throughout southern France and as far north as Le Mans in February 1096, then south to Languedoc.

4. Back into Italy in late summer 1096, reaching Rome late that year.

5. At Rome for much of 1097 into spring 1098, then to southern Italy, returning to Rome in late 1098 and dying there in July 29, 1099.

There is some reason to think, furthermore, that following the death on August 1, 1098, of his Crusade legate, Bishop Adhémar of Le Puy, Urban might have contemplated heading East to meet up at Antioch with the Crusaders, something that they had urged him to do.[9]

In the course of his extensive travels, as with Pope Leo forty years earlier, Urban II frequently presided over synods, and it is difficult to exaggerate the importance of these papal councils that occurred with great frequency after the middle of the eleventh century. They met throughout the western Church, but especially in Italy and when possible at the Lateran; and aside from offering venues for business of all kinds, their formal legislation, the conciliar canons, formed one of the chief building blocks of canon law and of papal monarchy in the High Middle Ages.[10] The pontificates of Urban II, Calixtus II, and Innocent II have all, for various reasons, been deemed crucial in the development of papal synodal ideas and practice, and Urban's assemblies in particular have been viewed as marking a transition toward increasing papal control over conciliar activity.[11]

Because the councils held after 1080 by Gregory VII and Victor III are very poorly documented, synodal continuities between Pope Urban and his immediate predecessors are difficult to assess. Leaving aside now the reforming conciliar traditions between Leo IX and Alexander II (1061–73), Gregory VII presided over at least eleven councils, Victor III over two, and Urban II probably held ten:[12] Melfi (September, 1089), Benevento (March, 1091), Troia (March,

---

[9] See Chapter 6, n. 58.

[10] In recent decades a number of these synods have been investigated but more deserve to be. No attempt will be made here to provide a full bibliography, but Gresser, *Synoden* xv–lxiv, offers an extensive list of literature; see esp. ibid., under Blumenthal and Somerville. Cf. Robinson, *Papacy* 121 ff., for papal general councils between 1073–1198, and cf. the recent remarks by Nathalie Kruppa, 'Einführung', in Nathalie Kruppa und Leszek Zygner (eds.), *Partikularsynoden im späten Mittelalter* (Göttingen 2006) 11–27, esp. 17.

[11] See Franz-Josef Schmale, 'Synodus-synodale concilium-concilium', AHC 8 (1976) 98 ff. (but cf. Wilfried Hartmann, 'Verso il centralismo papale (Leone IX, Niccolò II, Gregorio VII, Urbano II)', *Il secolo XI: una svolta?* [Annali dell'Istituto storico italo-germanico, Quaderno 35; Bologna 1993] 123); Robinson, *Papacy* 124–26; and Robert Somerville 'Observations on general councils in the Twelfth Century', AHC 40 (2008) 281–88.

[12] It is possible, but unlikely, that this number may change, although the tradition for a papal synod at Limoges in late 1095 was proven false (Somerville, 'French Councils' 59–60), and evidence for Urban's Lateran Council of 1097, which certainly did occur, is exceedingly thin and could easily have vanished (see Chapter 6, Sect. iv). The literature on Pope Gregory VII is vast and many works treat his councils: see, e.g., Cowdrey, *Gregory* 586 ff., and Blumenthal, *Gregor* VII 139 ff. Cf. Somerville, 'Gregory VII', passim, esp. 34, n. 2, and Gresser *Synoden* 115–257. For Victor III's synods at Capua in March, and at Benevento in August, 1087, see in JL, and Gresser, *Synoden* 259–60; and very briefly for Gregory's and Urban's councils, see Robert Somerville, 'Councils, Western (869–

1093),[13] Piacenza (March, 1095), Clermont (November, 1095), Tours (March, 1096), Nîmes (July, 1096), Lateran (1097), Bari (October, 1098), and St. Peter's, Rome (April, 1099).[14] Urban thus maintained a tradition of synodal frequency that would be continued into the early twelfth century by Paschal II and Calixtus II.[15] The Wibertine Schism accounted for the location of Urban's three southern Italian gatherings held between 1089 and 1093, and perhaps because their attendance was regional, it is debatable whether or not in the pontiff's view they warranted the label 'general council/synod'.[16]

Urban II celebrated no council, at least none that can be discerned, between the assemblies at Troia and Piacenza, that is for a two-year period. After Rome was accessible to him in late 1093 he remained there or in the vicinity for several months, but was on the road again in late summer, turning up at Pisa on September 12, 1094.[17] As late as autumn of that year, however, Urban seemed uncertain about the location for the council that he planned to convoke in Tuscany or Lombardy around the middle of February 1095, and to which he summoned Archbishop Rainaud of Reims.[18] The papal letter to Reims is lost, but the information is derived from a letter that Rainaud wrote to his suffragan, Bishop Lambert of Arras, announcing the pope's intention and pressing Lambert to attend the synod along with the abbots of his diocese.[19] Urban's chancery tendered similar invitations elsewhere. A contemporary source from Grenoble indicated that he invited 'Gallican bishops' (*Gallicanos episcopos*) to Piacenza.[20] Bernold of Constance in addition reported that letters of convocation were dispatched to bishops in Italy, Burgundy, France, Germany, Bavaria, and other provinces 'by canonical and apostolic authority' (*canonica et apostolica auctoritate*).[21] Ignoring such a canonical summons may have resulted in a suspension from office for Archbishop Hugh of Lyons, although

---

1179)', *Dictionary of the Middle Ages* 3 (1983) 633–39. Still informative despite its age is the narrative in Hefele–Leclercq, *Histoire*.

[13] See esp. Somerville–Kuttner, *Pope Urban*, Part II for Melfi, and Appendix II for Benevento and Troia.

[14] For a discussion of Pope Urban's synods after Clermont, see Chapter 6.

[15] Gresser, *Synoden* provides the most recent survey of early twelfth-century papal councils.

[16] The issue is murky: see Somerville–Kuttner, *Pope Urban* 181–85, and cf. the comments about conciliar terminology at the beginning of this section.

[17] See JL 5530. There are gaps in the information that JL offers for Urban's movements in 1094, and a fuller picture undoubtedly could be gained from investigating the sources for northern and central Italian history at the end of the eleventh century.

[18] JL 5531*; Gresser, *Synoden* 292, suggests Pisa as a possible location.

[19] For Rainaud's letter, see Kéry, *Arras* 186–87, no. [47], and Giordanengo, *Arras* 162 (G.36') (with a French translation). Urging Lambert to bring abbots of his church seems odd, for no particular reason suggests itself as to why Urban wished northern French monastic leaders to be on hand. Perhaps the text is corrupt, and has dropped a reference to other clergy from Arras also convoked to the synod: cf. the entourage from the church at Arras that accompanied Bishop Lambert to the Council of Clermont that is noted in Somerville, 'Society' 79–80.

[20] GaP 3. 1. 140, no. *193, a designation that included the archbishop of Vienne.

[21] Bernold; *Chronicon*, ed. Pertz 461 / ed. Robinson 518 (cf. GP 1. 393, no. *32).

whatever penalty actually was exacted in Hugh's case seems not to have been severe.[22]

Archbishop Rainaud's directive to Lambert is undated. JL calendared it between October 13 and December 19, two definite points in the papal itinerary for late 1094.[23] The letter from Reims to Arras could have been earlier, although probably not much later than December 1094. No information seems to be available to indicate when Pope Urban finally decided on Piacenza as the site of his planned assembly. On February 18, 1095, he still was in Cremona, which was the last fixed point before he opened the council on March 1 (a Thursday), at Piacenza.[24]

CIVITAS PLACENTINA/CONCILIUM PLACENTINUM

Why Piacenza? The evidence does not permit a clear answer for why Urban II selected this city, although its church and the region in the 1090s has been well studied.[25] Piacenza lies adjacent to the River Po, situated at the junction of many important routes for travel and commerce. It was a hub for pilgrim traffic, and without a doubt the location also recommended itself to the pope as a conciliar site because of its ecclesiastical situation. Piacenza was in the northeastern-most corner of the church province of Ravenna – home territory of Archbishop Wibert.[26] Yet despite its position 'de iure' in Wibert's province, a map reveals that Piacenza was three times closer to Milan than to Ravenna.[27] Bernold was certainly right when he wrote that Urban convened his synod 'among the schismatics', but the degree to

---

[22] Ibid., ed. Pertz 461 / ed. Robinson 519–20; cf. JL 5544, from March 9, immediately after the council, which seems to find Archbishop Hugh in possession of his legatine office.

[23] This is based on JL 5530, issued at Pisa on October 13, and JL 5532 (IP 3. 124, no. 3), issued on December 19.

[24] JL 5541; see Cheney, *Handbook* 90–1, for Easter on March 25 in 1095.

[25] Many works on medieval Italian urban and religious history treat Piacenza, and no effort has been made to list titles that do not deal with the council. For example, Luigi Canetti, *Gloriosa civitas: culto dei santi e società cittadina a Piacenza nel medioevo* (Cristianesimo antico e medievale 4; Bologna 1993), and Zumhagen, *Religiöse*, are valuable, but have little to say about Pope Urban's synod. The following selected works offer historical background and also pertain directly to the council: Fliche, *Réforme* 264 ff.; Becker, *Papst Urban* 1. 131 ff.; the studies by Pierre Racine, e.g., *Piacenza e la prima crociata* (Edizioni Diabasis, Reggio Emilia 1995), *Plaisance du Xe à la fin du XIIIe siècle, Essai d'histoire urbaine*, 3 vols. (Lille–Paris 1979), and id., 'Concile', and 'Civitas', both of which are in *Il concilio di Piacenza*; Rudolf Hiestand, 'Planung-Improvisation-Zufall: Politisches Handeln im 11. Jahrhundert oder noch einmal Piacenza 1076', in *Von Sacerdotium und Regnum, Geistliche und weltliche Gewalt im frühen und hohen Mittelalter: Festschrift für Egon Boshof zum 65. Geburtstag* (Cologne 2002), esp. 377–79. For religious establishments in Piacenza, see IP 5. 441 ff. Two collections of essays were published to commemorate the 900th anniversary of Pope Urban's synod of March, 1095, books very difficult to find even in Italy: *Concilio di Piacenza* has twenty-two articles, half of which concern the Crusade; *Piacenza e la prima crociata*, ed. Racine, has seven articles, all on the Crusade–the author is very grateful to Brian M. Jensen for providing a copy of the latter volume.

[26] Racine, 'Concile' 20–22, emphasizes this point; cf. id. 'Civitas' 14–15. For the importance of the location of the city, see Anna Zaninoni, 'La città che ospitò il Concilio: nodo viario e commerciale, tappa di pellegrinaggi nell'Italia padana', *Il concilio di Piacenza* 155–70. Gresser, *Synoden* 292, n. 155, provides useful information about the distribution of Gregorian/Urbanic versus Wibertine bishops in churches in northern and central Italy.

[27] Heidrich, *Ravenna* 199, provides a useful fold-out map showing the suffragan sees of Ravenna.

which Wibertine influence was to be felt at Piacenza in the mid-1090s is difficult to estimate.[28]

Between 1090 and 1091 Winrich of Trier assumed the title of bishop of Piacenza. He was still holding it in October 1095, although by then obviously gone from the city. Several factors contributed to his depature. Emperor Henry IV's power in northern Italy was broken in 1092 by the forces of Countess Mathilda of Tuscany. Subsequently, Milan, Cremona, Lodi, and Piacenza formed an anti-imperial alliance; local religious interests, especially the Pataria, fostered reforming/anti-imperial attitudes in Piacenza. These factors combined to make Winrich's presence in the city impossible.[29] His successor was Bishop Aldo, a reformer from an aristocratic family of the region, on whom more below. The tragic mutilation in 1089 of the ardent Gregorian bishop of Piacenza, Bonizo of Sutri, was still fresh in the memory in 1094–95, and it can be wondered how it might have influenced Pope Urban.[30] But that imponderable aside, by early 1095 the security offered by a combination of Mathildine forces and local partisans allowed the pontiff to plan and hold a large council in Clement III's backyard in the city of Piacenza.[31]

DATES – LOCATION OF SESSIONS – LITURGICAL ORDER

At the beginning of this chapter, Bernold's *Chronicon* was quoted to the effect that Urban II held his council at Piacenza 'around' mid-Lent. The synodal preamble that introduced the legislation, and which ultimately depended on papal chancery records, noted that the gathering 'was celebrated' (*celebrata est*) on the kalends of March, which points to a liturgical opening on March 1.[32] This preface also specified that these canons were approved on the seventh day, that is, March 7,

---

[28] Ibid. 114–15.

[29] Detlev Jasper, 'Winrich von Trier', *Die deutsche Literatur des Mittelalters, Verfasserlexikon* 10.3/4 (Berlin 1998) 1219–24, for Wenrich; and see also Ponzini, 'Situazione' 141–42, Zumhagen, *Religiöse* 173–74, and Glass, 'Bishops' 223, for Winrich. The literature on the political/ecclesiastical struggles in the early 1090s in northern Italy is vast, but especially useful are Becker, *Papst Urban* 1. 131–32, and more recently the following: Ponzini, 'Situazione' passim; Valerie Eads, 'The Geography of Power: Matilda of Tuscany and the Strategy of Active Defense', in Donald J. Kagay and L.J. Andrew Villaton (eds.), *Crusaders, Condottieri, and Cannon* (History of Warfare 13; Leiden 2003) 355–87, especially 382ff.; and Claudia Zey, 'Im Zentrum des Streit: Mailand und die oberitalienischen Kommunen zwischen *regnum* und *sacerdotium*', in Jörg Jarnut and Matthew Wernhoff (eds.), *Vom Umbruch zur Erneuerung?: Das 11. und beginnende 12. Jahrhundert - Positionen der Forschung* (MittelalterStudien 13; Munich 2006) 597ff. For Clement III/Wibert of Ravenna's prospects after the early 1090s, see Heidrich, *Ravenna* 161; for bishops loyal to him at the time of Piacenza, see Gresser, *Synoden* 292, n. 155.

[30] For Bonizo, see Bernold, *Chronicon*, ed. Pertz 449 / ed. Robinson 477. The literature on Bonizo is extensive, but see, inter al., Somerville–Kuttner, *Pope Urban* 50–1, especially n. 28, and Ponzini, 'Situazione' 137–41.

[31] Ibid. 146, although Racine, 'Concile' 22, speaks of Urban II's 'audace' in being willing to convene a council at Piacenza, 'en une terre sinon hostile, du moins peu sûre'.

[32] All copies of the acts of Piacenza are private accounts and none can be demonstrated to stem directly from Pope Urban's chancery, although the version that will be designated Φ, that survives in some manuscripts of the early twelfth-century canonical collection known as the *Polycarpus*, might go back to an official account. This will be treated in Chapter 4, Polycarpus Supplement (Φ).

'after lengthy deliberation' (*post tractationem diutinam*).[33] It is not said explicitly that the synod terminated on that day, but this might be assumed from the fact that legislation could be recited and formally published in a plenary session at the end of councils.[34] JL 5551 is a papal privilege issued for Cluny on March 16, in which Pope Urban wrote that this grant had been affirmed 'by us recently in the synod at Piacenza' (*a nobis nuper in Placentina [synodo]*). The implication is that by March 16 the council was over.[35]

According to the synod's preamble, on the first and on the third days the assembly met out of doors, 'in an open field' (*in campo*), because no church was large enough to contain the crowd (a statement then exegeted by reference to Moses and Christ legislating and preaching in the open).[36] It remains unclear, however, where the formal sessions met. A new cathedral was constructed only in the early twelfth century, in which Pope Innocent II held a council in June, 1132.[37] In March 1095, Urban II's synod probably used various churches throughout town in which to conduct business, and also convened in a field or plaza outside on March 1 and 3.[38]

Whatever else papal synods of the Reform era were – political conclaves (e.g., Reims, 1119), theological forums (e.g., Bari, 1098), launching pads for new initiative (e.g., Clermont, 1095) – these assemblies were conceived of as liturgical events (hence they are, as specified above, 'celebrated').[39] As liturgical moments they operated according to specific rules termed 'orders' (*ordines*).[40] It is, unfortunately, unknown which *ordo* or *ordines* governed the ceremonial procedures at the Council of Piacenza. Were local usages employed, or did the papal chancery provide material for the occasion? The paucity of surviving eleventh-/twelfth-century liturgical books from Piacenza makes the prospects of answering these question dim.[41]

---

[33] These statements will be analyzed in Chapter 2, *Enactment*, Sects. ii–iii.

[34] Cf. the comment in JL post 5541 for the view that March 7 was the conclusion. For promulgation of decrees at the end of councils see, inter al., Somerville, *Decreta* 39–41; Somerville–Kuttner, *Pope Urban* 228–45; Laudage, 'Ritual' 326 ff.; specific information ante JL 6311, for the end of Pope Paschal II's Lateran Council of March, 1112; and post JL 6759, for Pope Calixtus II's Council of Reims, in October, 1119.

[35] For JL 5551, see Armin Kohnle, *Abt Hugo von Cluny (1049–1109)* (Beihefte der Francia 32; Sigmaringen 1993) 123. Confirmation of this privilege was perhaps accompanied by a special papal encomium for Cluny akin to the *laudatio* of Gregory VII for the monastery delivered in the Lenten Lateran Council of 1080: see Somerville, 'Gregory VII' 52; and for the text, H.E.J. Cowdrey, *The Epistolae Vagantes of Pope Gregory VII* (Oxford 1972) 96–9. For a possible repetition at Piacenza see id., *Two Studies in Cluniac History, 1049–1126* (Studi Gregoriani 11; Rome 1978) 193, n. 31. See also in Chapter 2, (*Survival*, Sect. iii.b), the description of the text designated as MS V for the unique manuscript copy of the 1080 Gregorian sermon.

[36] For these Biblical images, see the commentary in Chapter 5.

[37] See IP 5. 461, no. +*1, and for the council in 1132 see post JL 7571.

[38] See, e.g., Racine, 'Civitas' 15, 'Concile' 22–3, and 'Santa Maria' 21, on the unresolved question of where the council met.

[39] See the discussion at the end of Gresser, *Synoden* 523 ff, esp. 559–63.

[40] See Schneider, *Konzilsordines* 623, sup. verb. *celebrare*. See also, in general for conciliar procedure, Martin Klöckener, *Die Liturgie der Diözesansynode* (Liturgiewissenschaftliche Quellen und Forschungen 68; Münster 1986) 29–32.

[41] For example, Schneider, *Konzilsordines* 57 ff., lists two *ordines*, nos. 7C and 8, that derive respectively from Italy around the year 1100, and from Milan in the eleventh century. Dr. Brian M. Jensen kindly informed the author that only fragments of liturgical books from Piacenza survive prior to the twelfth century.

ATTENDANCE

Piacenza was the 'general council' that Pope Urban hoped to convene from the early days of his pontificate, and attendance may well have been crucial to that designation (see n. 16). Participants came from both Italy and north of the Alps, including Germany, and the event would have brought a crowd of clergy and laity into town, although no reliable figures exist on the size of that crowd. In his *Chronicon*, Bernold reported that about (*fere*) 4000 clerics and more than 30,000 laity 'are reported to have been on hand', a general statement on Bernold's part that is probably an inflated estimate.[42] Racine notes that the population of Piacenza at the time of the assembly could scarcely have exceeded between 8000–9000 inhabitants. Drawing on early-modern sources, he comes up with an attendance of 200 bishops, 4000 clerics, and 30,000 laity, numbers that must have derived from a combination of Bernold and Ekkehard of Aura (see below).[43] It seems difficult to believe, although it cannot be disproven, that Piacenza's population could have expanded by 400 per cent for the week of the synod.

Considering the clergy, an important tradition for Pope Urban's earler synods spoke of seventy bishops and twelve abbots at Melfi, a crowd present at Benevento of bishops and abbots that 'could not easily be calculated' (*quorum numerus facile adnotari non potuit*), and about seventy-two bishops and twelve abbots in attendance at Troia.[44] If figures from the same source for the Council of Clermont are offered for comparison, twelve archbishops, eighty or eighty-two bishops, and innumerable abbots are given.[45] Sources for the Council of Bari in 1098 indicate between 130 to 185 bishops on hand; while Bernold spoke of 150 bishops and abbots at Pope Urban's last council, in 1099 at St. Peter's.[46] Thus Ekkehard's estimate of about (*fere*) 200 bishops at the Council of Piacenza appears somewhat high, although it is impossible to know for sure.[47]

A letter was issued by Urban II, on February 18, 1095 at Cremona (JL 5540), confirming a restitution by Count Raymond of Toulouse of possessions for the Benedictine monastery of St.-Gilles in the diocese of Nîmes. The document survives in a chancery original dated less than two weeks before the opening of the Council of Piacenza, but its form is curious. After the *datum* clause, both

---

[42] Bernold, *Chronicon*, ed. Pertz 462 / ed. Robinson 521: *In hac sinodo IIII fere milia clericorum et plus quam XXX milia laicorum fuisse perhibentur*. See also Ziese, *Wibert* 224–26.

[43] Racine, 'Concile' 22, and cf. id., 'Civitas' 3, with n. 6, where the unreliability of such numbers is admitted.

[44] These figures come from Φ (see n. 32), which may derive indirectly from papal chancery sources: see Somerville–Kuttner, *Pope Urban* 252, 302–5. A propos of abbatial participation in these gatherings, see the list of monastic privileges conceded by Urban II for houses in southern Italy in Spinelli, 'Urbano' 535–40.

[45] Somerville, *Decreta* 121; cf. Somerville, 'Society' 62–82, and id., 'Beyond Clermont'.

[46] For Bari, see Gresser, *Synoden* 322; for Rome, see Bernold, *Chronicon*, ed. Pertz 466 / ed. Robinson 537.

[47] *Frutoldi et Ekkehardi chronica necnon anonymi chronica imperatorum*, eds. Franz-Josef Schmale and Irene Schmale-Ott (Ausgewählte Quellen zur Deutschen Geschichte 15; Darmstadt 1972) 158.

preceding and following a list of witnesses, the text claims to have been read and confirmed in that synod. In his edition of the document, Etienne Baluze pointed out that the names of the witnesses were copied later than the main text, but he did not say how much later.[48] Autopsy shows that the subscriptions and the statements about confirmation are additions made to the charter in a different but contemporary hand, but perhaps were anticipated because the papal text per se, from protocol to *datum*, fills only about half of a large sheet of parchment. But putting aside these imponderables about form, it will be assumed that the churchmen listed as witnesses to this conciliar action for St.-Gilles were in fact on hand in the assembly.

The attendance information that follows is based primarily on the St.-Gilles charter, with names rearranged to show more readily rank and geographical distribution.[49] Two supplements are also brought to bear. In the first place, Bernold of Constance supplied names of a few more prelates, who will be designated in the tabulation by '[B]'. It is, furthermore, reasonable to assume that those who received benefits (such as Bishop Lambert of Arras; see JL 5546–5547), through letters written by Urban shortly after the council were on hand.[50] In the listing below, '[L]' signifies churchmen identified in papal letters dispatched in the days following the synod, who had most likely been there. In most cases personal names are Anglicized.

Cardinals

Cardinal-bishop John of Porto (whose name appears in the subscriptions to JL 5540 twice)[51]

Cardinal-priests Albert (of S. Sabina), Bonussenior (of S. Maria in Trastevere), Herman (of SS. Quattro Coronati), Richard (abbot of St.-Victor in Marseille), Teuzo (of SS. Giovanni e Paolo)

Cardinal-deacons Gregory (uncertain title), Hugh (uncertain title), John (of S. Maria in Cosmedin, and papal chancellor),[52] and Roger (uncertain titles)

---

[48] Etienne Baluze, *Miscellanea* 2 (Lucca 1761) 177=PL 151. 399, n. 32. See the information in Gresser, *Synoden* 294, n. 160, and also Leon Robert Ménager, 'Lanfranco, notario pontificio (1091–1093): la diplomatica ducale italo-normanna e la certosa di S. Stefano del Bosco', *Studi storici meridionali* 2 (1983) 8, 13, with a photo of the upper portion of the document which is preserved in Paris, BNF, Coll. Baluze 380, no. 6. Cf. Wilhelm Wiederhold, 'Papsturkunden in Frankreich IV', *Nachrichten Göttingen*, Phil.-hist. Klasse (1907) 39, n. 3 (repr. op. cit. [Acta Romanorum pontificum 7; Vatican City 1985] 285, n. 3); Leo Santifaller, 'Saggio di un Elenco dei funzionari, impiegati e scrittori della Cancellaria Pontificia dall'inizio all'anno 1099', *Bullettino dell'Istituto Storico Italiano per il medio evo* 56/57 (1940) 449; and Alfons Becker, 'Päpstliche Gerichtsurkunden und Prozessverfahren zur Zeit Urbans II. (1088–1099)', *Festschrift zum 65. Geburtstag von Hans-Walter Hermann* (Saarbrücken 1995) 41, n. 8.

[49] Cf. Gresser, *Synoden* 293–97, and Tangl, *Teilnehmer* 172–76, who remarked specifically (174) about the importance for Urban's prestige of having bishops at Piacenza from beyond Italy. These two works are the source of what follows when no other reference is provided.

[50] New editions of these letters are found in Kéry, *Arras* 187–88, nos.[49–50], and Giordanengo, *Arras* 164–67 (G.38 [*male* 5549]-39) (with French translations).

[51] Gresser, *Synoden* 295, n. 173.

[52] John was not listed among the witnesses in the supplement to the St.-Gilles letter, but was identified in the dating clause at the end of the document. As chancellor he would have played an important role in the synod: cf. Somerville–Kuttner, *Pope Urban* 199–202.

Archbishops

France. Peter of Aix, William of Auch, Amat of Bordeaux, Adelbert of Bourges, Rodulf of Tours.

Imperial Territory (Burgundy & Germany). Diemo of Salzburg [B], Guy of Vienne [L].

Italy. Patriarch Peter of Grado, Arnulf III of Milan,[53] Daimbert of Pisa, Rodulf of Reggio in Calabria.

Bishops

France. Lambert of Arras [L], Fulk of Beauvais, William of Couseran, Sancio of Lescar, Gottfried of Maguelonne, Radbod of Noyon [L], Otto of Oléron, Dodo of Tarbes.

Imperial Territory (Burgundy & Germany). Gebhard of Constance [B], Berengar of Fréjus, Hugh of Grenoble [L], William of Orange, Ulrich of Passau [B].[54]

Italy. Otto of Imola, Philip of Luni. A word is in order about Bishop Aldo of Piacenza. Aldo's precedessor was Winrich of Trier. Aldo del Gabrielli probably was consecrated either at the Council of Piacenza or shortly thereafter. As Racine notes, it is with Bishop Aldo that the city of Piacenza witnesses 'le passage au régime communal'.[55]

Spain. Representatives from King Alfonso VI of León-Castile were possibly at Piacenza, concerned with the transfer of an episcopal see from Oca to Burgos.[56]

Monastic leaders

Abbot Pons of Chaise-Dieu, Abbot Hugh of Cluny [L], Abbot Thoger of St. Georgen [L], Abbot Odilo of St.-Gilles [?],[57] Abbot Berengar of St.-Laurent in Liège [?],[58] Abbot Gebhard of Hirsau [L], representative of St. Peter im Schwarzwald [L],[59] Abbot Udalrich of Reichenau [B], Abbot Frothard of St.-Pons-de-Thomières, Abbot Tedbald of S. Stefano in Vercelli

---

[53] See Gresser, *Synoden* 295, n. 179, for Arnulf.

[54] The situation in the church at Cambrai at this time was complicated by a schism, and Gresser and Tangl have different views of the church's possible episcopal representation at Piacenza: ibid. 296, for the absence of Manassas, *electus* of Cambrai; cf. Tangl, *Teilnehmer* 175, for the presence of 'the bishop of Cambrai', on the basis of JL 5547, a letter addressed by Urban II to Gualcher, *Cameracensi electo*. The complications have been discussed by Kéry, *Arras* 287 ff.; see Somerville, 'Society' 86 (no. 6). Despite that letter to Gualcher, perhaps instigated by Bishop Lambert of Arras, present at the synod and well known for his eagerness to distance his newly restored see from Cambrai, there seems no reason to suppose that either candidate for Cambrai attended Piacenza.

[55] Racine, 'Civitas' 15. Aldo was bishop of Piacenza until 1121; for his reign, see Ponzini, 'Situazione' 141 ff., Simona Rossi, 'Il vescovo Aldo: Problematiche e linee interpretative del suo episcopato', *Concilio di Piacenza* 63–70, Zumhagen, *Religiöse* 175–76, and Glass, 'Bishops' 223 ff.

[56] See JL 5549; Gresser, *Synoden* 296–97, doubts the presence of the bishop of Burgos/Oca at Piacenza, suggesting that the matter was handled by Abbot Richard of Marseilles.

[57] See the discussion above about the St.-Gilles document (JL 5540), and cf. 5541 where Abbot Odilo is named. It would be odd, if he was at Cremona on February 18, if he did not continue on to Piacenza. Odilo or someone from St.-Gilles must have been the source of the list of witnesses appended to 5540.

[58] See JL 5538, discussed at the end of this chapter.

[59] See GP 2.1. 190–92, no. 1 [JL 5545]; no abbot is named in this privilege.

Others

Bernold offered pieces of information about other attendees at Piacenza.

- He reported the presence of the German Emperess Praxedis, who played a featured role at the synod (see Chapter 2, *Enactment*, Sect. iii).
- Bernold also noted that representatives [unnamed] of King Philip of France were on hand.[60]
- More important, in Tangl's estimation, than other bits of information on laity at Piacenza is Bernold's description of legates from the Byzantine Emperor Alexius I seeking assistance for his campaign in Asia Minor against the Turks.[61]
- Bernold's silence about Countess Mathilda of Tuscany at the council is puzzling, for her presence was attested by her lyrical biographer, the monk Donizo of Canossa.[62]

The churchmen and laity who can be, with a fair degree of certainty, located at Piacenza comprise a small number of those who were present. About thirty archbishops and bishops have been identified, and while there is no way to know how many prelates actually were in attendance, using the figures provided above for Clermont and Bari a very rough estimate of about 100 is not extravagant. That would mean that seventy bishops, more or less, remain invisible, most of whom represented churches in Italy and France.[63]

CONCILIAR CASES

The synod probably lasted for a week and concluded on March 7, but Pope Urban remained in Piacenza for a month, spending Holy Week and Easter (March 25; see n. 24) there. On April 4, he issued a privilege for Richard of Marseille, and then by April 10 was in Cremona.[64] For the period between March 8 and April 10 the calendar in JL registers nineteen papal letters and privileges, yet the total number

---

[60] For the marital problems of King Philip see *Chronicon*, ed. Robinson, n. 570; cf. Somerville, *Decreta* 5–6.

[61] Tangl, *Teilnehmer* 176.

[62] Donizo of Canossa, *Vita Mathildis* 2. viii, ed. Luigi Simeoni (Rerum Italicarum scriptores, nuova ed., 5.2 [Bologna 1930]) 80–1; id., *Vita di Matilde di Canossa* 2. viii, ed. Paolo Golinelli (Milan 2008) 180–83. For Donizo, of the Benedictine house of S. Apollonio in Canossa, see *Lexikon des Mittelalters* 3 (1986) 1247–48. Tangl, *Teilnehmer* 175, speculated that Mathilda's second husband, Duke Welf of Bavaria, was also on hand; for Welf V, see Robinson, *Henry* 279–81. For the venerable tradition found in the work of the seventeenth-century historian of Piacenza, P.M. Campi (not seen), that Pope Urban's gravely ill mother accompanied him to the synod where she died, see Racine, 'Santa Maria' 21. (Cf. Poggiali, *Memorie* 36, and in general on the pope's parents see the information gathered by Becker, *Papst Urban* 1. 27 ff.). Thomas Asbridge, *The First Crusade* (Oxford 2004) 60, writes that it is 'quite possible' that the Norman Crusader-to-be Bohemond was at Piacenza, but cites no evidence (for Bohemond see Chapter 6, Bari).

[63] Cf. n. 17 above.

[64] See JL 5560, and ante JL 5561 for the pope at Cremona.

promulgated was obviously larger.[65] Deliberations underlying those documents are mostly lost from view, and it is unknown how many reflect activity in the sessions of the council proper. Papal councils were magnets for disputes to be adjudicated before the Roman pontiff, but vignettes about procedures are not plentiful. Some of that activity was public and occurred in plenary sessions of the gathering (cf. the Grenoble–Vienne case, below), but the majority would have taken place in committees and private hearings, depending on the issue and the protagonist.[66]

Chapter 2 will present and analyze the remarkable descriptions of Piacenza found in Bernold's *Chronicon* and in the *Gesta Romanae aecclesiae contra Hildebrandum*. It might be expected that those works, written within five years of the event, would include information on ecclesiastical cases brought before the synod. By and large, however, this is not the case, and Bernold shows little interest, and the *Gesta* no interest, in church disputes adjudicated at the time. Bernold was a Gregorian south German monk, canonist, theologian, and chronicler who had much to tell his readers. His account of Piacenza was long, descriptive, included references to a handful of decrees, and also touched on a few canonical-institutional matters, such as consecration of a new abbot for the house of Reichenau, with reiteration of Constance's rights on the island, and Bishop Gebhard's part in consecrating Archbishop Arnulf of Milan.[67] But Piacenza's juridical activity was of minimal concern in the *Chronicon*, perhaps because most of the cases had little connection with Bernold's home church. The author of the *Gesta*, probably Cardinal Beno of SS. Martino e Silvestro, was a polemicist totally disenchanted with the canonical programs of Gregory VII and Urban II. Dripping with sarcasm and holding a jaundiced view of what transpired in the gathering, Beno offered a fascinating perspective on the synod but revealed nothing about cases ventilated therein.

Depite this paucity of information, three quarrels emerge with some clarity through papal letters issued soon after the council. These episodes, involving the chuches of Grenoble and Vienne, Liège, and Noyon, will be considered in alphabetical order. In each instance Piacenza represented only one moment in a longer history that cannot be delineated here.

---

[65] See, e.g., IP 6. 1. 393, no. *1, for mention of a papal privilege issued for the Cluniac priory of S. Giacomo di Pontida that is not listed in JL, and is dated by Kehr only to the year 1095. Cf. Spinelli, 'Urbano' 554–58, and 556 for a list of monastic privileges for Italian houses granted by Urban while the pope was at Piacenza. For papal documents issued at the time, see also the information in Santifaller, 'Elenco', esp. 436–73 (cf. 797–801). For a spurious papal indulgence for the church of S. Maria di Campagnola e S. Vittoria, supposedly proclaimed at Piacenza after the synod, see IP 5. 486–87, no. +1; but cf. Racine, 'Santa Maria' 22–23, who seemed to accept the indulgence as genuine.

[66] For a useful survey of information about cases in papal councils of the time, see Gresser, *Synoden*, supplemented inter al. by Somerville, 'Society' 82ff, Somerville-Kuttner, *Pope Urban* 245ff., and Blumenthal, *Early Councils*. The historian of eleventh/early-twelfth-century synods can envy what in comparison seems to be a flood of procedural information for councils in Antiquity: see, e.g., Ramsey MacMullen, *Voting About God in Early Church Councils* (New Haven 2006).

[67] For Reichenau see GP 2. 1. 157, nos. *26–*27; for Arnulf see GP 1. 19, no. *46, and IP 6. 53, no. *125.

Grenoble–Vienne

Urban II's letter addressed to Archbishop Guy of Vienne, dated March 12, recounted a complaint that was lodged at the council, 'in an open hearing' (*in communi audientia*), by Bishop Hugh of Grenoble against his metropolitan Guy.[68] The dispute was over possession of the territory (*pagus*) of Sermorens.[69] The partisan Grenoble cartulary recounted Guy's trickery in attempting to keep Hugh away from Piacenza. Only at the last minute did the bishop realize his error in trusting the archbishop, and finally grasped Guy's scheme to sidetrack him and to prevent a conciliar discussion about Sermorens before Urban II. With a headlong dash from the Rhône valley to Italy, Hugh arrived at Piacenza on the final day but nonetheless managed to present his case, according to the Grenoble cartulary, 'before the pope and the full council' (*coram papa et universo concilio*). Papal justice was on the bishop's side. Urban told Guy that Sermorens was long known to belong to Grenoble and was claimed by Vienne through the deceit of a false privilege, a deception that the pontiff branded as illegal and having no force of law. The *pagus* was confirmed to Hugh 'by synodal judgment' (*synodali judicio*).[70] Archbishop Guy would have been present through most of the council, but whether he remained to hear Hugh's accusation is uncertain, and perhaps he removed himself from the line of fire during the closing sessions.[71]

Liège

The situation of the church at Liège in the mid-1090s was complicated. Bishop Henry died in 1091. He was succeeded by a cleric named Otbert, appointed by Emperor Henry IV and consecrated in 1092 at Cologne. But Otbert was accused of being a simoniac, and dissent about his elevation roiled Liège for years. Among the bishop's opponents was Abbot Berengar of the Benedictine house of St.-Laurent, whom Otbert deposed.[72] Berengar sought refuge at Reims, and the dispute had came to Urban II's attention by the time of the Council of Piacenza, after which he

---

[68] JL 5548 (GaP 3. 1. 141, no. 195).

[69] For background on Sermorens and for the dispute, see Patrick J. Geary, *Aristocracy in Provence: the Rhône Basin at the Dawn of the Carolingian Age* (Monographien zur Geschichte des Mittelalter 31; Stuttgart 1985) 15 ff., GaP 3. 1. 136 ff. (nos. *183 ff.) and esp. Alfons Becker and Dietrich Lohrmann, 'Ein erschlichenes Privileg Papst Urbans II. für Erzbischof Guido von Vienne (Calixt II.)', DA 38 (1982) 71–73. The account from the Grenoble cartulary was edited by Jules Marion, *Cartulaires de la église cathédrale de Grenoble, dits Cartulaires de Saint-Hugues* (Collection de documents inédits sur l'histoire de France, Histoire politique 9; Paris 1869); see especially 56 (cf. *Recueil des historiens des Gaules et de la France* 14 [Paris 1877] 759–60).

[70] JL 5548 (GaP 3. 1. 141, no. 195): *Illam igitur subreptionem, per quam res sub querimonia positas quasi per privilegium vindicas, nos irritam esse, et vires nullas obtinere decernimus.*

[71] The controversy surrounding Sermorens was longstanding: see Beate Schilling, *Guido von Vienne-Papst Calixt II*. (MGH Schriften 45; Hannover 1998) 127–28, and 650, nos. 30 ff., and Mary Stroll, *Calixtus II (1119–1124): A Pope Born to Rule* (Studies in the History of Christian Traditions 116; Leiden 2004) 15 ff.; cf. Somerville, 'Society' 86, no. 11.

[72] Fliche, *Réforme* 263, called Berengar 'le pieux Bérenger'. For the situation at Liège see, inter al., ibid. 214, and 263–64, based on the fundamental work of Alfred Cauchie, *La querelle des investitures dans les diocèses de Liège et Cambrai* 2 (Louvain 1891) 7 ff. See also Maria Lodovica Arduini, *Non fabula sed res: Politische Dictung und dramatische Gestalt in den Carmina Ruperts von Deutz* (Temi e testi 33; Rome 1985), esp. 75 ff, and Kretzschmar, *Alger* 23–27.

issued a long letter to Berengar. The pontiff lauded the abbot's rectitude – 'We give thanks for you to God ... who illuminated the eyes of your mind for apprehending truth in this evil time when nearly all of France lies sunk under the gloom of error' – and also noted Otbert's condemnation:[73]

> Recently condemned by a decree of a council that we held, we already had excommunicated him by the authority of God, blessed Peter, and the holy Roman Church, to which under God's protection I serve; we had cursed him, along with his Wibert, because he is a simoniac...

Bishop Otbert had a long career, dying in 1119, and after the death of Henry IV in 1106 was reconciled with Paschal II. Pope Urban's notice of Otbert's synodal condemnation offers almost nothing about procedure, and because the name of the council in question was not provided, JL dated the letter only within the interval 1094–95.[74] Yet the assembly to which Urban referred must be Piacenza. The centerpiece of its legislation was a series of carefully formulated regulations that condemned simoniacs and schismatics. Otbert, guilty on both counts, was condemned *ipso facto* according to those decrees (see Chapters 4–5 for a new edition of the canons and a commentary on them). Whether or not the pope added a specific excommunication against him by name is unclear.

The wording in JL 5538 about Otbert's condemnation in one of Urban's synods is intricate.[75] The text could be read to imply a single excommunication, that is, Urban damned and excommunicated Otbert by a recent synodal decree, based on transcendent authorities, because he is a simoniac. But another, more nuanced, reading suggests that the passage is speaking of two condemnations, translating *iam* with the perfect tense *excommunicavimus* as 'we already had excomminicated' (as given above). If that possibility is adopted, the question arises as to when and where that earlier, pre-Piacenza excommunication of Otbert occurred. The matter remains uncertain, but one possibility can be suggested. Abbot Berengar was among those present on March 27, 1093, for the consecration of Bishop Poppo of Metz by the papal legate Hugh of Lyon.[76] Poppo's installation was accompanied by a

---

[73] JL 5538: *Gratias agimus Deo pro vobis ... qui in hoc malo tempore, cum omnis pene Gallia erroris caligine jacet immersa, oculos mentis vestrae ad cognitionem veritatis illuminavit. ... Quem [Otbertum] nos ex decreto concilii a nobis nuper acti damnatum auctoritate Dei et B. Petri, et sanctae Romanae Ecclesiae, cui auspice Deo deservio, jam excommunicavimus, et cum suo Wiberto ... portionem maledicitonis ei dedimus pro eo quod Simoniacus est. ...* The use of the first-person singular in Urban II's letter merits fuller study: cf. Somerville–Kuttner, *Pope Urban* 44. For the case of Otbert of Liège, see also Somerville, 'Society' 89–90.

[74] Perhaps the absence of the council's name indicated that, for a northern audience, 'Piacenza' per se meant little; what mattered was papal censure. Whether Abbot Berengar actually was at Piacenza is another matter; the text is not clear on that.

[75] The text is printed from PL 151. 397. The manuscript tradition for the letter has not been investigated.

[76] For Poppo, see Bernold, *Chronicon*, ed. Pertz 456 / ed. Robinson 501–2, and Franz-Reiner Erkens, *Die Trierer Kirchenprovinz im Investiturstreit* (Passauer Historische Forschungen 4; Cologne 1987) 168–85. It is surprising that no modern monograph has been published on Hugh of Lyon, although since 1973 three unpublished doctoral dissertations have been devoted to him: cf. Kriston Rennie, 'Hugh of Die and the Legatine Office under Gregory VII', *Revue d'histoire ecclésiastique* 103 (2008) 27–49, especially n. 3.

guarantee on Archbishop Hugh's part of papal support at Liège against Otbert, coupled with a warning against being in communion with him.[77] Excommunication is not mentioned, but as papal legate in Germany in 1085, Cardinal Odo of Ostia (the future Urban II) excommunicated a number of Henry IV's prelates.[78] Perhaps Otbert of Liège was hit with a similar legatine condemnation by Urban II's legate Hugh of Lyon in March, 1093.

Noyon
Three days before issuing his letter censuring Guy of Vienne, Pope Urban wrote to the clergy and people of Noyon about their bishop Radbod II.[79] He stated that in the council held at Piacenza no one had made accusations against Radbod. The pope referred to him as 'our brother' (*fratrem nostrum*), thus confirming that he too found no fault. Radbod served as bishop of Noyon for thirty years, from 1068 until his death in 1098. His career is at times murky, but in the 1070s he seemed to have been a confessed simoniac and was first censured by Pope Gregory VII's legate Hugh of Die (archbishop of Lyon from 1083–1106), and then by Pope Gregory himself. At Piacenza Urban II reinstated him to Noyon.[80] Information about that process at Piacenza is meagre to say the least, enough just to show that something of the sort occurred. Presumably Radbod came before the assembly as a penitent, and after questioning was given a 'clean slate' and reinstated by Pope Urban.[81]

PIACENZA AND THE FIRST CRUSADE

Bernold of Constance reported that at Piacenza Pope Urban received emissaries from Constantinople who were seeking recruits on behalf of Emperor Alexius I for his campaign against the Turks (*contra paganos*). These legates implored the pontiff and all the 'faithful of Christ' (*omnesque Christi fideles*) to provide assistance for defense 'of the holy church' (*sanctae aecclesiae*), which the 'pagans' had devastated up to the walls of Constantinople. Bernold continued and wrote that Urban urged many 'to promise under oath' (*iureiurando promitterent*) that they would go to the aid of Alexius.[82]

---

[77] Kretzschmar, *Alger* 25, n. 13, and 37, n. 61.
[78] Kuttner, 'Doctrine', Appendix I, and cf. ibid., Appendix IV, for the case of Poppo of Metz.
[79] JL 5544.
[80] See Dietrich Lohrmann, *Papsturkunden in Frankreich*, Neue Folge 7 (Anhandlungen Göttingen, phil.-hist. Klasse, dritte Folge, 95; Göttingen 1976) 96, Oliver Guyotjeannin, *Episcopus et comes: Affirmation et déclin de la seigneurie épiscopale au nord du royaume de France* (Mémoires et documents 30; Geneva 1987) 176–77, and Kéry, *Arras* passim.
[81] The acta of Urban II's Councils of Melfi and Clermont seem to contain no comparable situation, but a fuller study of his other synods could yield a parallel. Cf. mention of the situation of Bishop Arnulf of Cremona in Gregory VII's Lenten Council of 1078: IP 6. 1. 264, no. *3 (cf. Caspar, *Register* 369).
[82] Bernold, *Chronicon*, ed. Pertz 461 / ed. Robinson 520. See Becker, *Papst Urban* 2. 177, and especially 184 ff. The first section of Frederic Duncalf's chapter on Urban II's Councils of Piacenza and Clermont in Marshall Baldwin (ed.), *A History of the Crusades, I: The First Hundred Years* (Philadelphia

This episode is famous, and often cited in histories of the Crusades. It has been analyzed in some detail recently by Jonathan Shepard, who sees Bernold's comments as reflecting success on the part of Emperor Alexius by the mid-1090s in obtaining western military help.[83] There is no reason to question that Pope Urban allowed Byzantine agents to make such an appeal at Piacenza. There is no way of knowing when in the course of the synod they made their entrance, nor who they were, nor how they looked.[84] What Bernold described was one among other aspects of the council that he found noteworthy, such as the presence of Empress Praxedis, the *legatio* on behalf of King Philip of France, and the consecration of Archbishop Arnulf of Milan. These facets of the assembly might have recommended themselves not only because of their inherent interest, but also because Bernold saw them as confirmation of the wide-ranging importance of the synod that Pope Urban had convened at Piacenza.[85]

Following this introductory chapter the book will proceed as follows. Chapters 2–5 are devoted to Piacenza's legislative program. Chapter 2, 'Enactment, Circulation, and Survival of the Canons of Piacenza', is the longest in the volume. Its first part deals mainly with Bernold's *Chronicon* and the *Gesta Romanae aecclesiae*, looking at them especially in terms of the decrees; the second segment of the chapter will investigate how Piacenza's legislation has been preserved. Two appendices are added: the first contains the Latin text of Bernold's account of the gathering, with an English translation, and the second analyzes a provision attributed to Piacenza that survives outside the standard version of the canons. Chapter 3, 'Historiography', is based on information from the second section of the previous chapter and discusses the printed history of the decrees from the seventeenth to the late nineteenth century. Chapter 4, 'Transmission (with an edition & English translation of the canons)', explicates the need and the manuscript basis for a new edition. Chapter 5 offers a text-by-text commentary akin to that which accompanies the decrees of Melfi in Somerville-Kuttner, *Pope Urban*. Chapter 6, 'Legislation from the Councils of Urban II between Piacenza and Rome', opens with a recapitulation of the problem of 'the canons of Clermont', and then surveys what is known about the legislative traditions of Urban's later synods. His last council, held at St. Peter's in April 1099, is a gathering worthy of a separate study in its own right. The book closes with a short epilogue.

1958) 220–52, although out-of-date in several ways, offers a useful, general perspective on Piacenza and Bernold's report about the Greek agents' arrival in the synod.

[83] Jonathan Shepard, 'Cross-purposes: Alexius Comnenus and the First Crusade', in Jonathan Phillips (ed.), *The First Crusade: Origins and Impact* (Manchester 1997) 105–22, especially 113ff. Cf. Tyerman, *War* 61–2, 82–3.

[84] See the description of emissaries from Antioch who showed up at Paschal II's Council of Benevento in 1113: Rudolf Hiestand, *Papsturkunden für Kirchen im Heiligen Lande* (Vorarbeiten zum Oriens pontificius 3) (Göttingen Abhandlungen, dritte Folge 136; Göttingen 1985) 119–21 (no. 15).

[85] Tyerman, *War* 62, calls Piacenza 'the first international ecclesiastical assembly' of Urban II's pontificate.

2

Enactment, Circulation, and Survival of the Canons of Piacenza

ENACTMENT AND CIRCULATION

Introduction

The sketchy nature of evidence for the enactments from papal councils of the Gregorian period often has been noted.[1] The process by which popes of the time drafted and issued their decrees remains in many ways unclear. Urban II's Councils of Melfi, Benevento, and Troia seem to have promulgated canons over several days; the same is probably true in other instances such as Calixtus II's Lateran Council of 1123; and debate occurring on various questions in the early synods of Pope Urban was perhaps the basis for formal decrees.[2] Canons were commonly formulated as papal directives in the first-person plural (*decernimus*, *statuimus*, and so on), and their public recitation in synods is documented, for example, in the council at St. Peter's in 1099.[3] But caution is needed in drawing general conclusions about what happened in these gatherings, and the farrago of canonical traditions that erupted from the Council of Clermont impedes efforts to describe in a systematic manner how popes of the time transmitted legislation.[4] As Martin Brett writes, 'the tradition of the canons of Clermont makes it seem that they were never delivered at all in any formal sense'.[5]

As opposed to the chaos surrounding Clermont, two basic versions of the acts of Piacenza are known. An extended narrative account is woven into the *Chronicon* of Bernold of Constance, and lists exist, wholly or in part, of a set of decrees that circulated in manuscripts, in canon law collections, and in literary sources, namely the *Gesta Romanae acclesiae contra Hildebrandum*, Gerhoch of Reichersberg, and

---

[1] See, inter al., Blumenthal, 'Conciliar Canons', Brett, 'Lateran Council', and various works of Somerville listed in the bibliography.

[2] Somerville–Kuttner, *Pope Urban* 252–55 (cf. 240–45) for Melfi, and 302–5 for Benevento and Troia. For Lateran I, see Brett, 'Lateran Council' 23, n. 30.

[3] See Somerville-Kuttner, *Pope Urban* 268, for such first-person formulations at Melfi. Cf. Somerville, *Decreta* 20–41, and Laudage, 'Ritual' passim (321–22, for canons recited in synods). For Rome, see Chapter 6.

[4] For Clermont see Somerville, *Decreta*, passim, and 'Crusade and Canons', esp. 69 ff.; cf. Laudage, 'Ritual' 299–300, and 322–24.

[5] Brett, 'Lateran Council' 24.

the Annalista Saxo.[6] The lists of the canons sometimes are introduced by a preamble and usually include fourteen or fifteen provisions, plus in a few cases a notice about a liturgical development authorized at the synod.[7] Whether or not the preamble is attached, the text of the canons is similar and the decrees always are in the same order.[8] This rendition of the legislation, sometimes longer sometimes shorter, has been labelled the textus receptus.[9] Presenting the forms in which it survives and is diffused constitutes the major goal of the chapter that follows.

Bernold's narrative and the textus receptus share similarities, but each also contains things the other lacks. The *Chronicon* offers a wide-ranging discussion of Piacenza and includes that descriptive material that is missing from the textus receptus. Both of these accounts have been considered important witnesses for the council, but Bernold's has been especially valued. It was written within half a decade of the gathering, and obviously rests on testimony from eye-witnesses. Ludwig Weiland assumed that Bernold had the 'full acts of this council in front of him', from which he made an editorial selection, and that the textus receptus, which Weiland supposed existed in two or three versions (a conclusion seemingly based on the number of canons found in various copies), should be regarded as 'an abbreviation of the acts'.[10] These points will be considered in the section on Bernold below.

Gesta Romanae aecclesiae contra Hildebrandum

In addition to Bernold's *Chronicon* there is another source for Piacenza that was written between 1095 and the end of the eleventh century. The eighth tract in the *Gesta Romanae aecclesiae contra Hildebrandum* deals with the legislation from Piacenza, and includes information that claims to offer eye-witness glimpses into events at the synod. The *Gesta* are a set of polemical attacks against Gregory VII and Urban II written either by Beno, cardinal-priest of SS. Martino e Silvestro, or by someone else in the same circle of Roman dissonants. These treatises probably were published around the time of the council held against Urban II at Rome in summer

---

[6] Bernold, *Chronicon*, ed. Pertz 461–63 / ed. Robinson 518–22. For a very brief description of these two versions of the decrees, see Gossman, *Pope Urban* 3.

[7] A word is in order about the numbering of the canons. Decrees from councils at the time often are not numbered in manuscripts, and divisions for the same legislation often vary. The numbers assigned to canons here and throughout, including in the edition in Chapter 4, are editorial, following for convenience the enumeration in Weiland's edition.

[8] A sequence broken only by the selection of canons of Piacenza in Gerhoch of Reichersberg: see below in this chapter in *Survival*, Narrative, Sect. c.

[9] Somerville, 'Presentation' 196.

[10] Weiland 560: 'E Gestis huius concilii plura refert Bernoldus Constantiensis, qui ea integra ante oculos habuisse videtur, at canones eius suo modo variavit. Ea, que nobis in codicibus servata sunt, pro Breviario tantum Gestorum habenda sunt, quod in duobus vel fortasse tribus recensionibus ferebatur.' That Bernold had before him a full record of the acts of Piacenza was also assumed earlier by von Giesebrecht, on the basis of Bernold's access to a memorandum of a meeting after the council between Urban II and Henry IV's son, King Conrad. For this memo see below under Bernold, and Wilhelm von Giesebrecht, *Geschichte der deutsche Kaiserzeit*, 4th edn., 3 (Braunschweig 1876) 1178. Cf. Gerold Meyer von Knonau, *Jahrbücher des Deutschen Reiches unter Heinrich IV. und Heinrich V.* 4 (Leipzig 1893) 442, n. 6, for a similar view.

1098.¹¹ Tract viii, sarcastically labelled *decreta Turbani*, deals with Urban's canons and letters. The first texts given therein derive from Piacenza's textus receptus, that is, the synodal preamble and cc. 1–12, all prefaced by what could be taken as a general prologue for his treatise on the part of the author of the *Gesta*.

Piacenza's synodal preamble in the textus receptus speaks of debate during the conciliar sessions, and of formal approval for the legislation at the end. The text described 'A great inquiry [that] took place about those who bought churches and prebends, and about those who were ordained in the Wibertine schism', and succinctly concludes with a statement that 'Finally, on the seventh day [March 7] after lengthy deliberation, these chapters were presented and approved with the assent of the whole council'.¹² But what really happened? The *Gesta's* introduction to its presentation of the textus receptus tells a different story.¹³

> Here begin the decrees of 'Turbanus', in which he damned those things that are legitimate and confirmed those that are heretical. When these decrees were written down after the Council of Piacenza, secretly, at night, stars fell from the sky... to express how much illegality was committed.¹⁴

The preamble of the textus receptus and cc. 1–12 follow, in a rendition not wildly at variance with other witnesses, and after noting that these texts were burnt in protest at the synod in 1098 the author of the tract ridiculed the conciliar preamble, and in the process offered his own version of what occurred.

> How could decrees fabricated secretly under the name of the Council of Piacenza, long after the council was over, have been recited and approved by the assent of all in the

---

¹¹ For the manuscripts of the *Gesta* see below under *Survival*, Narrative, Sect. a; see also Somerville–Kuttner, *Pope Urban* 136 and 199, with bibliography; and Robinson, *Authority* 45 ff., and *Henry* 227, with bibliography, esp. for Beno. For the date and for the Roman synod see, inter al., Francke's introductory comments in MGH Lib. de lite 2. 366; Carl Erdmann, 'Gesta Romanae ecclesiae contra Hildebrandum', ZRG, Kan. Abt. 26 (1937) 433–36; Ziese, *Wibert* 242 and 247; Stoller, 'Councils' 315–21; and Gresser, *Synoden* 317–21. Joseph Schnitzer, *Gesta Romanae Ecclesiae des Kardinals Beno und andere Streitschriften der schismatischen Kardinäle wider Gregor VII.* (Historische Abhandlungen aus dem Münchener Seminar herausgegeben von Dr. K. Th. Heigel und Dr. H. Grauert 2; Bamberg 1892), did not have access to Kuno Francke's ed. of the *Gesta* in the MGH, Lib. de lite 2.

¹² Weiland 561: *Facta est autem magna consultatio de his, qui aecclesias vel praebendas emerant, sed et de his, qui in scismate Wibertino fuerant ordinati.... Septimo tandem die post tractationem diutinam haec sunt capitula prolata et assensu totius concilii approbata.* Cf. Saltet, *Réordinations* 247 ff. For the question of whether or not this was the last day of the council, and for the location of the sessions, see the previous Chapter, Sect. iii.

¹³ *Gesta Romanae aecclesiae*, ed. Francke, MGH Lib. de lite 2. 408: *Incipiunt decreta Turbani, in quibus ea quae sunt legitima dampnavit et quae sunt heretica confirmavit. Cum haec post concilium Placentinum noctu occulte scriberentur, factus est casus stellarum... ut exprimeretur, quantum nefas committeretur.* The *Gesta's* account of Piacenza has received very little attention, but see Stoller, 'Councils' 317–21, and Gresser, *Synoden* 302, and 319.

¹⁴ On a widely reported meteor shower that was seen in Western Europe on the night of April 4–5, 1095, see MGH Lib. de lite 2. 408, n. 7, plus the sources collected by Hagenmeyer, *Chronologie* 7. Cf. Jonathan Riley-Smith, *The First Crusade and the Idea of Crusading* (Philadelphia 1986) 33, and the *Vita* of Urban II in the *Liber pontificalis*, ed. Louis Duchesne, *Le Liber pontificalis* 2 (Bibliothèque des Écoles françaises d'Athènes & de Rome, 2e sér. 3; Paris 1892) 293: *Eodem vero anno quo iter ad eripiendum sepulchrum Domini gens illa arripuit, stellae vise sunt de caelo cecidisse.*

council? Under the name of the same council, for deception of the world [and] for subversion of the catholic faith, these decrees were spread throughout diverse parts of the world by a new method of betrayal. On the surface they have the appearance of honey and mercy, but on the inside they choke humanity with the poison of error. How, I ask, were those decrees which 'Turbanus' presented by novel arrogance with empty words alone[15] approved in the council? Publicly, in the very same hour, in the very same place, they were damned by the voice of the faithful, aroused to such an extent that 'Turbanus' barely avoided their violence and rage. I say that the faithful were so stirred up that they compelled him three times to condemn a statement of error which he had presumed to offer with words alone.[16]

The invective in these remarks clouds their credibility, and Fliche and Brett question their accuracy.[17] No other sources are at hand to control the details and to help in extracting whatever kernel of accuracy underlies the tirade against Pope Urban. Bernold of Constance reported a formal sentence of anathema, 'with burning candles', issued at Piacenza against Wibert of Ravenna and all his accomplices.[18] How does that formal condemnation of the schismatics fit with the *Gesta's* description of 'the faithful' rejecting Urban's decrees? No clear answer is possible.

What is clear, however, is how fundamentally Piacenza's decrees rankled Urban's opponents, and this displeasure is intensified in the *Gesta's* attempt, brimming with sarcasm, to refute them.[19]

... who can admire in sufficient measure the blasphemies of 'Turbanus', who condemns sacred laws and perversely attacks those ordained without simony by simoniacs?... A new order, a new dispensation, a new form of power – on the

---

[15] The Latin *cum solis et nudis verbis* could mean that what Urban proposed was simply announced, without supporting authorities.
[16] *Gesta Romanae aecclesiae*, ed. Francke, MGH Lib. de lite 2.410: *Quomodo in concilio sunt recitata vel assensu omnium comprobata, que longe post peractum concilium furtim sub nomine Placentini concilii fabricata, sub nomine eiusdem concilii ad deceptionem orbis, ad subversionem fidei catholicae novo prodicionis genere per diversas mundi partes sunt diffusa, in facie quidem speciem mellis et misericordiae habentia, interius vero erroris veneno humanum genus subfocantia? Quomodo, inquam, in concilio sunt comprobata, quae, cum solis et nudis verbis Turbanus nova presumptione protulisset, ore fidelium ibidem publice eadem hora sunt dampnata, fidelibus adeo commotis, ut vix evaderet Turbanus eorum impetus et iras? fidelibus, inquam, ita concitatis, ut cogerent eum ter condempnare sententiam erroris, quam solis verbis proferre presumpserat.*
[17] Fliche, *Réforme* 265, n. 7, and Brett, 'Lateran Council' 23–4.
[18] Bernold, *Chronicon*, ed. Pertz 462 / ed. Robinson 521: *sententia anathematis sinodali iudicio cum ardentibus candelis*. For a similar ritual of excommunication at Calixtus II's Council of Reims in 1119, see Hesso, *Relatio*, ed. Wattenbach 28. For early-medieval use of candles in ceremonies of excommunication, see Roger E. Reynolds, 'Rites of separation and reconciliation in the early Middle Ages', *Segni e Riti nella Chiesa Altomedievale Occidentale* (Settimane di studio del Centro italiano di studi sull'alto medioevo 33; Spoleto 1987) 414–15 (repr. in id., *Law and Liturgy in the Latin Church, 5th-12th Centuries* [Variorum Collected Study Series CS457; Aldershot 1994]); and cf. Cyrille Vogel and Reinhard Elze, *Le Pontifical Romano-Germanique du Xe siècle* 1 (Studi e testi 226; Vatican City 1963) 310–11, Ordo lxxxv.
[19] *Gesta Romanae aecclesiae*, ed. Francke, MGH Lib. de lite 2. 410–11: *... quis satius admirari potest blasphemias Turbani, sacras leges condempnantis, ordinatos non symoniace a symoniacis perverse abdicantis?... Novus ordo, nova discretio, novum genus potentiae, immo nova perversitas, nova canonici iudicii perver sio!... Spiritu erroris omnia, Turbane, turbasti in quantum potuisti.... Haec testantur maiora concilia et doctores orthodoxi, contra quos spiritu avaritiae delatrans, Turbane, os tuum posuisti in coelum.*

contrary, a new perversity, a new perversion of canonical judgment!... By the spirit of error, 'Turbanus', you confused everything as much as you could.... Railing against the great councils and the orthodox teachers who testify to these things, 'Turbanus', with the spirit of greed 'you set your mouth against heaven'.[20]

Notwithstanding the bombast, can it be assumed that the *Gesta* include some truth about Piacenza? They were composed very shortly after the event, and gross fabrication about a gathering attended by many important people who were still alive would have been poor strategy, even in a polemic.

Two key points emerge. In the first place, both the preamble to the textus receptus and the *Gesta* indicated a lively debate in the council over the crucial issues of simoniacal and schismatic ordinations. But in the *Gesta* Urban is depicted as very much on the defensive, compelled to admit three times that statements he put forth without convincing support from the tradition were wrong. What the pope's arguments were and who his opponents were is not stated. Secondly, the *Gesta* imply that the process described at the end of the synodal preamble – that of the decrees being presented and unanimously approved in the assembly, 'on the seventh day after lengthy deliberation' – did not occur. Rather, Urban is accused of fabricating the legislation in secret after the synod ended, and then circulating it in the name of the council.

No information is available beyond the preamble of the textus receptus and the polemic of the *Gesta* about how Urban and his advisers formulated and presented Piacenza's decrees. If, however, the council's participants, or some group of them, balked at what was set forth and were even able to make Urban backtrack in some way, it would not be the first or the last time that debate and disagreement took place in a church council, or even when an uproar forced a pope's hand. In the face of stiff opposition at Reims in 1119, for example, Calixtus II altered a decree against lay investiture. In an earlier case, Peter Damiani reported that Leo IX faced stormy protest in one of his synods when he invalidated simoniacal ordinations, and consequently retreated on the matter.[21] Furthermore, although no retraction of a decree is mentioned, the summary in Gregory VII's papal Register of the acts of the Lenten Synod of 1079 reveals an intense struggle over the doctrine of the Eucharist.[22] As noted above, debates occurred in the early synods of Urban II. For Melfi in 1089 the following is noted (ante c. 11): 'At length on the sixth day, after it was debated more extensively about the customs of the church, he [Urban] added...' And ante c. 1 of Troia: 'finally, with everyone consenting, this chapter was

---

[20] The author is grateful to Carmela Vircillo Franklin for pointing out that the end of this passage derives from Ps. 73[72]:9.
[21] Hesso, *Relatio*, ed. Wattenbach 27; Kurt Reindel, *Die Briefe des Petrus Damiani* 1 (MGH, Die Briefe der Deutschen Kaiserzeit 4.1; Munich 1983) no. 40, 498–99. See also Somerville, 'Reims' 42–3, and the discussion in Laudage, 'Ritual' 331 (although Peter Damiani's text said nothing about a decision being deferred overnight, and the council in question seems not to be Vercelli but Rome, 1049).
[22] Caspar, *Register* 425–26.

promulgated'.[23] These examples suggest that the *Gesta's* description of Urban under attack at Piacenza may be simply an exaggerated portrayal of the sort of give and take that is seen elsewhere in councils of the time.

What of the charge that the canons were disseminated 'long after the council was over'? One instance can be cited of a situation a few years after the Council of Piacenza in which decisions were held out of circulation for revision after a synod ended. Anselm of Canterbury was reluctant to distribute a final text of the rulings from his Council of Westminister in 1102 because they were proposed too hastily, the assembly being unable to treat them thoroughly. He felt that changes might be needed, and that the bishops who attended should be consulted before a final version was sent to the churches throughout England.[24] In denouncing how the canons from Piacenza were issued, perhaps the *Gesta* vilified a process of revision similar to that contemplated by Anselm, although it seems unlikely that Urban planned to reconvene any significant number of the bishops who had been at Piazenza to consider a revised text.[25]

The *Gesta* complain that the canons were widely distributed 'by a new method of betrayal', *novo prodicionis genere* – perhaps a pun was intended at that point, with *prodicionis/productionis*. Furthermore, the statement that the decrees were drawn up after the Council of Piacenza ended could mean that something different had been submitted for approval at the synod. Bernold of Constance revealed that Piacenza dealt with an array of matters beyond those found in the *textus receptus*, and as will be suggested below, the assembly might have repromulgated legislation from Urban's earlier councils. But the fact that one slate of legislation survives in several dozen copies as 'the canons of Piacenza' implies that Urban and his chancery had a mechanism for spreading a single canonical program whose diffusion was considered crucial.[26] What that process of distribution might have been, and the degree to which the rulings, which thus could have been spread, resembled what was presented to the participants during the synodal sessions, remain open to question.[27] Perhaps the distinction was between a version of repromulgated canons

---

[23] Somerville–Kuttner, *Pope Urban* 255: *Sexto demum die postquam diutius est de moribus ecclesie disputatum adiunxit*; and 304: *tandem consentientibus omnibus hoc... capitulum promulgatum est*.
[24] See *Councils & Synods* 1.2. 668ff., esp. 670, and bibliography given there, and cf. Laudage, 'Ritual' 323–24.
[25] In fact, Anselm was unable to do so: see Somerville, *Decreta* 20.
[26] No process for producing copies of a unified canonical program is discernible for the acts of Melfi: see Somerville–Kuttner, *Pope Urban* 229. Cf. Leidulf Melve, *Inventing the Public Sphere: The Public Debate during the Investiture Contest (c. 1030–1122)* 1 (Brill's Studies in Intellectual History 154; Leiden 2007) 96–97 (but with a faulty reference to Somerville–Kuttner, *Pope Urban*).
[27] Cf. the discussion in Chapter 4, Transmission beyond Φ, Sect. d, on MS Vat. lat. 1208 (= MS V). It is possible that Urban disseminated the canons of Piacenza by means of letters addressed generally and in some way circulated to many places. None survives, but in the twelfth-century canon law collection found in Montecassino, Archivio dell'Abbazia, MS 216, p. 197, Piacenza c. 14 is inscribed *Urbanus papa omnibus Christianis*. (see Reynolds, *Collectio* 99). This is slender evidence, and the possible use of such letters by popes of the time is a foggy topic deserving further study. See, e.g., Brett, 'Lateran Council' 27, Somerville, 'Crusade and Canons' 70–4, and in Chapter 6 on Urban's Councils of Clermont and Tours. Could Countess Mathilda of Tuscany have facilitated a 'new method' of disseminating Urban's legislation? Her acta reveal that in April 1095 she was at Piadena, which is roughly halfway between Cremona and Mantua, certainly in the vicinity of Piacenza; even if she had no

from earlier synods that had come Bernold's way, and rulings that were new at Piacenza, that is, the possibly revised program in the textus receptus. Bernold's account thus may have combined both old and new elements, providing a narrative based on a canonical program from Piacenza that was different from the textus receptus but, nonetheless, not inaccurately labelled canons of Piacenza.

It is too simple to portray the schismatic cardinals as opposed to Urban II merely because they had forsaken the Gregorian camp in the 1080s. Aside from the obvious governmental issues that divided the Henricians and Urban's supporters, fundamental canonical and theological questions were at stake in the *Gesta*. Urban II's canons of Piacenza were only one important element in a debate that raised old questions about ordinations carried out by 'schismatics' and 'heretics', whoever they were deemed to be, and also about ecclesiastical power.[28] Urban's pontificate is riddled with decisions about orders and about the religious life that could be called into question by traditionalists, particularly those with a conception of papal authority different from that which was developing in the last years of the eleventh century among the reformers.[29] The diatribe in the *Gesta* notwithstanding, the widely circulated decrees of Piacenza represented crucial formulations in the canon law tradition, a story that begins to unfold in the second part of this chapter and develops in Chapters 4–6.

A final point involves the connection proposed in the *Gesta* between Piacenza's legislation and the widely reported meteor shower on April 4–5, 1095 ('When these decrees were written down... secretly, at night, stars fell from the sky'). The heavenly disapproval is rhetorical, but the following can be suggested. As discussed in Chapter 1, Dates, the council probably ended on March 7. Urban then remained at Piacenza throughout March and was still there on April 5, but by April 10 he had moved to Cremona.[30] With both the *Gesta's* opprobrious comment and the meteor shower in mind, it can be speculated that a revision of the canons was made within approximately a month of the council, at Piacenza or nearby. Certainly seven months later, by the time of the Council of Clermont in mid-November, a slate of legislation was attributed to Piacenza, and both Bernold and the Cencius–Baluze version of Clermont's canons reported its reiteration at Clermont.[31] In fact the

---

clearly organized chancery, she was surrounded by 'giudici e cappellani', to quote Roberto Ferrara, who might have been recruited for papal scribal service. See Elke and Werner Goez, (eds.), *Die Urkunde und Briefe der Markgräfin Mathilde von Tuszien* (MGH Laienfürsten- und Dynastenurkunden der Kaiserzeit 2; Hannover 1998) 9–10 (for the quotation from Ferrara), 143–45 (no. 45), for Mathilda at Piadena, and 577 ('Platena') for Piadena's location.

[28] See the assessment of Robinson, *Authority* 175: 'The synodal decisions of Urban II and the propaganda of the papal party during these years, with their insistence on the invalidity of the ordinations of the *Wibertistae*, provided the rationale for the abandonment of the antipope and the anti-bishops by the imperial government'.

[29] See, e.g., in addition to Piacenza's canons, the texts in Somerville–Kuttner, *Pope Urban* 41 ff., JL 5383 (IP 3. 119, no. 2, and 320, no. 6), JL 5760 (see Somerville, 'Inspired Law'), etc. See also the discussion in Chapter 5, esp. about Piacenza cc. 10–12.

[30] See ante JL 5561.

[31] Bernold, *Chronicon*, ed. Pertz 463 / ed. Robinson 526; Somerville, *Decreta* 123.

Collectio Caesaraugustana includes several canons repeating nearly verbatim decrees of Piacenza from the textus receptus but ascribed to Clermont.[32]

Bernold of Constance

The *Gesta* and Bernold's *Chronicon* are the earliest sources for Piacenza. Bernold (+1100), a cleric at Constance and later a monk of St. Blasien and finally of Allerheiligen at Schaffhausen, was an important thinker and prolific writer in support of the reforming popes, 'der bedeutendste süddeutsche Kanonist im Investiturstreit', as he recently has been characterized.[33] He was interested in canon law, theology, liturgy, and history, and wrote several polemical tracts dealing with the great issues of his day. Ordained a priest in 1084 by Gregory VII's legate to Germany, Cardinal-bishop Odo of Ostia (from 1088 Pope Urban II), a day later Bernold would have seen Odo consecrate Gebhard of Zähringen as Bishop Gebhard III of Constance. The monk-scholar and his bishop developed a close working relationship, with Bernold, supplying Gebhard with opinions and writings on theological and canonical issues.[34]

The *Chronicon* reflects many of Bernold's interests, including study of church councils.[35] More space is devoted therein to Piacenza than to any of Urban II's other synods, but it is overwhelmingly unlikely that Bernold attended the gathering. At Bishop Gebhard's urging he composed a work, *De reordinatione vitanda et de salute parvulorum, qui ab excommunicatis baptizati sunt*, that served as a 'position paper' for the bishop with a view toward Piacenza.[36] The first of the questions handled in the tract is schismatic ordinations, but Bernold devoted a good amount of space to another matter that in his view also belonged on the synod's agenda: the question of children who were baptized *in excommunicatione*.[37] At both the beginning and the end of the *De reordinatione* he observed that he rushed to complete it, obviously with Gebhard's departure for Italy looming. Those would be odd statements if Bernold were going along, and his absence is virtually certain when, in the last line, he wished Bishop Gebhard Godspeed and a safe return *nobis cito*.[38]

What Bernold knew about the Council of Piacenza therefore must have come secondhand from Gebhard and others in the bishop's entourage. The degree to

---

[32] For the *Collectio Caesaraugustana*, see below under *Survival*, Canon Law, Sect. c.

[33] Bernold, *De excommunicatis*, ed. Stöckly and Jasper 2. For Bernold in general see the introduction to that volume, esp. pp. 2–9, on which the remarks to follow are based. Beyond the bibliography given there, of special importance are Robinson, 'Bernold', the introduction to Robinson's edition of the *Chronicon*, and for Bernold's conciliar ideas Hermann Josef Sieben, *Die Konzilsidee des lateinischen Mittelalters (847–1378)* (Paderborn 1984), Ch. 3, 'Konzilien in der Sicht des Gregorianers Bernold von Konstanz (+1100)'.

[34] Robinson, 'Bernold' 185.

[35] Bernold, *De excommunicatis*, ed. Stöckly and Jasper 6.

[36] Ibid. 9, refers to the work as 'eine Art Materialsammlung für Bischof Gebhard III. von Konstanz zur Synode von Piacenza'. The treatise is available, ed. Thaner, in MGH Lib. de lite, 2. 150–56.

[37] Ibid. 154–56.

[38] Ibid. 151 and 156.

which the recommendations made in the *De reordinatione*, although not adopted, were nonetheless influential at Piacenza is difficult to say. Based on the synodal preamble, Saltet rightly noted the lengthy debate that occurred about simony and schismatic orders (see the preceding section on the *Gesta*). He also believed that Bishop Gebhard presented his ideas about baptism of children in schism, although rightly observed that evidence is lacking.[39] Yet Saltet's views on Bernold's treatment of orders probably are too critical and anachronistic. Robinson's assessment is more nuanced, putting the monk from Constance back into the intellectual environment of the late eleventh century.[40] Even if Bernold's stance on baptism of children made no impact on the council's legislation, and even if his formulations about ordination were not followed, his 'position paper' drawn up for Gebhard could have helped to clarify issues that were on the table in March 1095, even potentially divisive questions that were hammered out *post tractationem diutinam*, as the synodal preamble put it.

The *Chronicon's* account of Piacenza will be printed below in Appendix I of this chapter, but a summary is in order here.[41] It opens with clear echoes of the preamble to the textus receptus;[42] but whereas that introduction states that the synod met out of doors on the first and third days, the *Chronicon* implies that all sessions were in the open air.[43] Bernold then describes the complaint *In hac sinodo* by Empress Praxedis against sexual abuses at the hand of her husband Emperor Henry IV. He offers comment, perhaps not fully accurate, about the situation of King Philip of France and Archibishop Hugh of Lyon,[44] and follows with mention of the arrival of the representatives from the Byzantine Emperor Alexius I seeking assistance against the Turks, noting Pope Urban's support of their plea (see the end of Chapter 1).

Those snapshots are supplemented by selections of the legislation ('Among others, however, these things were decided in that synod'. [*Haec autem inter alia in illa sinodo constituta sunt*]): who should be denied penance; that priests should offer penance only with the approval of their bishop; that communion be offered to those who, confessing properly, live among excommunicants 'in body alone and not in mind' (*solo corpore non mente*); portions of cc. 2–4 are cited from the textus receptus;[45] condemnation of 'the heresy of the Nicolaitans' (*heresis Nicholaitarum*) including a statement that laity should not receive ministry from incontinent clergy; condemnation of the eucharistic teaching of Berengar of Tours; notice about the solemn excommunication of Wibert of Ravenna and his supporters (see n. 18). A short digression on the large attendance precedes quotation of nearly

[39] Saltet, *Réordinations* 247–249, and see 249, n. 3.
[40] Bernold, *Chronicon*, ed. Robinson, 522, n. 582, and see also Robinson, 'Bernold', esp. 188.
[41] Bernold, *Chronicon*, ed. Pertz 461–63 / ed. Robinson 518–22, and the text will be printed from the latter. Cf. Hefele-Leclercq, *Histoire* 388–91.
[42] Bernold, *Chronicon*, ed. Robinson, 518 ff., uses different typefaces to make this point.
[43] Bernold: ... *ad quam sinodum multitudo tam innumerabilis confluxit, nequaquam in qualibet aecclesia illius loci posset comprehendi*. Piacenza, ed. Weiland, 561: *Et primo quidem ac tercio die in campo concilium sedit. Tantus enim convenerat populus, ut nulla eos aecclesia caperet*.
[44] See Bernold, *Chronicon*, ed. Robinson 520, n. 572, and Becker, *Papst Urban* 1. 195.
[45] See the edition in Chapter 4.

all of cc. 13–14 from the textus receptus. Bernold then concludes with information about specific participants, about Bishop Gebhard's part in the consecration of Archbishop Arnulf III of Milan, and about Pope Urban's consecration of Abbot Udalrich II of Reichenau and the interdiction to Udalrich of episcopal power over the clergy and people of the island of Reichenau (which belonged to the bishop of Constance).[46]

Other than pieces of cc. 2–4 and cc. 13–14, none of what Bernold included appears in the textus receptus. Similar to the *Gesta*, moreover, for some of his account Bernold's *Chronicon* is a unique source: for example, condemnation of Nicolatians and of the teachings of Berengar of Tours, and the arrival of the Byzantine legation. He paraphrased the synodal preamble of the textus receptus, but the edition in Chapter 4 shows that his version of cc. 2–4 and 13–14 contains few differences from that account. Although he chose to quote only a few decrees, it can be suggested, nonetheless, that Bernold probably knew the textus receptus in full. Immediately following the conciliar narrative, a report is inserted into the *Chronicon* describing a meeting at Cremona on April 10–15, between Pope Urban and Emperor Henry IV's son, King Conrad.[47] Bernold's description of that encounter incorporated segments of what has been considered a papal chancery *aide-mémoire*.[48] That memorandum is known to survive in two manuscripts, in both of which it follows the conciliar preamble and cc. 1–15 of the textus receptus of Piacenza. Those manuscripts – MSS Lh and Sta described below – were written in the very early twelfth century in southwestern Germany, and one of them can be placed specifically at the monastery of Zwiefalten in the diocese of Constance. It is impossible to establish a firm link between either book and Bernold;[49] but the presence of these codices in Bernold's vicinity, and the fact that the Cremona memo appears therein and nowhere else – except underlying the *Chronicon*'s report about the meeting between Urban and Conrad – suggests access not only to the memorandum but also to the texts with which it travelled, that is, Piacenza cc. 1–15.

What can be said, however, about the material on Piacenza in the *Chronicon* that is lacking in the textus receptus, much of which occurs nowhere else? Unless Bernold simply were assigning to the council decisions for which he wished the stamp of papal authority, regardless of whether they formed part of the synodal proceedings or not, Weiland's assumption that the textus receptus contains only part of the council's acts would seem correct. Somehow Bernold obtained a more detailed picture of aspects of the council, and Robinson assumes that he used papal documents 'fast wörtlich'.[50] Fliche also values Bernold's text highly, considering the

---

[46] See in Chapter 1, Conciliar Cases. See also Robinson's notes to Bernold's text, 522, n. 583, which indicate that Bernold is the sole source for Arnulf's consecration.
[47] Bernold, *Chronicon*, ed. Pertz 462 / ed. Robinson 523.
[48] See the discussion of MS Lh, and the references given.
[49] Prof. Herrad Spilling of the Württembergische Landesbibliothek in Stuttgart kindly informed the author that it is impossible to connect either manuscript to Constance, St. Blasien, or Allerheiligen at Schaffhausen.
[50] Robinson, 'Bernold' 187.

inclusion of decrees from the textus receptus a guarantee against the claim about their suspicious origin in 'ce pamphlet haineux et partial', meaning the *Gesta*.[51] How Bernold gained access to both the textus receptus and to some or all of the rest of the *acta* can only be guessed. His interest in councils could have been known to associates from Constance who attended Piacenza, and upon returning they might have put at his disposal decrees, notes, and even a copy of the Cremona memo. Thoroughly digested, this material then constituted the basis for the discussion of the council found in the *Chronicon*.[52]

Another perspective on Bernold's sources can be gained from considering the possibility, as suggested above, that at Piacenza Urban II repromulgated acts from his early synods in southern Italy. This process of repetition is well known and could have happened at Piacenza, although no evidence is known to this author that confirms it.[53] If it occurred, those who supplied Bernold with information certainly could have reported it. Urban's councils at Melfi, Benevento, and Troia were mentioned at appropriate points in the *Chronicon*, although none of their canons were listed.[54] Nonetheless, some of Bernold's information about Piacenza could be based on Urban's earlier synods, for example Melfi: clerical celibacy; proper confession and penance; those excommunicated by one bishop should not be received by others; Benevento: condemnation of the Guibertines; regulations for Lent.[55] Not everything about Piacenza that is unique in Bernold's report is readily explained thus, and even when the parallels are tolerably close, Bernold's formulations can differ in detail. For instance, Melfi cc. 1–3 on celibacy indicate nothing about a refusal on the part of the faithful to be served by incontinent clergy, and Melfi c. 16 is considerably longer than the comment on proper penance in the *Chronicon*.[56] If,

---

[51] Fliche, *La Réforme* 265, n. 7.
[52] See Somerville, *Decreta* 32–41, more recently id., 'Crusade and Canons' 70–74, and Blumenthal, 'Conciliar Canons' 372, on records that participants in councils might have obtained.
[53] See, e.g., Laudage, 'Ritual' 327; also Somerville-Kuttner, *Pope Urban* 202–3, for the decrees of Melfi repeated in later councils. The issue of the re-promulgation of Urban II's decrees is, however, complicated: cf. the discussion about the *Collectio Caesaraugustana* below under *Survival*, Canon Law Collections, Sect. c, and also the discussion at the end of Chapter 6 about the repetition of canons of Piacenza and Melfi at the Council of Rome in 1099.
[54] Bernold, *Chronicon*: for Melfi, ed. Pertz 449–50 / ed. Robinson 479; for Benevento, ed. Pertz 451 / ed. Robinson 484; for Troia, ed. Pertz 456 / ed. Robinson 502.
[55] Somerville–Kuttner, *Pope Urban* 253, for Melfi cc. 1c-3 (celibacy); 257, for cc. 15–16 (bishops, and penance); 303, for Benevento c. 4 on Lenten observances.
[56] Cf. Bernold, *Chronicon*, ed. Pertz 462 / ed. Robinson 520, with Melfi c. 16 (Somerville–Kuttner, *Pope Urban* 257). Bernold: . . . *constituta sunt, ut ad penitentiam nullo modo reciperentur, qui concubinas, vel odium ex corde vel quodlibet mortale peccatum dimittere nollent*. Melfi, c.16: *Sane quia inter cetera unum est quod sanctam maxime perturbat ecclesiam, false videlicet penitentie, confratres nostros episcopos et presbiteros admonemus ne falsis penitentiis laicorum animas decipi et in infernum pertrahi patiantur. Falsam autem penitentiam esse constat cum spretis pluribus de uno solo penitentia agitur, aut cum sic agitur de uno ut non discedatur de alio. Unde scriptum est, 'Qui totam legem observaverit, offendit autem in uno, factus est omnium reus', scilicet quantum ad vitam eternam. Sicut enim si peccatis esset omnibus involutus ita si in uno tantum maneat eterne vite ianuam non intrabit. Falsa etiam fit penitentia cum penitens ab officio, vel curiali vel negotiali, non recedit, quod sine peccatis agi ulla ratione non prevalet, aut si odium in corde gestetur, aut si non offenso cuilibet satis fiat, aut si non offendenti offensus indulgeat, aut si arma contra quis iustitiam gerat.*

therefore, Bernold used earlier synodal *acta* that were recycled at Piacenza, he no doubt edited them.[57]

If these speculations are feasible and if Bernold had access both to fifteen canons from the textus receptus and to repromulgated acts from Melfi, Benevento, and Troia, the question should not be why there is so much about Piacenza in the *Chronicon* but rather why Bernold reported so little, and specifically so few decrees. The answer to that question can only be a guess about a speculation. Perhaps the actual texts from Urban's earlier conciliar legislations were not transmitted but only a sense of the regulations. Bernold is known to have selected for his chronicle material on subjects that interested him personally, and items that might have special relevance for the church in Constance.[58] Consider, for example, the legatine synod that Bishop Gebhard convened at Constance in April 1094. The *Chronicon* inserted details of that gathering along with information about its legislation. The assembly condemned both incontinent priests and simoniacs, adding a statement to the effect that laity were barred from their ministrations (*ab eorum officio*). A decree about the Ember Days was also issued, and complaints were heard from Empress Praxedis about her husband Henry's abuse of her.[59]

All of these items are found in Bernold's report on Piacenza, including a boycott of the Nicolaitians, which might have resulted from the editing of Melfi's decrees on celibacy to produce a statement congruent with the 1094 synod. Furthermore, the *Chronicon*'s omission of segments of the textus receptus about ordination of schismatics and symoniacs could reveal Bernold's disappointment that Piacenza did not adopt his position on reordination as set forth in the *De reordinatione vitanda*.[60] Along the same lines, personal interest could explain his mention of condemnation of the *heresis Berengariana*. Bernold attended Gregory VII's Lenten Council of 1079 where Berengar was condemned in person for the last time, and he also wrote a treatise against Berengarian views on the eucharist.[61] Finally, although the appearance of the Greek ambassadors at Piacenza had no parallel in the legatine council of April 1094, nor in Urban's earlier synods, as far as is known, it made an impression on Bernold, and his interest in the development of the Crusades is clear in various entries inserted in the *Chronicon* between 1096 and 1100.[62]

Summary

A summary is in order at this point about the information on Piacenza in the *Gesta* and the *Chronicon*. The treatment of the council by both sources is both tantalizing

---

[57] Weiland 560, wrote that Bernold 'canones... suo modo variavit'.
[58] Bernold, *De excommunicatis*, ed. Stöckly and Jasper 6; cf. in Chapter 1, Conciliar Cases.
[59] Bernold, *Chronicon*, ed. Pertz 458 / ed. Robinson 511–12. For legislation about the Ember Days, see the commentary in Chapter 5; for Praxedis' charges, see Robinson, 'Bernold' 184, and *Henry* 289–90, where earlier bibliography is found.
[60] Robinson, 'Bernold' 188, and Bernold, *Chronicon*, ed. Robinson 522, n. 582.
[61] Ibid. 162, and 178.
[62] Bernold, *Chronicon*, ed. Pertz 464, 466–67 / ed. Robinson 527–29, 534–35 and 540; see also in Chapter 1, Piacenza-Crusade.

and frustrating. Each was composed soon after the synod by someone possessing extensive information about what happened there, and each is a witness to early use of the widely circulated record of the synodal acts that has been termed the textus receptus. The *Gesta* cited the preamble and cc. 1–12, and accused Pope Urban of manufacturing the canons in secret after the council ended and passing them off as decrees approved in the assembly. Trying to locate a historical core within the rhetoric of the *Gesta*, it was suggested that perhaps Urban revised the enactments presented at the synod before putting them into circulation. Based on what the *Gesta* wrote about 'falling stars', a revision might have been done within about a month of the synod, soon after a widely reported meteor shower was visible over western Europe in early April. Yet apart from the meteors and use of the textus receptus, the information about Piacenza in the *Gesta* cannot be corroborated.

To a lesser degree the same is true of much that Bernold wrote about the council. He was very interested in its details, had direct access to information from people who attended, and probably also was familiar with the textus receptus. What Bernold wrote about Piacenza that did not derive from that source could have come from participants' notes and memories, and from repromulgation of legislation from earlier synods. It is conceivable, and maybe even likely, that he also had at his disposal, as Weiland supposed, the now lost 'gesta integra' of Piacenza. Bernold's choices about what he included would have been influenced by his personal interests and those of the church in Constance, for example, the theology of Berengar of Tours, and the issues treated in the assembly of April 1094.[63] In conclusion, however, what can be said emphatically about much that both the *Gesta* and the *Chronicon* relate about Piacenza is 'non liquet'.

SURVIVAL

Introduction

The textus receptus of Piacenza's legislation is, completely or in part, found in a variety of medieval witnesses. Many of those canons also were reissued in Urban II's later synods at Clermont, at Rome in 1099, and perhaps elsewhere although the evidence for that is unclear. Repromulgation of the *capitula* from Piacenza at Clermont is well attested, although details are opaque, as will be discussed below under Canon Law Collections, Sect. c, and for the councils between 1096 and 1099 see Chapter 6. But setting aside questions about Piacenza and Urban's later synod, the survival of the decrees of March 1095, will be described under the following categories.

1. *Polycarpus Supplement* (= Φ).
2. Series of decrees appearing in twenty-eight manuscripts of various sorts, virtually all of which date from the twelfth century. Most of these texts begin

---

[63] Perhaps decisions from local synods might help to account for the proliferation of 'canons of Clermont': cf., e.g., Somerville, 'Crusade and Canons' 70.

with the long synodal prologue (*Anno Dominice incarnationis mxcv*...), as in Φ, followed by a set of canons, usually fourteen or fifteen items. Six of these manuscripts constitute a distinct subset that contains fourteen canons and replaces the formal prologue with a short inscription.

3. Two canons are quoted by Urban II himself in a letter sent to the clergy and people of Bologna within two to three years of Piacenza (JL 5694 [IP 5. 248–49, no. 14]).

4. Five canons appear in Gerhoch of Reichersberg's *Liber de simoniacis*, and five others are included in the chronicle known by the name of its compiler, the Annalista Saxo. Both works date from the mid-twelfth century.

5. Groups of decrees lacking the prologue are found within several twelfth-century canon law collections. If all known copies of these works were listed, however, including Gratian's *Decretum*, the number of exemplars would be huge and it would be impractical if not impossible to provide descriptions of them all. Thus only a selection of manuscripts of these compilations will be given.

The goal of the second part of this chapter is to identify the manuscripts and literary sources in which significant portions of the legislation of Piacenza survive. The result is more descriptive than analytic, accumulating and describing information rather than evaluating it, which will be the task in Chapter 4. In his edition of the canons published in 1893, Weiland grouped the manuscripts he used according to the number of canons that they contained. The same procedure will be adopted here for the lists of decrees calendared in *Polycarpus* Supplement, and Lists of Canons, below.

Polycarpus Supplement (Φ): preamble + fifteen canons + concluding notice on tenth preface for the mass

The well-known early twelfth-century canon law collection in eight books titled the *Polycarpus* remains unedited.[64] The work was assembled by a cleric named Gregory, about whose career little is known.[65] He was archdeacon at Lucca, and mentioned there for the last time in September 1109. Between 1109 and 1111 Gregory was made cardinal priest of the church of St. Grisogono, and died on November 30, 1113. He would have worked on the *Polycarpus* over a period of time, and the compilation was dedicated to Bishop Diego Gelmírez of Santiago de Compostela (1101–39/40). It is impossible to specify when the work was finished, although Cardinal Gregory was a supporter of Pope Paschal II and the project could have been completed after the tumultuous events at Ponte Mammolo in April 1111.

---

[64] See Horst, *Polycarpus* passim, Somerville–Kuttner, *Pope Urban* 187 ff., and Kéry, *Collections* 266–69; all, especially the latter, with bibliography. The edition of the *Polycarpus* by Carl Erdmann, supplemented by Horst Fuhrmann and Uwe Horst, is now available electronically through the MGH website.

[65] See Horst, *Polycarpus* 1 ff. for what follows.

Three manuscripts from the *Polycarpus*' 'French Manuscript Group' include near or at the end of the eighth book a noteworthy supplement that is an important source for papal councils of the time. It contains seven accounts in chronological order of synods of Urban II and Calixtus II: Melfi, Benevento, Troia, Piacenza, Clermont, Toulouse (1119), and the Lateran (1123).[66] In most cases these entries open with a formal preamble, followed by decrees occasionally interspersed with notices of conciliar acts and procedure. The accounts of Piacenza are written continuously, with ¶ signs indicating divisions which are consistent across the three manuscripts, with one exception.[67]

ΦPa = Paris, BNF, lat. 3881, fols. 182v-83r.

Twelfth-century, of uncertain origin, perhaps from southern France, northern Spain, or even Italy.[68] In the eighteenth century the book was at the monastery of St.-Sauveur in Aniane, whence Étienne Baluze edited several texts from the conciliar supplement.[69]

ΦVp = Città del Vaticano, BAV, Reg. lat. 987, fols. 165r-66r.

Twelfth- or early thirteenth-century, French and perhaps southern French, owned in the year 1647 by Alexandre Petau, then councillor to the Parlement of Paris.[70] This was Weiland's MS 3.

ΦVr = —————————————Reg. lat. 1026, fols. 209va-10rb.

Early thirteenth-century, French and perhaps southern French.[71]

ΦVa = —————————————Barb. lat. 860 (XVI.67), fols. 68r-71r (according to the modern enumeration at bottom of the pages).

ΦVa is a sixteenth-/seventeenth-century paper manuscript containing a *mélange* of information assembled by or for Antonio d'Aquino (+1627), to be used for the Roman Edition of the ecumenical councils. Conciliar material of Urban II belonging to the Φ tradition is included, and collations show that to an

---

[66] Ibid. 12, places these manuscripts in 'die französische Handschriftenfamilie'; Kéry, *Collections* 267, puts the Parisian book and Reg. lat. 987 in a 'Sub-Group of French Manuscripts'. See also Somerville–Kuttner, *Pope Urban* 187–88, esp. 187, n. 8, with further bibliography; ibid. 252–58, for Melfi, and 302–5, for Benevento and Troia. For Clermont, see Somerville, *Decreta* 121–24, and for Lateran I Leonardi in COD 188 ff., and Brett, 'Lateran Council' 19.

[67] See the apparatus criticus to the edition, 'ante c. ⟨8⟩', for a ¶ sign missing at that point in Φ Vr.

[68] Somerville-Kuttner, *Pope Urban* 188. The discussion there in n. 11 of Paul Fournier's belief that Φ Pa was Italian in origin should have included the fact that this opinion obliquely was carried over into Fournier-LeBras, *Histoire* 2. 169 (see Paul Fournier, 'Les deux recensions de la collection canonique romaine dite le "Polycarpus"', *Mélanges d'archéologie et d'histoire de l'École français de Rome* 37 [1918/19] 60, n. 4 [*Mélanges de droit canonique* 2. 708, n. 4]). Following the *Polycarpus*, MS Φ Pa contains, fols. 191–235, the *Liber sententiarum Magistri A*. See Paule Maas, *The Liber sententiarum Magistri A*. (Middeleeuwse Studies 11; Nijmegen 1995) 36–38, and passim, who provides a full description of the manuscript, and believes that it was written 'in a French hand' in the first half of the twelfth century.

[69] Somerville–Kuttner, *Pope Urban* 188.

[70] Opinions vary on the date of this book, e.g., ibid. 188, called it twelfth-century. See also Gassó and Batlle, *Epistulae* lv, although Fournier, 'Deux recensions' 58 (*Mélanges de droit canonique* 2. 706) said early thirteenth-century, as does Kéry, *Collections* 267. Fournier-LeBras, *Histoire* 2. 169, locate the home of all French manuscripts of the *Polycarpus* in southern France.

[71] Fournier, 'Deux recensions' 60 (*Mélanges de droit* 2.708); Kéry, *Collections* 267.

overwhelming degree of probability the source was ΦVr.[72] The text of Piacenza was written by a scribal hand, with variants and a few comments added in the margins by d'Aquino. ΦVa was Weiland's MS 4.[73]

ΦVb = ——————————————— Reg. lat 399, fol. 71r.

ΦVb is placed at the end of this section because although it is not related in a demonstrable way to the *Polycarpus*, its account of Piacenza derives from a source containing much or perhaps all of the material found in Φ. MS Vb is the *Liber provincialis* of Archbishop Hugo Guidardi of Benevento (1365–85), including the acts of a provincial synod held at Benevento in 1374. Other items on church discipline are added, and among them on fol. 71v-r (the page is misbound) is a set of excerpts from papal and Roman law texts dealing mainly with money and simony. Many of these selections appear to derive from the canonical collection of Cardinal Deusdedit (completed in the mid-1080s), but others are conciliar decrees from Urban II and Calixtus II, all of which occur in Φ. For Piacenza this includes an abbreviated form of the preface, cc. 1–2, 4–5, 13–15, and the concluding notice, and the text offers unique readings. Whether the compiler of ΦVb had access to all of the synods found in Φ is unknown because only a single leaf of the book survives and nothing from the Councils of Troia and Clermont is included. The evidence is slender and foggy, but ΦVb raises the possibility that Φ or something akin to Φ was known independently of the *Polycarpus*.[74]

Lists of Canons in Medieval Manuscripts beyond Φ

Apart from Φ, lists of decrees of Piacenza have been discovered, as indicated above in the introduction, in about thirty twelfth-century manuscripts. Some, in whole or in part, are canon law collections (as indeed is Φ, but this is treated throughout as a special case). The decision to place such manuscripts either here or in Canon Law Collections below, requires explanation. Categorizing canon law manuscripts prior to Gratian's *Decretum* is often not a straightforward matter. The short works, for example, in MSS O and Os (see below), and the compilation following Bonizo of Sutri's *Liber de Vita Christiana* in MS Fc, are seemingly unique legal/theological/liturgical *mélanges*, not organized in any readily discernible way and not attributable to any compiler. MS W offers further ambiguity. Does its account of Piacenza occur within a collection, that is, an expanded version of the *Collection in Seventy-Four*

---

[72] See Somerville–Kuttner, *Pope Urban* 189–90, for Φ Va, with bibliography. The Editio Romana of the ecumenical councils, *Concilia generalia Ecclesiae catholicae*, 4 vols., was published 1608–12. Collating the canons of Piacenza leaves little if any doubt about the dependence on Φ Vr. It cannot be proven that both Φ Va and Φ Vr did not depend on a third exemplar which would have been used by each, 400 years apart, yet the former's apparent misreading in the account of Piacenza of specific abbreviations in the latter suggests that this is even more unlikely than the discussion in Somerville–Kuttner, made it.

[73] The author is grateful to Consuelo Dutschke and to Susan L'Engle for information about Φ Va.

[74] For Φ Vb see Robert Somerville, 'Cardinal Deusdedit's *Collectio canonum* at Benevento', in Katherine G. Cushing and Richard F. Gyug (eds.), *Ritual, Text and Law: Studies in Medieval Canon Law and Liturgy Presented to Roger E. Reynolds*, (Aldershot 2004) 281–92.

Titles, or should it be deemed as one of a series of supplements to the compilation? Other examples could be given.[75]

In the canonical collections that will be listed in Canon Law Collections, below, blocks of decrees from Piacenza can be said to be integrated into the works in question. They are also generally prefaced by short inscriptions identifying Pope Urban, and sometimes but certainly not always the synod itself, for example, *Urbanus papa*, or *Urbanus papa ii. ex synodo Placentie habita* and *Urbanus in Placentino concilio*. The canons presented in this way are, therefore, highlighted as papal legal statements rather than elements in historico-canonical narratives that consist of synodal protocol plus decrees.[76] Placing manuscripts that contain Piacenza's legislation either in this category or below in Canon Law Collections might be seen as a fine distinction but it is not arbitrary, and has been determined by the form of conciliar records that originated close to the time of the assembly.[77]

The descriptions of manuscripts to follow contain information about date, origin, and general content. An effort has been made to describe how Piacenza's decrees are situated within the book in question, for example, what is found before and after. A complete list of all texts found in these codices has not been attempted, but an effort has been made to provide references where this information and further bibliography is available. The copies that were known to Weiland will be noted.

a) **Preamble + cc. 1–15**
B = Brussels, Bibliothèque royale Albert Ier, 495–505 (cat. 2494), fols. 16va-17rb.
B contains the *Collectio Dionysio-Hadriana* (18–207), written in northeastern France in the late ninth century, and was later amplified both at the beginning and end. Conceivably at some point it migrated to Italy, and it also passed through the hands of Rather of Verona/Liège, as a formula for excommunication written in his hand may be found within (204rb-204v). By the fifteenth century B was at the abbey of Orval in the diocese of Trier. Piacenza was added before the *Dionysio-Hadriana* in the twelfth century, as were, in a different hand, extracts on ordination and usury from the *Panormia* and the *Decretum* of Ivo of Chartres. The account of Piacenza is written continuously, with ¶ signs indicating divisions. This was Weiland's MS 5, but cited with an incorrect shelfmark.[78]

---

[75] e.g., MS Li, an expanded copy of the *Panormia* of Ivo of Chartres; and cf. the placement of the canons of the Council of Rome (1099) in the two manuscripts of the Thérouanne *Collection in Nine Books* (see Chapter 6).

[76] Gaudemet, 'Sources' 258, n. 10, noted that inscriptions for texts of papal councils that dropped the name of the synod focus attention 'sur la qualité de législateur du Pontife'.

[77] The term 'fine distinctions' is borrowed from Linda Fowler-Magerl, 'Fine Distinctions and the Transmission of Texts', ZRG, Kan. Abt. 83 (1997) 146–86. See also the perspicacious discussion by Martin Brett, 'Editions, Manuscripts and Readers in Some Pre-Gratian Collections', in Cushing and Gyug (eds.), *Ritual, Text and Law* 205–24 (see n. 74 above).

[78] B was described by Gérard Fransen, 'Les manuscrits canoniques de l'abbaye d'Orval', *Aureavallis: Mélanges historiques réunis à l'occasion du neuvième centenaire de l'abbaye d'Orval* (Liège 1975) 115–19, see also 111, who emphasized the need for a full paleographical study of all segments of this book. See now the details provided by Bernhard Bischoff, *Katalog der festländischen Handschriften des neunten Jahrhunderts* 1 (Wiesbaden 1998) 150, and id., *Anecdota Novissima: Texte des vierten bis sechzehnten*

Lh = London, BL, Harley 3001, fols. 80v-82r.

Lh, containing mainly texts of Gregory the Great, was written in southwestern Germany (but not at Zwiefalten; see the description below of Sta), in the first quarter of the twelfth century by five primary hands (a sixth, slightly later, added a chapter list at the beginning of the manuscript for the *Regula pastoralis*). Piacenza occurs toward the end of the manuscript, preceding a report about the meeting between Henry IV's son King Conrad and Pope Urban II at Cremona in mid-April 1095. The account of Piacenza is written continuously, with ¶ signs indicating divisions. This was Weiland's MS 1, whence he also edited the account of the papal-royal meeting, a text which has been considered an official chancery memorandum. See above in **Enactment**, at **n. 48**, for Bernold of Constance's knowledgement of the memorandum.[79]

Mid = Milan, Biblioteca Ambrosiana, A.46 inf., fols. 151r-v.

The core of Mid is an assembly of canonical texts and Frankish capitularies put together in the vicinity of Reims at the end of the ninth century. Texts in Mid and perhaps the book itself are important for the changing forms of the canonical collection of Anselm of Lucca in the late eleventh/early twelfth century. Mid thus may have been in northern Italy by the end of the eleventh century, and was at the Benedictine house of S. Dionigi in Milan perhaps no later than the twelfth. The entry for Piacenza is added in a twelfth-century hand in empty space on fol. 151. It is written continuously, with ¶ signs indicating divisions.[80]

O = Oxford, Bodleian Library, Canon. Pat. lat. 39 (S.C. 19025), fol. 86r-v (correct numbering at top of the pages).

O contains three separate manuscripts, all written in Italy and possibly central Italy in the mid-twelfth century or slightly later. Piacenza occurs in the last of the three, an assemblage of theological and canonical texts, and is preceded by texts of Gregory VII's Lenten Council of 1078 (85r, cc. 14–16 according to Caspar's edition), and followed by the acts of Paschal II's Lateran Council of 1112 (87r), all in different hands. The account of Piacenza is written continuously, without ¶ signs.[81]

Jahrhunderts (Quellen und Untersuchungen zum lateinischen Philologie des Mittelalters 7; Stuttgart 1984) 11. The author is also grateful to Hubert Mordek, *bonae memoriae*, for information about B.

[79] The memo and part of Piacenza'a conciliar protocol was edited from Lh (but with an incorrect shelfmark) by G.H. Pertz, (MGH Scriptores 8; Hannover 1848) 474, in a note to the edition of the *Chronicon* of Hugh of Flavigny. Weiland wrote (564), that the memorandum 'a curiali quodam scripta esse videtur'. Becker, *Papst Urban* 1. 20, n. 60, called the text a 'Registernotiz?' and at 134, n. 477, noted Bernold of Constance's description of the meeting between Urban and Conrad, 'offensichtlich in Kenntnis der gleichzeitigen kurialen Aktenaufzeichnung (Registernotiz?)': see Bernold, *Chronicon*, ed. Pertz 463 / ed. Robinson 523. Goez, 'Thronerbe' 33, n. 229, speaks of 'Der wie eine kuriale Registernotiz anmutende Bericht'; Robinson, *Henry* 291, calls the notice 'An official memorandum intended for the papal register'. The author is grateful to Michael Gullick and to Prof. Herrad Spilling for information about Lh.

[80] Mordek, *Bibliotheca* 233–40, gave a complete description of Mid. See also Kéry, *Collections* passim, but especially 178–79, and Klaus Zechiel-Eckes, 'Eine Mailänder Redaktion der Kirchenrechtssammlung Bischof Anselms II. von Lucca (1073–1086)', ZRG, Kan. Abt. 81 (1995) 137–47; 144 for S. Dionigi.

[81] The author is grateful to the late Albinia de la Mare for information on this book. See H.O. Coxe, *Catalogi codicum manuscriptorum Bibliothecae Bodleaianae* 3 (Oxford 1854) 308–9 (with old folio numbers). For the texts of Gregory VII see Caspar, *Register* 372–73, and for those of Paschal II see

Pm = Paris, BNF, lat. 3187, fols. 123r-24r.

Pm is an eleventh-/twelfth century book containing the late eleventh-century canonical *Collection in Four Books*, to which parts of two other manuscripts of the same age were added. Piacenza, lacking in c. 15 the last sentence, *Sique tamenprevideat.*, is the first among these additions, followed by a variety of canons that the modern catalogue equates to texts in Anselm of Lucca's collection. This may point to an Italian origin for the manuscript from which this fragment was drawn. The account of Piacenza is written in several paragraphs.[82]

Sta = Stuttgart, Württembergische Landesbibliothek, Cod. theol. et phil. 4°254, fols. 123r-25r.

Sta was written by five hands in the first quarter of the twelfth century at the Benedictine double monastery of Zwiefalten in the diocese of Constance. It contains the same set of texts as Lh through the *conventus* between Urban and Conrad, but then adds a version of JL 5456, a papal letter known hitherto only from a shorter excerpt in Bernold of Constance's *Chronicon*. Both Lh and Sta end with a few items not found in the other. Textual variants preclude direct dependence between them, but they obviously are closely related both textually and in point of origin, and perhaps drew on a common source for the texts up to and including the items from Urban II. The account of Piacenza is written continuously, with ¶ signs indicating divisions.[83]

MSS Mub and Pb are placed at the end of this section because, although they have significant gaps, both are witnesses to c. 15.

Mub = Munich, Bayerische Staatsbibliothek, clm. 5129, fols. 85v-86r.

Mub, although lacking cc. 8–14, contains both the preamble and c. 15. The book is a late twelfth-century copy of the *Opusculum de aedificio Dei* of Gerhoch of Reichersberg, to which Piacenza was added, probably in the same hand. Its immediate provenance was the house of regular canons at Beuerberg in the diocese of Freising. Classen stated that the manuscript was written at Reichersberg in Gerhoch's lifetime (+1169), although Elisabeth Klemm lists either Beuerberg or Reichersberg as its place of origin, perhaps copied at Beuerberg from an exemplar from Reichersberg. Piacenza's preamble and c. 1 are written continuously, with *Primum capitulum* in the margin opposite the latter. A majuscule Q begins cc. 2–7, written continuously without ¶ signs, and c. 15 begins with a majuscule S, a (nineteenth-century?) hand adding 'Cap. xv' in the margin. This was Weiland's MS 14.[84]

Weiland 571–73. A few lines of theological notes on 85v-86r, and at the bottom of 86v, are inserted between the canons from 1078, Piacenza, and those of 1112.

[82] See *Catalogue général des manuscrits latins* 4 (Paris 1958) 325–330; Jasper, *Papstwahldekret* 92; Kéry, *Collections* 211–12. *Catalogue général* used for its reference to Anselm of Lucca the early-modern Anselmian *mélange* put together by Luc d'Achery, found in BNF, lat. 12450–51. For this 'Kunstprodukt des 17. Jahrhunderts' see Peter Landau, 'Die Rezension C der Sammlung des Anselms von Lucca', BMCL 16 (1986) 19, n. 20 (repr. Id., *Kanones und Dekretalen* 45*, n. 20).

[83] The author is grateful to Prof. Herrad Spilling (see n. 79) for her interest in the connection between Lh and Sta. See Borries-Schulten and Spilling 43–44, and Mews 'Zwiefalten' 184–89 (a reference kindly pointed out by Alison Beach). The author plans to take up the question of JL 5456 in a separate study; the fragment in the *Chronicon* is found ed. Pertz 453 / ed. Robinson 491.

[84] See Classen, *Gerhoch* 407, and 312, n. 26, for the derivation from Reichersberg. For his ideas and those of others on the origin of the book, see Elisabeth Klemm, *Die Romanischen Handschriften der*

Pb = Paris, BNF, Baluze 7, fol. 244r.

Pb is placed at the end, and although aberrant in various ways it preserves a witness for c. 15. Pb offers, furthermore, a decree found nowhere else (see also below for Pj). The papers of Étienne Baluze are well known for their scholarly value. Pb presents a wealth of information, mainly concerning councils, e.g., transcriptions from manuscripts, various notes often with corrections inserted later, and commentaries. The texts of Piacenza on fol. 244r were taken *Ex veteri codice MS bibliothecae Colbertinae* – a book which remains unidentified – and provide in a form not found elsewhere cc. 13–14 and the end of c. 15, followed by the otherwise unattested *Presbiteros et diaconos*, which will be printed at the end of the edition in Chapter 4. The account is written continuously, without ¶ signs.[85]

b) **Preamble + cc.1–14**

C = St.-Claude, Bibliothèque municipale, 17(3), fols. 283vb-84ra.

Long considered a copy of Burchard of Worms' *Decretum*, C contains a twelfth-century, perhaps early-twelfth-century, copy of the early eleventh-century *Collection in Twelve Parts*. The book was at St.-Claude from at least the late fifteenth century and could have been written there. Piacenza is the last item in a group of texts which follow the main collection, and is preceded immediately by forgeries attributed to Boniface IV (JE+1996), and to Gregory I (JE+1366) (*partim*). Piacenza, probably written in a different hand than the forgeries, is presented continuously, with ¶ signs indicating divisions.[86]

E = El Escorial, Real Biblioteca de San Lorenzo, A.I.6, fol. cxxi(ra-b).

E is a fourteenth-century manuscript of Gregory the Great's letters, followed by a letter of Archbishop Richard II of Bourges (+c.1090), and Piacenza. E is the latest of the known medieval witnesses for the textus receptus, and the only text

---

Bayerischen Staatsbibliothek 2: Die Bistümer Freising und Augsburg, verschiedene Deutsche Provenienzen (Katalog der illuminierten Handschriften der Bayerischen Staatsbibliothek in München 3: Die Romanischen Handschriften 2; Wiesbaden 1988) 72–3, no. 81. Cf. Günter Glauche, *Katalog der lateinischen Handschriften der Bayerischen Staatsbibliothek München: Die Pergamenthandschriften aus Benediktbeuren Clm. 4501–4663* (Catalogus codicum manu scriptorum Bibliothecae Monacensis 3, Series nova 1; Wiesbaden 1994) 85–6, and XII–XIII, especially for Munich, Clm. 4556 (Weiland's MS 15) as a copy of Mub from the year 1460. MS 4556 will not be collated for the edition below. For an older description of Mub see *Catalogus codicum Latinorum Bibliothecae Regiae Monacensis* 1.2, ed. altera (Catalogus codicum manu scriptorum Bibliothecae Monacensis 3.2; Munich 1894) 268. It can be pointed out that above *Primum capitulum* is written, probably by the same hand that wrote 'Cap. xv', 'xx p. 805', indicating where the decrees of Piacenza are found in Mansi, *Amplissima collectio*, vol. 20. For Gerhoch see also in Narrative Sources, Sect. c, below.

[85] See post JL 5541 for Pb (a text known to Weiland, 561, n. 1), and also L. Auvray and R. Pourpardin, *Catalogue des manuscrits de la collection Baluze* (Paris 1921) 13–19. For Baluze in general see Robert Somerville, 'Baluziana', AHC 5 (1973) 408–23 (repr. Id., *Papacy, Councils, and Canon Law*); see also Patricia Gillet, *Étienne Baluze & l'histoire du Limousin* (Hautes études médiévales et modernes 92; Geneva 2008).

[86] Jörg Müller, *Untersuchungen zur Collectio Duodecim Partium* (Abhandlungen zur Rechtswissenschaftlichen Grundlagenforschung 73; Ebelsbach 1989) 37–38, provides a detailed description of C. Émile Van Balberghe, 'La Préface du Décret [de Burchard de Worms] et la "Collectio XII Partium"', BMCL 3 (1973) 7–8, wrote that 'Ce manuscrit pourrait être originaire de Saint-Claude et date du début du xiie siècle.'

to survive in Spain, although it is not clear that it was written there. The decrees are written in paragraphs, each beginning with a ¶ sign. Weiland knew of this manuscript but did not use it.[87]

Fc = Florence, Biblioteca Medicea Laurenziana, S.Croce23, dext.5, fols. 183r-84r.

Fc contains Gezo of Tortona's work on the Eucharist (late tenth-century) as does Mip below, and, beginning on 91r, a partial copy of Bonizo of Sutri's *Liber de Vita Christiana*. Piacenza is the first item in a set of supplements following the *Liber* but in the same hand. Fc was written in Italy (perhaps in the vicinity of Brescia), probably in the second quarter of the twelfth century but possibly as late as mid-century. The account of Piacenza is written continuously, without ¶ signs.[88]

Lu = Lucca, Biblioteca Capitolare Feliniana 124, fol. 196ra-rb.

Lu, a book which often has been used and cited, contains Burchard of Worms' *Decretum*, followed by the *Collectio Novariensis*, followed in turn by supplements copied by different scribes, including Piacenza and immediately thereafter, on fol. 196v, JL 5290 in the same hand. The main portion of Lu was written in central Italy in the last quarter of the eleventh century. The book probably was at Lucca from around the year 1100, and the texts at the end could have been added there. Piacenza is written in paragraphs that commence with majuscule letters of varying size. This was Weiland's MS 8.[89]

Mic = Milan, Biblioteca Ambrosiana, H.48 sup., fols. 162v-63v.

---

[87] See the description in G. Antolin, *Catálogo de los Códices Latinos de la Real Biblioteca del Escorial* 1 (Madrid 1910) 13–16, but fuller information is given by Paul Ewald, 'Reise nach Spanien im Winter von 1878 auf 1879', *Neues Archiv* 6 (1881) 223–24. See Weiland 561, n. 1. For the letter of Richard of Bourges see Robert Somerville, 'A Letter from Archbishop Richard II of Bourges to Bishop Pons Stephani of Rodez concerning the Abbey of St.-Amans de Rodez', in Oliver Münsch and Thomas Zotz (eds.), *Scientia veritatis: Festschrift für Hubert Mordek zum 65. Geburtstag* (Ostfildern 2004) 294–309.

[88] Fols. 91 ff. are described by Ernst Perels, *Bonizo, Liber de vita christiana* (Texte zur Geschichte des römischen und kanonischen Rechts im Mittelalter 1; Berlin 1930) lv–lvii; see lvi for Perels' speculation that the entire book may be written in the same hand. For the full codex, see Bandini, *Catalogus* 4. 635–47; Jasper, *Papstwahldekret* 126 (who calls the material after the *Liber* a 'kanonistischen Materialsammlunng'), and Kéry, *Collections* 234. For a seventeenth-century copy of Fc in Paris, BNF, lat. 12391 (not seen), see Gabriella Braga, 'La fortuna di un errore: la "Definitio brevis de Eucharistia"', *Bollettino dell'Istituto storico Italiano per il Medio Aevo e Archivio Muratoriano* 89 (1980–81) 408–9, and Walter Berschin, 'Zwei neue Bonizo-Handschriften', *Scriptorium* 41 (1987) 89–90 (cf. id., *Bonizone di Sutri, la vita e le opere* [Medioevo-traduzioni 1; Spoleto 1992] 29). Braga, op. cit., 405, n. 73, notes that Fc's date has been a matter of conjecture, and confirms the mid-twelfth-century date based on an examination of the manuscript by Armando Petrucci. For the book's origin perhaps in the 'area breciana', see Daniela Mazzuconi, 'La diffusione dell'opera di Gezone de Tortona in Italia settentrionale', *Aevum* 57 (1983) 189–214.

[89] See Schneider, *Konzilsordines* 233–34, Kéry, *Collections* 32, and esp. 139, and Roberto Bellini, 'Un Abrégé del Decreto di Burchardo di Worms: La Collezione canonica in 20 libri (Ms. Vat. lat. 1350)', *Apollinaris* 69 (1996), esp. 131. Laudage, 'Ritual', found Lu especially interesting and discussed it at several points. See 295, especially n. 19, for a description of the supplements and speculation that the account of Piacenza therein was 'die direkte Abschrift' of a text which belonged to Bishop Rangerius of Lucca. (For Rangerius [+1112] at the Council of Rome see Chapter 6.) See also 324–26, for further speculations regarding the presence of JL 5290 in Lu, and 329, n. 109, and the photo on 330, for a representation on fol. 4v of the Council of Nicaea in the year 325 (for JL 5290 see also Somerville, 'Gregory VII' 50). For the possible use of Lu in the compilation of the *Polycarpus* see Horst, *Polycarpus* 19–20. Kery, Collections 139, notes a close connection between the supplements in Lu and Florence, Bibl. Laurenz., Calci 11 (9), but the canons of Piacenza are not found in that book

Mic is made up of three twelfth-century manuscripts which contain works of Richard of St.-Victor, Bernard of Clairvaux, and others. The first two were copied in Italian Cistercian scriptoria, the first perhaps at Morimondo in the archdiocese of Milan. The third, containing a variety of texts, has been described as written 'in area milanese'. Piacenza follows directly and in the same hand a work titled *Pauca ex eruditorum virorum voluminibus excerpta de catholica ecclesia, eius ministri et baptismi officio*, and is written continuously, without ¶ signs.[90]

Mip = ——, M.79 sup., fols. 248va-49ra.

Mip is a 'massive theological compendium' containing, among many other things, eighth-century Biblical commentaries from the Canterbury school. It was copied by two principal hands in the second half of the eleventh century, and based on a calendar containing saints venerated specifically at Piacenza, an origin in that city is suggested. That the Council of Piacenza is the first of a group of later additions by various scribes, including the acts of Paschal II's Lateran Council of 1112 (fols. 249rb-49vb), might confirm this. Mip was later in Brescia. The division of the account of Piacenza is not easy to decipher, but probably is intended to be in paragraphs, some of which are preceded by ¶ signs.[91]

Os = Oxford, Bodleian Library, Selden supra 90 (S. C. 3478), fols. 24v-25r.

Os is made up of segments of several manuscripts from the twelfth century to the sixteenth. Fols. 22–29, from the early twelfth century, offer the *Donation of Constantine*, JL 4269, a liturgical chant, Piacenza, a unique account of Urban II's Council of Clermont, and a long decree attributed to Urban II, *De ieiunio quatuor temporum*, all copied without any breaks other than new inscriptions by the same or very similar hands. The origin of these pages is unknown, but fols. 30–37 are late twelfth-century and derive from St. Augustine's Abbey at Canterbury. Piacenza is written continuously, without ¶ signs.[92]

(information kindly provided by Hubert Mordek). For MS Lc, see also now Blumenthal and Jasper, passim.

[90] See the description by Mirella Ferrari, 'Bibliothece e scrittori Benedettini nella storia culturale della diocesi Ambrosiana: Appunti ed episodi', *Ricerche storiche sulla Chiesa Ambrosiana* IX (Archivio Ambrosiano 11; Milan 1980) 284–85, who did not identify the text preceding Piacenza.

[91] Mip is described in detail in Bernhard Bischoff(+) and Michael Lapidge, *Biblical Commentaries from the Canterbury School of Theodore and Hadrian* (Cambridge Studies in Anglo-Saxon England 10; Cambridge 1994) 275–87, and 283 for the Council of Piacenza (see 278, and cf. 275, n. 2, where the need for 'the attention of a professional cataloguer' is indicated for this collection of texts). Piacenza and the Lateran Council of 1112 (see Weiland 571–73), are separated (fol. 249ra) by a column of what those authors call 'notes on the eucharist', written in a different hand from either conciliar account. In addition to Piacenza and the synod of 1112, Mip contains the acts of Gregory VII's Lenten Synod of 1078 in an earlier section of the book (fol. 155r-v): see Caspar, *Register* 368–73. For texts of these same three synods very close together see MS O above. Mip also transmits Gezo of Tortona's work on the Eucharist (see Bischoff–Lapidge 282), as does Fc above. (The author is grateful to Olivia Remie Constable for providing information about Mip.)

[92] See Somerville, *Decreta* 112–17, where further bibliography is given. These folios, and especially the concluding text on the Ember Days, will be the subject of a separate study (cf. in Chapter 6, in the commentary on c. 14). The author is grateful to Prof. Susan Boynton of Columbia University for her views about the musical notation on fols. 23v-24r. That notation is typical of the neumes in many early twelfth-century French, and some northern French, manuscripts. In that period musical notation in England was naturally heavily influenced by French books and traditions, and the neumes could conceivably be English. The chant itself is a responsory sung at Matins on feasts of the Virgin Mary,

Enactment, Circulation, and Survival of the Canons of Piacenza   39

V = Città del Vaticano, BAV, Vat. lat. 1208, fols. 127r-28r.

V contains Paul the Deacon's Life of Pope Gregory I, followed by other texts, and was written in Italy in the twelfth-century continuously by one scribe copying an earlier manuscript in which the various pieces found in MS 1208 already were assembled. The supplements to the Life of Gregory include what professes to be a papal *laudatio* of Cluny from Gregory VII's Lenten Synod of 1080, inscribed *Decretum domni Gregorii pape de Clunicensi monasterio* (125v-26v) (see also in Chapter 1, n. 35). The decrees of Piacenza are written continuously and divided into four sections numbered [*i*]-*iiii*, with the following verse copied before the preamble: *Vrbani papae decretum pontificale. Conditur hic scripto formoso denique dicto.* Canons of the Council of Melfi in 1089 follow those of Piacenza (128r-29v), inscribed *Ex synodo eiusdem Urbani pape apud Melfiam.*, numbered in sequence with Piacenza as *v-xv* (omitting *vii*). This was Weiland's MS 6.[93]

Va = ——Vat. lat. 629, fols. 269va-70ra.

Va contains an amalgamation of the Pseudo-Isidorian Decretals and the *Liber pontificalis*, with other items appended in various hands. It derives from southern Tuscany, perhaps from the Benedictine house of San Antimo near Montalcino in the diocese of Chiusi. A papal list on fol. 121ra where Urban II's dates are added in a second hand suggests a date before 1099 for much of the book. Piacenza is the last text in Va, copied in the same hand as the immediately preceding entries from Gregory VII, including canons of the November synod of 1078. Piacenza is written continuously, without ¶ signs. This was Weiland's MS 9, but cited as *codex quidam Vaticanus*, and is the exemplar from which Holste prepared the 'editio princeps' of the canons (see the discussion in Chapter 3).[94]

Vm = ——Vat. lat. 1364, fols. 189v-90v.

Vm contains the B recension of Anselm of Lucca's *Collectio canonum*, and was copied, perhaps at Mantua, around the year 1100. Piacenza is the first of a set of additions at the end of bk. 7 (after *c.* 209) of the collection, but in the same hand as what precedes. Piacenza is divided into numbered capitula. This was Weiland's MS 7.[95]

---

and is numbered 6725 in R.-J. Hesbert, *Corpus antiphonalium officii* 4 (Rerum ecclesiasticarum documenta, Series maior, Fontes 10; Rome 1970) 183. Further study could point to a locale where this text was sung, and hence suggest the place of origin of the manuscript from which these pages were taken. Cf. *Councils & Synods* 1.2. 648, n. 1, where it is stated that Os 'may well' not be of English origin. See also Barker-Benfield, *St. Augustine's* 2062, for the sections of Os from St. Augustine's.

[93] For this manuscript, designated there as MS Vq, see Somerville–Kuttner, *Pope Urban* 192–93. The items following the Life of Gregory I appear in all probability to be copied from MS V, in the sixteenth-century miscellany found in MS Vat. lat. 6197, with Piacenza at fols. 340v-41v: see Somerville–Kuttner, *Urban* 193, and Weiland 561, n. 1, for what certainly is a reference to MS 6197 but with an incorrect shelfmark ('6196'). See also the discussion of MS V in Chapter 4.

[94] MS Va is described, with bibliography, in Kuttner-Elze, *Catalogue* 1. 16–20, where the provenance is given as 'Montalcino, Monastery of Sant' Antonio'; but see Schneider, *Konzilsordines* 154, who, correcting the name of the house, writes that the book was written in 'südliche Toskana (San Antimo bei Montalcino?)'. For the canons of Gregory VII from the synod in November, 1078, see Caspar, *Register* 402–6.

[95] MS Vm is described, with bibliography, in Kuttner-Elze, *Catalogue* 1. 137–38. That Piacenza is an addition to bk. 7 seems clear from the fact that it is not numbered 'c. 210'. For the content of bk. 7

Y = New Haven, Yale University, Beinecke Rare Book and Manuscript Library, Marston 158, fol. 1r.

Y contains St. Ambrose's commentary on the Gospel of Luke, and was written in northen Italy around the year 1100. The main text begins on fol. 1v, with Piacenza added by another hand on 1r. The book was at the Cistercian abbey of Hautecombe in the diocese of Geneva not long after it was written, but whether the canons of Piacenza were added before Y moved north or not seems to be an open question. They are written continuously, without ¶ signs.[96]

Pj = Paris, BNF, lat. 18083, fols. 149v-50v.

Pj is placed at the end of this section because it offers a decree found nowhere else (see also above for Paris, BNF, Baluze 7). After c. 14 the text *Siquis decimam* is copied, which will be presented at the end of the edition. Pj contains a twelfth-century copy of works of St. Augustine, perhaps from the first quarter of the century and perhaps originating in the vicinity of Chartres or Orléans. Monastic forgeries attributed to Gregory I, including JE +1366, follow the last Augustinian text (*De dono* [here *bono*] *perseverantie*) but in a different hand, and Piacenza follows the forgeries in yet another hand. The immediate provenance of Pj is the Couvent des Jacobins de la rue Saint-Honoré in Paris. The account of Piacenza is damaged, written continuously, without ¶ signs.[97]

c) **Preamble + varia**

F = Florence, Biblioteca Medicea Laurenziana, Plut. xviii.14, fol. 114vb.

F contains a late eleventh-century copy of Gregory the Great's *Homiliae* on Ezechiel, damaged at the end. Piacenza is added immediately, in the last column of the manuscript in another hand. The text is damaged and breaks off in the middle of c. 4. F is one of a small group of manuscripts that refer to the account of Piacenza as a *Decretum*, and the only one that uses the adjective *beati* in describing Urban – *Decretum beati Urbani pape* – probably indicating that the text, written continuously without ¶ signs, was transcribed after the pope's death.[98]

Li = Lincoln, Cathedral Library, 192, fols. 110v-11r.

---

of Anselm B, see John Gilchrist, 'The Collectio canonum of Bishop Anselm II of Lucca (d.1086): Recension B of Berlin, Staatsbibliothek Preussischer Kulturbesitz Cod. 597', *Cristianità ed Europa: Miscellanea di studi in onore di Luigi Prosdocimi* 1.2, ed. Cesare Alzati (Rome 1994) 388–94, where only 208 canons are indicated.

[96] See Barbara A. Shailor, *Catalogue of the Medieval and Renaissance Manuscripts in the Beinecke Rare Book and Manuscript Library, Yale University 3: Marston Manuscripts* (Medieval and Renaissance Texts and Studies 100; Binghamton 1992) 304–5. The author is grateful to Robert Babcock of the Beinecke Library who noted that Piacenza was written in a charter hand and not a book hand.

[97] Léopold Delisle, 'Inventaire des manuscrits latins de Notre-Dame et des divers petits fonds conservés à la Bibliothèque Nationale sous les numéros 16719–18613 du fonds latin', BEC 31 (1870) 539–40 (also separately, with slightly different title [Paris 1871] 79–80). Delisle wrongly attributed the Gregorian texts to Gregory VII. The author is grateful to Dr. Patricia Stirnemann for information about MS Pj.

[98] Bandini, *Catalogus* 1. 467–68, who comments that the added material is not found in the printed conciliar editions, is incorrect. MS F is not listed by M. Adriaen in the critical edition of the *Homiliae* in *Corpus Christianorum*, Ser. Lat. 142 (1979).

Li, written all in one hand in France, owned by the Celestines of Marcoussis in the diocese of Paris in the fifteenth century, is a twelfth-century copy of Ivo of Chartres' *Panormia*, with supplements, including an account of Piacenza, written continuously without ¶ signs, and contains cc. 1–7, although lacks the last line of c. 7. That was all that the scribe planned to copy, for following immediately, inscribed *Ex dictis Ieronimi presbiteri*, is the canon *Mensuram temporis* that occurs at various points: see, e.g., Gratian, *Decretum* D. 1, c. 86, de pen.[99]

d) **Lacking the preamble, containing cc. 1–14**
G = Göttweig, Stiftsbibliothek, 85 (8), fols. 1v-2r.

G contains a twelfth-century copy of Augustine's *Liber de fide et operibus*, and books from the New Testament (the Acts of the Apostles, and the Canonical Epistles). Piacenza is at the beginning of the manuscript, fols. 1–2, followed by c. 4 of Paschal II's Council of Guastalla (1106), in a different hand. Weiland knew of this manuscript but did not use it.[100]

Mup = Munich, Bayerische Staatsbibliothek, clm. 11316, fols. 115–16r.

Mup contains a late-twelfth-century copy of Ivo of Chartres' *Panormia* from the house of Augustinian Canons at Polling in the diocese of Augsburg. The *Panormia* ends at fol. 111v, and is followed by a remarkable supplement of papal conciliar texts, i.e., Reims (1119), Pisa (1135), Piacenza (1095), Reims (1148), and Lateran III (1179), all written in one hand. The account of Piacenza is written continuously, without ¶ signs.[101]

Muw = ――clm. 22011, fol. 1r.

Muw is one of a set of manuscripts from the Benedictine double monastery of Wessobrunn in the diocese of Augsburg that contains the works of Gregory the Great – here bks. 23–27 of the *Moralia* – which were copied early in the twelfth century by the nun-scribe Diemut. The account of Piacenza is added in another early twelfth-century hand at the beginning of the book, written continuously, without ¶ signs.[102]

---

[99] Rodney M. Thomson, *Catalogue of the Manuscripts of Lincoln Cathedral Chapter Library* (Woodbridge 1989) 154. Brett '*Panormia*', 263, calls MS Li 's.xii/xiii.', and see also id., 'Margin and Afterthought: the *Clavis* in Action', in Martin Brett and Katherine G. Cushing (eds.), *Readers, Texts and Compilers in the Early Middle Ages: Studies in Medieval Canon Law in Honour of Linda Fowler-Magerl* (Farnham 2009) 155–56.

[100] See J. Friedrich Schulte, 'Die Rechtshandschriften der Stiftsbibliotheken von Göttweig…', *Sitzungsberichte der kaiserlichen Akademie der Wissenschaften*, philosophisch-historische Classe 57 (1867) 560, who said that the canons at the beginning of the book precede theological works, but did not identify them. The author is grateful for that information to Matthew Heintzelmann of the Hill Museum and Manuscript Library at St. John's University, Collegeville, Minnesota. For c. 4 of Guastalla in MS G, see Blumenthal, *Early Councils* 55. Weiland 561, n. 1, was confused about which canons of Piacenza are found in this book.

[101] See Robert Somerville, 'The Council of Pisa, 1135: A Re-examination of the Evidence for the Canons', *Speculum* 45 (1970) 98–114 (repr. Id., *Papacy, Councils and Canon Law*), and Peter Landau, 'Die Rubriken und Inskriptionen von Ivos Panormie', BMCL 12 (1982) 48 (repr. Id., *Kanones und Dekretalen* 114*).

[102] For this manuscript see Elisabeth Klemm, *Die Romanischen Handschriften der Bayerischen Staatsbibliothek* 2 (Katalog der illuminierten Handschriften der Bayerischen Staatsbibliothek in München 3; Wiesbaden 1988) 164–65, no. 237; and for Diemut see ibid. 163, and Alison I.

Stb = Stuttgart, Württembergische Landesbibliothek, Cod. theol. et phil. 2°210, fols. 134r-35r.

Stb contains Ambrose of Milan's *Hexaemeron*, copied early in the twelfth century at the Benedictine double monastery of Zwiefalten in the diocese of Constance. Piacenza was added by the same or a very similar hand, and the decrees were written continuously, without ¶ signs.[103]

VB = Vyssí Brod (Hohenfurt), Klásterni knihovna, CXIX, fols. 30r-v.

The manuscripts of the former Cistercian monastery of Vyssí Brod are now owned by the Krajská vedecká knihovna (Episcopal Library) in Ceské Budejovice (Budweis). VB is a short twelfth-century manuscript written in one hand and containing the *Micrologus* of Bernold of Constance, followed, fols. 28v-30r, by the Carolingian *Admonitio synodalis*, and then Piacenza as the last item in the book, written continuously, without ¶ signs.[104]

W = Vienna, Österreichische Nationalbibliothek, lat. 2153 (Iur. can. 38), fols. 67v-69r. W contains two separate manuscripts. The second, fols. 95ff., is the *Compilatio tertia* of Innocent III's decretals. The first is an early twelfth-century copy of the *Collection in Seventy-Four Titles* (1–41v), with other material appended that was transcribed without any gap, probably by one scribe copying an earlier exemplar where the texts found here were assembled over time. Piacenza is preceded by canons of Gregory VII's Lenten Council of 1078, and followed immediately in the middle of a line, without a break or a new inscription, by Pope Gregory's November Synod of 1078. W was at the abbey of St. Pölten in the diocese of Passau in the late Middle Ages. Gassó and Batlle thought it could have been copied in that vicinity or elsewhere in Lower Austria or Northern Italy. The account of Piacenza and the subsequent Gregorian council is written continuously, without ¶ signs. This was Weiland's MS 13, cited following Mansi as *codex quidam Vindobonensis*.[105]

Beach, *Women as Scribes: Book Production and Monastic Reform in Twelfth-Century Bavaria* (Cambridge Studies in Palaeography and Codicology 10; Cambridge 2003) 49. The author is grateful to Prof. Beach, and to Dr. Dieter Kudorfer of the Bayerische Staatsbibliothek in Munich, for kindly answering questions about Muw.

[103] Borries-Schulten and Spilling 43. See also Mews, 'Zwiefalten' 185–87.

[104] See Raphael Pavel, 'Beschreibung der im Stifte Hohenfurt befindlichen Handschriften', *Xenia Bernardina, Pars secunda: Handschriften-Verzeichnisse* 2 (Vienna 1891) 207–8; and for the present location see Paul Oskar Kristeller, *Iter Italicum* 6 (London 1993) 461, and id. and Sigrid Krämer, *Latin Manuscript Books before 1600*, 4th edn. (MGH Hilfsmittel 13; Munich 1993) 346. Taylor, 'Inventory' 188–89, did not see VB but suggests that this copy of the *Micrologus* may be incomplete. For the *Admonitio* see Schneider, *Konzilsordines* 430, n. 52; the edition by R. Amiet, 'Une "Admonitio Synodalis" de l'époque carolingienne: Étude critique et édition', *Mediaeval Studies* 26 (1964) 18–82, did not use VB. The author is grateful to Prof. Jiri Kejř for assistance in obtaining photos of this text.

[105] MS W is described in detail by John Gilchrist, *Diversorum patrum sententie siue Collectio in LXXIV titulos digesta* (Monumenta iuris canonici, Corpus Collectionum 1; Vatican City 1973) lviii–lx, with bibliography; note also is Gassó and Batlle, *Epistulae* xlvi–xlviii. For the texts of Gregory VII, i.e., cc. 14–16 of the Lenten Synod of 1078, and the account of the November council of the same year, see Caspar, *Register* 372–73, and 402–6.

JL 5694 (IP 5.248–49, no.14) – c. 8, and c. 9 partim

No chancery original of this letter is known, and it survives at the end of a twelfth-century manuscript of St. Augustine's sermons, Città del Vaticano, BAV, Vat. lat. 478, fol. 143r, copied after a list of the canons from Urban II's Council of Melfi, and before JL 5670 (IP 5. 248, no. 14). Both letters are addressed to Bologna, probably indicating where the manuscript was written. Jaffé's date for JL 5694 was April 17, 1097–98, but Kehr narrowed the year to 1097. The letter was edited by L. Savioli in the late eighteenth century from a early-modern Bolognese copy of Vat. lat. 478, and the printing in PL 151.500 follows Savioli's edition.[106] Since the text was edited more than two hundred years ago on the basis of an early-modern transcription, it will be re-edited here (with the manuscript's spelling retained, but with editorial capitalization and punctuation). For the excommunication of Wibert of Ravenna by Gregory VII (February 1078), see Caspar, *Register* 369; and see also the Council of Rome (1099), c. 8 (Mansi 20. 963; cf. Chapter 6).

>   Urbanus episcopus servus servorum Dei venerabili fratri
>   B<ernardo> Bononiensi episcopo salutem et apostolicam
>   benedictionem. De ordinationibus ab heresiarcha Guiberto
>   factis postquam a beatae memoriae Gregorio papa et a Romana
> 5 aecclesia dampnatus est, quaeque etiam a <p>seudoepiscopis
>   per eum postea ordinatis perpetrate sunt, Placentinae synodi
>   generale[107] iudicium definitum est ut irritae habeantur nisi
>   probare valuerint se cum ordinarentur eos nescisse dampnatos.
>   Quia vero fratres super quibus rogas religiosos asseris, et
> 10 omnino vim passos et tractos ad ordinandum confiteris, magnam
>   etiam acclesiae tuae necessitatem conquereris, utrum eis in
>   sacerdotali ordine condescendendum[108] sit tuae prudentiae pro
>   graviori oportunitate committimus. Vestra vero experientia
>   caveat ne in eos aut scandalum aut infamiam aecclesia
> 15 paciatur. In aliis, qui non eadem religionis gratia et
>   violentiae illatione excusabiles sunt, omnino synodalis
>   iudicii sententiam persequeris. Si quos tamen propensiori
>   necessitate restitueris, non sine penitentiae cotidianae
>   remedio pacieris, et ipsos autem inter eos quibus ordinandis
> 20 manum imponis dum orationum sollemnitas agitur interesse
>   praecipito. Quod tamen omnino praecipimus ne sine graviori
>   aecclesiae necessitate et personarum merito ullatenus
>   praesumatur. Data Laterani XV Kal. Maii.

>   6–7 synodi gene generale MS 8 nescissae MS
>   11 conquaereris MS persequaeris MS 20 imponis *sup.*
>   *lin.* MS

---

[106] For Vat. lat. 478, see Marcus Vatasso and Pius Franchi de'Cavalieri, *Codices Vaticani Latini* 1 (Rome 1902) 357–58, and Somerville–Kuttner, *Pope Urban* 192; for the printings of the letter, see IP 5. 249.

[107] *gene generale* MS.

[108] For this verb in Urban II's acts see Somerville, 'Pseudo-Council' 27, where the occurrence in the present text is not indicated.

The detail offered in this letter is reminiscent of JL 5409, in which Pope Urban cited and interpreted canons from Melfi for Bishop Pibo of Toul.[109] There must have been other papal replies that are now lost to similar inquiries about conciliar decrees and especially about the canons of Piacenza. Unfortunately in JL 5409, and even more so here, only a very small portion of the legislation is cited.

Canon Law Collections

This section will indicate the collections where lists of the decrees of Piacenza have been found.[110] The intent is essentially descriptive, noting which texts appear where, and providing some historical background and bibliography. The compilations will be treated in three sections: *Variae* (of undetermined origin); Italian collections; and the *Collectio Caesaraugustana* (cf. Chapter 4 Canon Law Collections, Sect. c).

a) Variae collectiones

T = Turin, Biblioteca Nazionale Universitaria, D.IV.33 (Pasini 239), fols. 135v-36r.
  T is the unique mid-twelfth-century copy of the Turin *Collection in Seven Books*, composed c.1100, although, as Linda Fowler-Magerl writes, 'it is difficult to say where', perhaps in northern Italy, or Poitou, or elsewhere.[111] The book provides an interesting array of texts from Pope Urban II, including a significant account of the Council of Melfi in 1089. Piacenza cc. 1–14, constituting the latest databale items in the codex, occur in bk.7 as *cap. i.-iv* of the synod but also as cc. 208–211 of that seventh book. The synodal prologue is absent, as are ¶ signs dividing the texts.

L = London, British Library, Add. 11440, fol. 67r-v.
  L contains copies from the second or third quarter of the twelfth century of two canonical collections probably written in northern France or the Low Countries. Fols. 1–72, all in one hand, is an unanalyzed compilation, including Piacenza cc. 1–12 (lacking the last line of c. 12); fols. 73–112 offer a very abbreviated text of Ivo of Chartres' *Panormia*. The account of Piacenza is written continuously, without ¶ signs.[112]

---

[109] Somerville–Kuttner, *Pope Urban* 186.

[110] For canonical collections, see the remarks above in *Survival*, Introduction, and also at the beginning of Lists of Canons.

[111] See, in general, Somerville–Kuttner, *Pope Urban* 190–92, with earlier bibliography, Fowler-Magerl, *Clavis* 163–66, and Kéry, *Collections* 265–66. Neither Paul Fournier, 'De quelques collections canoniques issues du Décret de Burchard', *Mélanges Paul Fabre* (Paris 1902) 208–13 (repr. *Mélanges* 1. 224–29), nor Fournier-LeBras, *Histoire* 2. 163–67, indicated that the Turin Collection had influence on later compilations, but Fowler-Magerl (165), shows that it was influential in southern France or Catalonia, and in the region of Milan.

[112] See the very brief notices in *List of Additions to the Manuscripts in the British Museum, 1836–1840* (London 1843) 14, for 1838, and Z.N. Brooke, *The English Church and the Papacy* (Cambridge 1931) 245, who indicated that MS L is twelfth-century but 'does not appear to have been in England at that time'. For the second part of L, see Brett, '*Panormia*' 263. The author is grateful to Michael Gullick for additional information on the book.

b) Italian Collections

Canons from Piacenza were not originally part of Ivo's *Panormia*.[113] But a set of decrees, cc. 5–7 and 9, is added to bk. 3 of two manuscripts of the work, in the margin of Vp and incorporated into the text of the collection in Fv. These two copies of this set of decrees clearly are related – see the apparatus criticus, and the discussion below in Chapter 4, Canon Law Collections, Sect. c – but the details are a matter for further investigation.

Vp = Città del Vaticano, Vat. lat. 1360, fol. 38v.

> A twelfth-century book, with the texts from Piacenza inscribed simply *Urbanus.*, transcribed in the lower margin of 38v in a hand different from the main text. This page comprises bk. 3, cc. 119–27 (see the printing of the *Panormia* in PL 161. 1155–58). The added decrees are written continuously, without ¶ signs. Perhaps an indication of Vp's origin in the province of Aquileia appears in the addition of a full text of JL 8289 (GP 1. 402–3, no. 7), with addressees and datum on 88v, at the end of the book.[114]

Fv = Florence, Biblioteca Nazionale Centrale, Conv. sopp. G.1.836, fols. 43v–44r.

> Fv is a twelfth-century book from Vallombrosa. the canons from Piacenza are incorporated into bk. 3, between cc. 121 and 122, again inscribed simply *Urbanus.*, with c.9 separated by a ¶ sign and inscribed *Eiusdem*.[115]

The following collections of Italian origin dating from the first decades of the twelfth century contain significant blocks of legislation from Piacenza: the *Polycarpus* (Poly.), the *Collection in Seven Books* (7L), the *Collection in Three Books* (3L) along with its derivative, the *Collection in Nine Books* (9L), and the two versions of Gratian's *Decretum* (Grat. 1 & Grat. 2).[116] Urban II's authorship of these decrees is well attested in the inscriptions found in those works, but in only two cases is the Council of Piacenza named; before c. 1 in 7L, and before c. 15 in Gratian 2. Coupled with the well-known practice in canonical collections of authors abbreviating rubrics and dropping attributions, while the evidence is meagre it suggests that these rulings derived from Piacenza rather than from another of Pope Urban's synods.[117] The table below shows the distribution of Piacenza's legislation in these compilations, with the italicized entries under Grat. indicating the canons that

---

[113] This is a reason for dating the collection before 1095, but see now Martin Brett, 'Urban II and the collections attributed to Ivo of Chartres', in Stanley Chodorow (ed.), *Proceedings of the Eighth International Congress of Medieval Canon Law* (Monumenta iuris canonici, Subsidia 9; Vatican City 1992) 27–46, esp. 30.

[114] Kuttner–Elze, *Catalogue* 1. 129–30, but with no information about the book's origin.

[115] MS Fv occasionally has been mentioned by scholars, e.g., Fournier, 'Collections Yves de Chartres', BEC 58. 27, n. 1 (*Mélanges* 1. 506, n. 1), Brett, "*Panormia*" 262, and Jasper, *Papstwahldekret* 10, n. 36, and 92.

[116] For details about these works, see the following: in general Kéry, *Collections*, and more recently Fowler-Magerl, *Clavis*; for 7L Somerville–Zapp, '"Eighth Book"', and Peter Landau, 'Die Quellen der mittelitalienischen Kanonessammlung in sieben Büchern (MS Vat. lat. 1346)', in Katherine G. Cushing and Richard F. Gyug (eds.), *Ritual, Text and Law: Studies in Medieval Canon Law and Liturgy Presented to Roger E. Reynolds* (Aldershot 2004) 255–68; Motta, *Coll. can. 3L*; and for the recensions of Gratian, Winroth, *Making*.

[117] See, e.g., Somervile–Kuttner, *Pope Urban* 194ff., and in general, Gaudemet, 'Sources' 255–58. For Urban's Council of Rome, from which decrees at times identical to those of Piacenza survive in northern canon law collections, see Chapter 6.

	Piacenza	Poly.[118]	7L	3L	9L	Grat.
<1>	Ea-firmamus.		4.9.9[119]	2.9.11[120]	3.5.1[121]	1.3.5a[122]
<2>	Quicquid-censemus.		ditto	ditto	ditto	ditto(b)
<3>	Siqui-commendat.		ditto	ditto	ditto	*1.1.108a*
<4>	Qui-decernimus.		ditto	ditto	ditto	*ditto(b)*
<5>	Quicumque-inveniuntur.		ditto	2.9.12	3.5.2	*1.5.1*
<6>	Illi-auctoritate.		ditto	ditto	ditto	*ditto*¶*1*
<7>	Siqui-patimur.		ditto	ditto	ditto	*ditto*¶*2*
<8>	Ordinationes-iudicamus[123].	om.	om.	om.	om.	om.
<9>	Similiter-dampnatos.	7.15.2[124]	add.[125]	2.9.13	om.	9.1.5
<10>	Qui-commendat.	ditto	ditto	ditto	om.	ditto¶1
<11>	Amodo-habeatur.	ditto	ditto	ditto	om.	ditto¶2
<12>	Quamvis-severitati,	ditto	ditto	ditto	om.	ditto¶3
	ut-caritati.	om.	om.	om.	om.	om.
<13>	Illud-exigatur.	3.10.29	5.25.2[126]	3.7.71	7.6.48	om.
<14>	Statuimus-fiant.	3.25.16	[6.72.5][127]	3.8.41	7.7.28	76.4
<15>	Sanctorum-prevideat.					70.2
<Notatio>	In-nostrum.					70 dict.p.c.2

appear in both the first and the second versions of Gratian. This information must be evaluated with care, however, and readers should not be deceived by the symmetry. The discussion below in Chapter 4 will show that the transmission of these texts among the six collections noted is not as linear as the chart might suggest.

[118] This table excludes the lists of canons of Piacenza found in the particular version of the *Polycarpus* that has been designated as ΦVa and ΦVb.

[119] The enumeration is drawn from Gossman, *Urban* 35–38, who uses 7Lv, which represents the earliest form of the collection: see Somerville–Zapp, '"Eighth Book"' 163. The vagaries of trying to keep track of titles and canons in 7L is illustrated by the fact that in 7Lw these canons are at 4.11.16.

[120] Cf. the previous note for the problem of treating canons in unedited collections. The information for 3L in Gossman, *Urban* 42–43, is flawed because fols. 33–34 of the Vatican manuscript of the work are misbound. See now Motta, *Coll. can. 3L*, for the correct enumeration (cf. Picasso, 'Tradizione canonistica' 119, n. 31, whose table is based on Motta's edition).

[121] The enumeration is taken from Motta, *Coll. can. 3L* 1. 193–94, and 2. 73, and 88.

[122] Three numbers refer to the second section of the *Decretum Gratiani*, i.e., *Causa, questio*, and *canon*; italics indicate texts also found in Gratian 1. Of the known sources of Gratian (see Winroth, *Making* 15–17), Poly. and 3L contain decrees of Piacenza.

[123] The possibility that *homoioteleuton* is at work in the texts of cc. 8–9 in the collections listed here will be taken up in Chapter 4, Canon Law Collections, Sect. b.

[124] The enumeration is from Horst, *Polycarpus* 218. Gossman, *Urban* 34 and 42 (cf. 105), and Picasso, 'Tradizione canonistica' 119, n. 31, write that the *Polycarpus* and 3L include c. 8. The situation is complicated, as the discussion in Chapter 4, Canon Law Collections, Sect. b indicates, but the substance of that canon is missing in both collections.

[125] These texts are additions after bk.7 in 7Lv, but have been integrated into the collection in other copies. e.g., in 7Lw they are added immediately after the first seven canons of Piacenza, at 4.11.17, with the inscription *Urbanus* of 7Lv changed to *Idem* (see Somerville–Zapp, '"Eighth Book"' 172). For the statements in Gossman, *Urban* 38 and 105, that 7L contains c. 8, see the previous note.

[126] See the previous note; this text appears in 7Lv in the margin of 109v, but at 5.25.2 in 7Lw.

[127] In 7Lw c. 14 is copied on fol. 252r and ascribed *Paschalis papa ii.*, as is also the case in the version of 7L found in Cortona, Biblioteca Comunale e dell'Accademia Etrusca, MS 43, fol. 226v. (Neither of these 'Paschal' occurrences was noted in Somerville–Zapp, '"Eighth Book"' 171–72.) This attribution of Piacenza c. 14 to Paschal II could simply be a mistake, or Paschal might have re-promulgated the text at one of his synods: see Blumenthal, *Early Councils* 113–14.

Leaving aside Gratian, according to the latest information available the other four works survive as follows in manuscript copies:[128] *Polycarpus* 13 MSS; 7L 4 MSS; 3L 2 MSS; 9L 2 MSS. The following manuscripts have been collated for the edition in Chapter 4.

POLYCARPUS
Poly.m = Madrid, Biblioteca nacional, lat. 7127, fols. 336r, 354v, 442v.
Poly.p = Paris, BNF, lat. 3881, fols. 56r, 78r, and 170v-71r.

7L
7Lv = Città del Vaticano, BAV, Vat. lat. 1346, fols. 88r, 109v, 188r.
7Lw = Vienna, Österreichische Nationalbibliothek, 2186, fols. 152r-v, 196v.

3L
The manuscripts of 3L and locations of the canons of Piacenza therein are as follows; 3L is now available in the edition by Motta, *Coll. can. 3L*.
3Lp = Pistoia, Archivio Capitolare del Duomo 135 (109), fols. 37v-38v, 177v, 186r.
3Lv = Città del Vaticano, BAV, Vat. lat. 3831, fols. 34v-33r,[129] 103v-4r, 106v-7r.

9L
BAV, Città del Vaticano, Archivio d: S. Pietro C.118, fols. 31r, 91r, 92v.

GRATIAN
Knowledge of Gratian's *Decretum* has advanced significantly with the discovery of a version (Gratian 1) earlier and sigificantly shorter than the well-known text that circulated throughout Europe from the mid-twelfth century onward (Gratian 2).[130] The first version appears in several manuscripts which are described in detail in Anders Winroth's book in which the discovery was announced.[131] The appearance of Piacenza varies considerably in the two versions, as indicated in the tabulation above (a full account of the contents of Gratian 1 is provided in the Appendix of Winroth's study). All manuscripts of this version that have canons of Piacenza were collated and are listed below. It should be pointed out that Grat.1a, Grat.1b, and Grat.1f also contain, added later in supplements or in the margins,

---

[128] This information is taken from Kéry, *Collections* 266–72 (adding what is given in Somerville–Zapp, '"Eighth Book"' 163–64, for 7L); partial manuscripts are included in the count.

[129] For suspicion about misbinding of the manuscript see Gossman, *Urban* 42, where 33r should be read for 34r.

[130] See in general the special volume of the *Revue de droit canonique* 48.2 (1998), dedicated to articles concerning this discovery: *Le Décret de Gratien revisité (Hommage à Rudolf Weigand)*. The labels 'Gratian 1' and 'Gratian 2' will be followed, although questions about the utility of these titles have been raised: see José Miguel Viejo-Ximénez, 'La recepción del derecho Romano en el derecho canónoco', *Ius Ecclesiae* 14 (2002) 386.

[131] Winroth, *Making* 23ff.

second-recension texts missing in the first. The process by which those additions penetrated the first version of the *Decretum* has yet to be clarified.

Grat.1a = Admont, Stiftsbibliothek 23, fols. 104v, 107v.

Grat.1b = Barcelona, Archivo de la Corona de Aragón, Ripoll 78, fols. 109vb-110ra, 115vb-16ra.

Grat.1f = Florence, Biblioteca Nazionale Centrale, Conv. sopp. A.1. 402, fols. 23ra, 25rb.[132]

Grat.1p = Paris, BNF, nal 1761, fols. 95ra, 101vb-2ra.

Grat.2 = Friedberg, *Decretum*.[133]

Discussion on the origin of the early version of the *Decretum Gratiani* has focused new attention on yet another manuscript: St. Gallen, Stiftsbibliothek 673. As with some copies of the first recension, this manuscript too was long thought to contain an abbreviation of the standard text of Gratian's work, but closer examination now has established a clear connection between this book and the first version, although the details of the relationship are debated.[134] For present purposes it will be sufficient to indicate the presence of the canons of Piacenza found therein (cc. 3–7), although in an unusual form, and to include these texts in the collations.[135]

Grat. 1s = St. Gallen, Stiftsbibliothek 673, pp. 40–41.

c) Collectio Caesaraugustana and the Councils of Piacenza and Clermont

The important collection known as the *Caesaraugustana* (named by Antonio Agustín for the charterhouse in Saragossa in northeastern Spain where the earliest manuscript was discovered), awaits a thorough study. The work exists in several recensions, and its place of origin and date of compilation have been characterized thus: 'Any date between 1108 and 1140 is possible, but a date after 1120 is more probable... [composed in] Northern Spain, Aquitaine or Burgundy; Eastern Pyrenees?'[136] The collection does not contain any canons of Piacenza labelled as such, but includes cc. 1–7, most of c. 12, and c. 13, all

---

[132] For this book, see ibid. 31–32, and in more detail, id., 'Le Manuscrit florentin du Décret de Gratien. Critique des travaux de Carlos Larrainzar sur Gratien I', *Revue de droit canonique* 51 (2001) 211–31.

[133] For Gratian 2 Friedberg's edition is used. This is not an ideal solution but works tolerably well to show the difference between Gratian 1 and Gratian 2. For Friedberg's text, see Regula Gujer, *Concordia discordantium codicum manuscriptorum* (Forschungen zur Kirchlichen Rechtsgeschichte und zum Kirchenrecht 23; Cologne 2004) 5 ff.

[134] Larrainzar, 'Borrador' passim. Debate about the nature of this manuscript is found in articles in *Revue de droit canonique* 51.2 (2001); more recently see José Miguel Viejo-Xieménz, 'La composición del Decreto de Graciano', *Ius canonicum* 45 (2005) 431–85, Anders Winroth, 'Recent Work On The Making of Gratian's *Decretum*', BMCL 26 (2004–6) 1–29, and Sommar, *Correctores* 4, esp. n. 4.

[135] Larrainzar, 'Borrador' 623, notes the placement of Piacenza cc. 3–4 after cc. 5–7 in this manuscript. See also the tabulation in the Appendix, ibid., 652 ff.

[136] Kéry, *Collections* 260–62; see also Fowler-Magerl, *Clavis* 239 ff., and most recently, ead., 'The Version of the *Collectio Caesaraugustana* in Barcelona, Archivo de la Corona de Aragón, MS San Cugat 63', in Cushing and Gyug (eds.), *Ritual, Text and Law*, 269–80 (see n. 116 above for the full ref.)

inscribed as canons of Urban II's Council of Clermont.[137] Are these provisions from Piacenza or from Clermont?

The answer is not simple. Bernold of Constance wrote that Clermont confirmed what had been done at Piacenza, and the Φ version of the acts of Clermont stated that the *capitula* of all of Urban's earlier synods were confirmed at Clermont, and those gatherings were named: Melfi, Benevento, Troia, and Piacenza.[138] It is noteworthy that, inscribed *Item post alia*, the text of Melfi c. 8, prohibiting lay investiture of bishoprics and abbeys, appears in the *Caesaraugustana* immediately after Clermont/Piacenza c. 13.[139] That could suggest that Melfi was further down a list of earlier conciliar legislation, including the canons of Piacenza, that was re-enacted at Clermont. But whatever the situation, as Stefan Beulertz has written, the matter 'läßt sich kaum klären'.[140]

It would, however, be rash simply to discount the inscription for Clermont and to assume that it was a copyist's error and was meant to read *Urbanus papa in concilio Placentino*.[141] Churchmen from southern France and northern Spain attended Clermont, and re-promulgated texts from the Italian councils bearing inscriptions to Clermont could have been taken home by those participants. Whatever their origin, whoever preserved these decrees in the *Collectio Caesaraugustana* excluded cc. 8–11, which deal specifically with the Wibertine Schism, and focused instead on the rulings about simony. The reason is unknown, but perhaps the dispute about schismatic orders was a less burning issue either in the environment of the Council of Clermont, where these canons were reiterated, or in southern France or northern Spain, where the collection was assembled.[142]

Variants among the Clermont/Piacenza decrees from the *Caesaraugustana* will be listed separately in the apparatus to the edition. The following manuscripts have been used, with Pc1, S, and Pc2 representing successive stages of the compilation.[143]

Pc1 = Paris, BNF, lat. 3875, fols. 21v-22r.
S = Salamanca, Biblioteca Universitaria, 2644, fols. 23r-v.
Pc2 = Paris, BNF, lat 3876, fol. 17v.

---

[137] Somerville, *Decreta* 125–26. These decrees were edited by Étienne Baluze from Paris, BNF, lat. 3875, in his annotations to Pierre de Marca, *De concordia sacerdotii et imperii* (Rovereto 1742) 396.

[138] Bernold, *Chronicon*, ed. Pertz 464 / ed. Robinson 526; for the text from Clermont, see Somerville, *Decreta* 123 (c. 5).

[139] This is the source of the confusion about an investiture canon enacted at Piacenza: see the discussion of MS ΦVa in the following chapter.

[140] Beulertz, *Verbot* 48.

[141] See the tradition that Clermont reiterated the inauguration at Piacenza of a tenth preface for the mass (see Somerville, *Decreta* 130, and Chapter 5), and cf. the information found in some versions of the *Collectio Caesaraugustana* that this was renewed by Pope Urban at the Council of Nîmes in 1096, where Clermont's legislation was re-enacted (Somerville, 'French Councils' 62–4 [repr. Id., *Papacy, Councils and Canon Law*]).

[142] Assuming that the decrees in question in the *Caesaraugustana* are canons of Piacenza that were reissued at Clermont, the situation is thus analogous to what occurred at the Council at Rome in 1099, i.e., a significant part of the canonical program from Piacenza was taken up by a later synod of Urban II. No evidence is at hand that Piacenza's legislation was repeated in councils between Clermont and Rome, but it seems feasible. For those assemblies see Chapter 6.

[143] See the references in n. 136.

Narrative Sources

Canons from Piacenza appear in the following works composed between the time of the synod and the mid-twelfth century. Other decrees inserted here and there in similar sources may have been missed, especially in works written in the second half of the twelfth century and later.

a) The *Gesta Romanae aecclesiae contra Hildebrandum* – cc. 1–12

These polemics were discussed in detail at the beginning of this chapter. Tract viii contains the preamble and cc. 1–12 from Piacenza. The *Gesta* were edited by Kuno Francke using two manuscripts.[144] These were Weilland's MSS 10–11.

Bg = Brussels, Bibliothèque Royale Albert Ier, 11196–97.

Bg is an early twelfth-century miscellany, including the *Gesta*, and the Register of Pope Gregory I, from the Hospital of St. Nicholas near Kues, and once was owned by Nicholas Cusanus. Piacenza is at fol. 8r-v.[145]

Hg = Hannover, Niedersächsische Landesbibliothek, XI.671 (110).

Hg is a sixteenth-century composite manuscript, including in addition to the *Gesta*, the 'Hannover Letter Collection', and once was used by the Magdeburg Centurions. Piacenza is at fols. 124v-125v.[146]

Hg is an inferior text to Bg but not derivative from it, and both manuscripts are collated for the edition below.[147]

b) Bernold of Constance, *Chronicon* – varia

Bernold's elaborate treatment of Piacenza was considered in detail in the first part of this chapter. The autograph of the *Chronicon* survives in Munich, Bayerische Staatsbibliothek, clm. 432. Bernold's account includes snippets of Piacenza cc. 2–4, and virtually all of cc. 13–14. The general diffusion of cc. 13–14 offers little variation, and Bernold's texts will not, therefore, be included in the apparatus criticus. But given the importance of Bernold's account for the history of Piacenza, this narrative will be printed in full from the new edition by I.S. Robinson, and translated below, in Appendix I to this chapter.

---

[144] MGH Lib. de lite 2. 366ff., with Piacenza at 408–9.

[145] See Joseph Van den Gheyn, S.J., *Catalogue des manuscrits de la Bibliothèque Royale de Belgique* 2 (Brussels 1902) 237, no. 1235, and Werner Krämer, 'Cod. Brux. 11196–11197 Lib. de lite Beno, Gesta Romanae ecclesiae; Nikolaus II., Briefe; Gregor I., Register', *Mitteilungen und Forschungsbeiträge des Cusanus-Gesellschaft* 14 (1980) 182–97. Blumenthal, *Early Councils* 116–17, and Claudia Märtl, *Die falschen Investiturprivilegien* (MGH Fontes iuris Germanici antiqui in usum scholarum 13; Hannover 1986) 123, also offer useful information and bibliography.

[146] See Carl Erdmann(+) and Norbert Fickermann, *Briefsammlungen der Zeit Heinrichs IV.* (MGH Die Briefe der Deutschen Kaiserzeit 5; Weimar 1950) 1ff., and 249–52, I.S. Robinson, 'The "Colores Rhetorici" in the Investiture Contest', *Traditio* 32 (1976) 209–10, and Heidrich, *Ravenna* 150–51.

[147] Martin Steinmann, 'Eine neue Handschrift der "Gesta Romanae ecclesiae contra Hildebrandum"', *Deutsches Archiv* 27 (1971) 200–202, announced the discovery of a new exemplar of the *Gesta* (Basel, Universitätsbibl. A.V.13), a late-medieval paper manuscript closely related to Hg although not its source, and presenting a more corrupt text. It has not been collated for this edition.

c) Gerhoch of Reichersberg, *Libellus de eo, quod princeps mundi huius iam iudicatus sit* (Liber de simoniacis) – c. 15 partim, followed by cc. 1–4

Gerhoch's *Libellus* was composed in 1135 and dedicated to Bernard of Clairvaux. It survives in three manuscripts, one of which, Klagenfurt, Studienbibliothek 10, fols. 81 ff., contains an autograph, with Piacenza at 94r-v; this manuscript was collated alongside Sackur's edition for the texts of Piacenza.[148]

d) Annalista Saxo – cc. 8–12

The 'Saxon Annalist' is a title bestowed in 1723 by the first editor, Johann Georg von Eckhart, on the compiler of a extensive German chronicle for the years 741 to 1139. The work survives in Paris, BNF, MS lat. 11851. This is the original exemplar, written by several hands in the middle of the twelfth century in eastern Saxony, perhaps in the vicinity of Magdeburg. No medieval copies or excerpts are known. Piacenza appears under the year 1100, within a discussion of Urban II's condemnation of ordinations performed by Wibert of Ravenna. For the collation below the recent edition by Klaus Nass has been followed.[149]

Conclusion

The survival of the legislation from Piacenza rests on several dozen manuscripts, virtually all of the twelfth-century, that present essentially the same canons, notwithstanding textual variants. Not all copies include all the decrees, but most contain the texts about simony and ordinations that were prompted by the Wibertine Schism. That program was conceived as a unit and more or less survives as one, including in systematic canon law books. Canons attributed to Piacenza seem to turn up in isolation less frequently than for other councils of Urban II, and only a small number has been discovered, although this is a preliminary result that requires further attention.[150]

---

[148] The information presented here is drawn from Classen, *Gerhoch* 408–9, and 465. Ernst Sackur edited the *Libellus* in Lib. de lite 3. 239–72 (see the remarks of Classen, op. cit. 409), with Piacenza at 253. The author is grateful to the Hill Museum and Manuscript Library at St. John's University, Collegeville, MN, and especially to Matthew Heintzelmann, for expediting a copy of the relevant pages of the manuscript from Klagenfurt. For Gerhoch see also MS Mub above in *Survival*, Lists of Canons Sect. a.

[149] See Klaus Nass, *Die Reichschronik des Annalista Saxo und die sächsische Geschichtsschreibung im 12. Jahrhundert* (MGH Schriften 41; Hannover 1996), esp. 1–3, 14–21, 31–32, and 330–31, specifically for Piacenza, and 365–75 for a discussion of date, location, and author. Nass' edition is available in *Die Reichschronik des Annalista Saxo* (MGH Scriptores 37; Hannover 2006), with Piacenza at 502–3. The author is grateful to Dr. Nass and to Dr. Detlev Jasper of MGH for information about the Annalista.

[150] See the two texts, in MSS Pj and Pb, given at the end of the edition in Chapter 4, and see also Appendix II below. For purposes of comparison, see individual canons from Melfi and Benevento noted in Somerville–Kuttner, *Pope Urban* 204–14, and 274, Gossman, *Urban* 106, and Roger E. Reynolds, 'Patristic "Presbyterianism" in the Early Medieval Theology of Sacred Orders', *Mediaeval Studies* 45 (1983) 338 (repr. Id., *Clerics in the Early Middle Ages* [Variorum Collected Studies Series CS669; Aldershot 1999]). For Clermont, see Somerville, *Decreta* 139–41. Piacenza cc. 14–15 plus the concluding liturgical notice have been discovered standing alone as follows (and no doubt elsewhere too): c. 14 – inscribed *Urbanus papa omnibus Christianis*, in the twelfth-century canonical collection in Montecassino, Archivio dell'Abbazia, MS 216, p. 197 (Reynolds, *Collectio* 99); inscribed *Urbanus papa*

As described at the beginning of Chapter 1, Urban's desire in light of the Wibertine Schism to legislate about ordination and orders was a pressing issue. Earlier sections of the present chapter suggested that the pope and his chancery were determined to circulate widely a series of decisions on these questions. The procedures employed for doing so remain largely a mystery, but whatever the process entailed, the result was broad dissemination of a suprisingly unified canonical agenda that became an important building block of the legal structure of the medieval Church. The uniformity of what survives as the canons of Piacenza is all the more striking when compared with the vast number of different traditions stemming from the Council of Clermont nine months later. Whatever mechanisms Pope Urban had for disseminating the rulings from Piacenza in March, 1095, those same methods seem to have been either unavailable or unsuccessful at Clermont in November of that year.

Although a surprisingly large circulation has been documented for texts from the Council of Melfi, Piacenza's decrees survive far more widely than any of Urban's earlier councils.[151] That Pope Paschal II emphasized the importance of Piacenza may have helped in the distribution, although Bernold of Constance and the *Gesta* show that the process was well under way before 1100.[152] Aside from a small number of later exemplars, moreover, no list of the provisions was copied directly from any other, and thus what survives rests on dozens of lost witnesses made closer to the time of the synod. With extensive absorption into canon law collections, and taking into account reiteration in the Councils of Clermont and Rome, the fortuna of texts from Piacenza is a very impressive phenomenon.

---

ii., in the twelfth-century *Collectio Pragensis* in Prague, Národni Knihovna České Republiky, MS VIII. H.7, fols. 22vb-23ra (see Kéry, *Collections* 286–87, and Fowler-Magerl, *Clavis* 244–45 [called by Kéry '*Collectio Pragensis*', and by Fowler-Magerl '*Collectio canonum Pragensis I* or the *Collectio CCXCIV capitulorum*']); with same inscription in the margin of fol. 52r in the twelfth-century copy of the *Panormia* found in BAV, Vat. lat. 1359 (see Kuttner–Elze, *Catalogue* 127–28). A slightly different form of c. 14 appears on fol. 83v of the Turin *Collection in Seven Books* (bk. 5, c. 204), inscribed *Urbanus papa de ⟨ieiunio⟩ quatuor temporum.* (this is MS T [see above, *Survival*, Canon Law Collections], containing Piacenza cc. 1–14 at fols. 135v-36r). One instance of c. 15 and one of the concluding notice have been found: c. 15 – inscribed *Urbanus papa ii in Placentina synodo dixit.*, added to bk. 2 of the partial, thirteenth-century copy of the *Panormia* in Cambridge, Pembroke College 103 (fol. 32r) (see Brett, '*Panormia*' 262); notice – Paris, Bibl. de l'Arsenal, MS 713, fol. 19r (*In Placentina synodo ab Urbano papa ii antiquis novem prefationibus decima est addita que sic se habet*), added to a late twelfth-century *Panormia* (see ibid. 267, for this manuscript); the notice also occurs ascribed to the Councils of Clermont and Nîmes (see n. 141 above). Martin Brett has pointed out to the author in addition that c. 15 and the notice are found as supplements in a copy of the *Panormia* (from Padua) in Paris, BNF, MS lat. 10742 (see Brett, '*Panormia*' 266). For part of JL 6436 (IP 5. 367, no. 7) (= C.30, q. 2, c. 5), inscribed to the Council of Piacenza see Uta-Renata Blumenthal, 'Decrees and decretals of Pope Paschal II in twelfth-century canonical collections', BMCL 10 (1980) 19, n. 24 (repr. Ead., *Papal Reform and Canon Law in the 11th and 12th Centuries* [Variorum Collected Studies CS618; Aldershot 1998]), and cf. Motta, *Coll. can. 3L* (pars altera) 150, for 3.12.[121], wrongly inscribed to Piacenza.

[151] Somerville–Kuttner, *Pope Urban* 186–214.
[152] See Blumenthal, *Early Councils* 32, and especially n. 14 for JL 6050 (GP 4.4. 119, no. 208), and most recently ead., 'Pasquale II e il concilio di Guastalla del 1106', Glauco Maria Cantarella and Daniela Romagnoli (eds.), *1106. Il Concilio di Guastalla e il mondo di Pasquale II* (Alessandria 2006) 29–30.

The greatest number of copies of the textus receptus derive, not surprisingly, from Italy and especially northen Italy, but Germany, France, and perhaps northern Spain also contributed manuscripts where the canons were transcribed. None is known from Britain or from the frontiers of Latin Christendom in eastern or northern Europe, but not every manuscript has been tied to a place of origin (see, for example, the discussion above about MS Os), and no doubt additional exemplars remain undetected.[153] Furthermore, if Piacenza as mediated through the decrees of the Council of Rome is taken into account (see Chapter 6), a significant diffusion via canon law books which circulated in northwestern France and across the Channel comes into play.[154]

The survival of the canons from a number of papal councils between Popes Leo IX and Eugene III remains to be investigated, and for some of those gatherings the canonical tradition is substantial. The legislation from Gregory VII's Roman Synod of November, 1078, for example, is included in many canon law books throughout western Europe, yet those provisions do not survive outside of such books to the extent that Piacenza's do.[155] How the fortuna of Piacenza compares with the legislative traditions of popes from later in the twelfth century such as Calixtus II and Innocent II remains to be determined. The Lateran Councils of 1123 and 1139 each contributed a slightly larger group of texts to the second version of Gratian's *Decretum* than did Piacenza. But a place in Gratian for Piacenza's rulings assured their survival, and later commentaries on Gratian provide insight about how those canons were understood in the High and late Middle Ages and on into early-modern times.[156]

---

[153] Brett, 'Lateran Council' 14–15, remarks on the absence of manuscripts that were written in England or brought there early on containing the canons of Piacenza.

[154] The distribution of canons of Rome is not readily apparent from the tables in Gossman, *Urban* 104–8, since no differentiation was made between the common decrees of Piacenza and Rome. The Roman provisions occur inter al., as will be discussed below, in the early-twelfth-century northern French *Collection in Ten Parts*, a copy of which is found in Cambridge, Corpus Christi College 94. This book is clearly English (communication of Martin Brett), although it may or may not originate at Canterbury. N.R. Ker, *Medieval Libraries of Great Britain*, 2nd edn. (Royal Historical Society Guides and Handbooks 3; London 1964) 39–40, rejected his earlier attribution to Canterbury Cathedral, but tentatively suggested that it might have been written at Canterbury in St. Augustine's Abbey (cf. 337). That attribution is presented without question by Richard Gameson, *The Manuscripts of Early Norman England (c.1066–1130)* (Oxford 1999) 60, and affirmed by Barker-Benfield, *St. Augustine's* 2045.

[155] John Gilchrist, 'The Reception of Pope Gregory VII into the Canon Law (1073–1141)', ZRG, Kan. Abt. 59 (1973), 35–82; op. cit. Part II, ibid. 66 (1980) 129–229 (repr. Id., *Canon Law in the Age of Reform, 11th-12th Centuries* [Variorum Collected Studies Series CS406; Aldershot 1993]). See also now Blumenthal, 'Conciliar Canons' 367–68.

[156] For a succinct account of the development of the collections of high medieval canon law, and for the use of that material in the later sixteenth century, see Sommar, *Correctores*, Introduction.

Appendix I: English Translation of Bernold of Constance's Description of the Council of Piacenza[157]

Domnus papa, Deo et sancto Petro prosperante, iam pene ubique praevaluit et in media Longobardia, in civitate Placentia, inter ipsos scismaticos et contra ipsos, generalem sinodum condixit. Ad quam episcopos Italiae, Burgundiae, Franciae, Alemanniae, Baioariae, aliarumque provinciarum canonica et apostolica auctoritate, missis literis, convocavit.

Facta est autem haec sinodus circa mediam quadragesimam Placentiae, ad quam sinodum multitudo tam innumerabilis confluxit, ut nequaquam in qualibet aeclesia illius loci posset comprehendi. Unde et domnus papa extra urbem in campo illam celebrare compulsus est. Nec hoc tamen absque probabilis exempli auctoritate. Nam ipse primus legislator Moyses populum Dei in campestribus legalibus praeceptis, Deo iubente, instituit et ipse Dominus non in domibus, sed in monte et in campestribus discipulos suos evangelicis statutis informavit. Missas quoque nonnunquam extra aeclesiam satis probabiliter, necessitate quidem cogente, celebramus, quamvis aeclesias earum celebrationi specialiter deputatas non ignoremus.

In hac sinodo Praxedis regina, iam dudum a Heinrico separata, super maritum suum domno apostolico et sanctae sinodo conquesta est de inauditis fornicationum spurciciis, quas apud maritum passa est. Cuius querimoniam domnus papa cum sancta sinodo satis misericorditer suscepit, eo quod ipsam tantas spurcicias non tam

By the favor of God and St. Peter, the lord pope now prevailed almost everywhere, and in central Lombardy, in the city of Piacenza among those schismatic and against them he prepared for a general synod. By sending out letters he convoked to this gathering by canonical and apostolic authority bishops of Italy, Burgundy, France, Germany, Bavaria, and of other provinces.

This synod occurred around the middle of Lent, and such an innumerable multitude convened to that synod that it simply could not be contained in any church in town. Whence the lord pope was compelled to celebrate it outside the city in an open field. He did not do this without the authority of a credible example, for with God's permission that first legislator, Moses, taught legal precepts to the people of God on a plain, and the Lord instructed his disciples in the teachings of the gospel not in a dwelling but on the mount and on the plain. Sometimes also we celebrate masses when necessary very adequately outside of a church, although we are not ignorant of the fact that it is churches particularly that have been designated for those celebrations.

In this synod Queen Praxedis, long separated from Henry, complained to the lord pope and the holy synod about her husband, regarding the unheard-of filth of fornication that she suffered at his hands. The lord pope with the holy synod received her complaint very mercifully, since he recognized for certain

---

[157] Printed by kind permission of Hahn Verlag from Bernold, *Chronicon*, ed. Ian Robinson (Germany: Hahnsche Buchhandlung, 2003), 518–22. The account in ed. Pertz, is found in 461–62. The paragraph divisions of Robinson's edition have been followed in the translation. For this text see above in *Enactment*, Bernold.

commisisse, quam invitam pertulisse, pro certo cognoverit. Unde et de penitentia pro huiusmodi flagiciis iniungenda illam clementer absolvit, quae et peccatum suum sponte et publice confiteri non erubuit.

Ad hanc sinodum Philippus rex Galliarum legationem suam direxit, seque ad illam iter incepisse, sed legitimis soniis se impeditum fuisse mandavit. Unde indutias sibi usque in pentecosten apud domnum papam, sinodo intercedente, impetravit. Domnus autem Hugo Lugdunensis archiepiscopus ad eandem sinodum vocatus, ab officio suspenditur, eo quod ipse non venerit nec legatum cum canonica excusatione illuc pro se direxerit.

Item legatio Constantinopolitani imperatoris ad hanc sinodum pervenit, qui domnum papam omnesque Christi fideles suppliciter imploravit, ut aliquod auxilium sibi contra paganos pro defensione sanctae aeclesiae conferrent, quam pagani iam pene in illis partibus deleverant, qui partes illas usque ad muros Constantinopolitanae civitatis obtinuerant. Ad hoc ergo auxilium domnus papa multos incitavit, ut etiam iureiurando promitterent, se illuc, Deo annuente, ituros et eidem imperatori contra paganos pro posse suo fidelissimum adiutorium collaturos.

Haec autem inter alia in illa sinodo constituta sunt, ut ad penitentiam nullo modo reciperentur, qui concubinas, vel odium ex corde vel quodlibet mortale peccatum dimittere nollent. Item ut nullus presbiter aliquos ad penitentiam reciperet, nisi cui proprius episcopus hanc curam commisisset. Item ut quibuslibet rite ad confessionem venientibus eucharistiam non denegemus, quos solo corpore, non mente, inter

both that she had not initiated such filthiness and also had endured it unwillingly. Whence with clemency he absolved her of the penance that ought to be imposed for disgraces of this sort – she who willingly and publicly was not ashamed to confess her sin.

Philip, king of France, sent a legation to this synod and had set out himself on that journey, but reported that he had been prevented from appearing for legitimate reasons. Whence from the lord pope, with the synod interceding, he gained a delay for himself until Pentecost. The lord Hugh, archbishop of Lyon, having been called to the same synod was suspended from office because he did not appear nor send a representative with a canonical excuse on his behalf.

Likewise a legation came to this synod from the Constantinopolitan emperor, who humbly implored the lord pope and all the faithful of Christ that they offer help to him against the pagans for the defense of the holy church which they already had almost annihilated in these parts, occupying those regions up to the walls of the city of Constantinople. The lord pope induced many men to offer this help, so that they promised indeed by oath that they will journey there with God's help and, to the best of their ability, will provide help to the same emperor.

Among others, however, these things were decided in that synod. That those who are unwilling to relinquish concubines, hatred in their heart, and any mortal sin whatsoever should by no means be received to penance. Likewise, that no priest, except to whom his own bishop committed that duty, should receive anyone to penance. Likewise, that we

excommunicatos manere nec tamen eorum sacramentis communicare cognoscimus.

In hac quoque sinodo heresis simoniacorum penitus damnata est, ut quicquid vel in sacris ordinibus vel in aeclesiasticis rebus data vel promissa pecunia adquisitum simoniace videretur, pro irrito haberetur, nullasque vires habuisse vel habere iudicaretur. His tamen qui non simoniace et nescienter a simoniacis ordinati sunt, misericordia in servando ordine concessa est. Qui vero scienter ab huiusmodi ordinati sunt, cum suis ordinatoribus inrecuperabiliter damnati sunt. Item heresis Nicholaitarum, id est incontinentium subdiaconorum, diaconorum et praecipue sacerdotum, inretractabiliter damnata est, ut deinceps de officio se non intromittant, qui in illa heresi manere non formidant, nec populus eorum officia ullo modo recipiat, si ipsi Nicholaitae contra hęc interdicta ministrare praesumant. Item heresis Beringariana, iam ab antiquo sepissime anathematizata, iterum damnata est et sententia catholicę fidei contra eandem firmata est, videlicet quod panis et vinum, cum in altari consecrantur, non solum figurate sed etiam vere et essentialiter in corpus et sanguinem Domini convertantur. Item in Guibertum heresiarchen, sedis apostolicae invasorem, et in omnes eius complices sententia anathematis sinodali iudicio cum ardentibus candelis iterum promulgata est. In hac sinodo IIII fere milia clericorum et plus quam XXX milia laicorum fuisse perhibentur.

should not deny the eucharist to anyone at all properly seeking penance whom we recognize to remain among the schismatics in body alone, not in mind, nor to share their sacraments.

Also in this synod the heresy of the simoniacs was absolutely damned, so that whatever either in sacred orders or in ecclesiastical possessions has been gotten with money either given or promised is considered simoniacal, held to be illegal, and judged to have had and to have no power.[158] To those, however, who were ordained unwittingly by simoniacs, mercy was conceded for the order to be retained.[159] But those who knowingly were ordained in this way were irretrievably damned with their ordainers.[160] Likewise the heresy of the Nicolaitans, that is of incontinent subdeacons, deacons, and especially priests, was damned irrevocably, so that henceforth those who do not fear remaining in that heresy should not appropriate for himself an office, nor should the people in any way accept their services if they, contrary to these prohibitions, presume to minister. Likewise the Berengarian heresy, already for a long time very often anathematized, again was damned and the opinion of the catholic faith confirmed against it, namely that the bread and wine, when they are consecrated on the altar, not only figuratively but even in truth and in essence are converted into the body and blood of the Lord. Likewise a sentence of anathema by synodal judgment, with burning candles, again was promulgated against the heresiarch Guibert, the invader of the apostolic see,

---

[158] Cf. c. 2 of the textus receptus, ed. at the end of Chapter 4.
[159] Cf. ibid. c. 3.
[160] Cf. ibid. c. 4.

In hac sinodo constitutum est, ut pro crismate et baptismo et sepultura nichil unquam exigatur. Item, ut ieiunia IIII[or] temporum hoc ordine celebrentur, scilicet primum in prima epdomada quadragesimae, secundum in epdomada pentecostes. Tercium vero et quartum in Septembri et Decembri solito more fiant.

Huic sinodo reverentissimi antistites interfuerunt, de Baioaria quidem Diemo Salcburgensis archiepiscopus et Ŏdalricus Pataviensis episcopus, eius suffraganeus, de Alemannia vero Gebehardus Constantiensis episcopus. Qui et Arnoldum Mediolanensem archiepiscopum, diu quidem electum sed nondum consecratum, eodem tempore ex concessione domni papae Mediolani consecravere. Ipse quoque domnus papa Ŏdalricum Augiensem abbatem eo tempore consecravit, qui itidem praedictae sinodo interfuit. Cui in praesentia Constantiensis episcopi omnem episcopalem potestatem in clerum et populum Augiensis insulae interdixit, quam dudum Constantiensi episcopo concessit. Abbas tamen ille non multo post de illa potestate se intromisit. Unde quaerimonia facta ab episcopo, domnus papa illum, missis literis, ab huiusmodi praesumptione iterum compescuit.

and against all his accomplices. In this synod nearly 4000 clergy and more than 30,000 laity are reported to have been on hand.

In this synod it was decided that nothing ever should be exacted for chrism, baptism, and burial.[161] Likewise, that the Ember Days should be celebrated in this order, namely, the first in the first week of Lent, the second in the week of Pentecost, but the third and fourth should be made in September and December in the accustomed manner.[162]

At this synod [these] most reverent bishops were present: from Bavaria Archbishop Diemo of Salzburg, and his suffragan Ulrich of Passau; from Germany Bishop Gebhard of Constance. At the same time at Milan, with the permission of the lord pope, they consecrated Archbishop Arnulf of Milan, elected a long time ago but not yet consecrated. At this time also the lord pope himself consecrated Abbot Udalrich of Reichenau who likewise was present at the afore-said synod. The pope, in the presence of the bishop of Constance, forbade him all episcopal power over the clergy and people of the island of Reichenau, which not long ago he [the pope] conceded to the bishop of Constance. Soon after, nevertheless, that abbot appropriated for himself that power. Whence, a complaint having been made by the bishop, the lord pope, with letters having been sent, again restrained him from a presumption of that sort.

---

[161] Cf. ibid. c. 13.
[162] Cf. ibid. c. 14.

Appendix II: Vagrant Canons

As noted in the last section of this chapter, in comparison with other papal synods of the time Piacenza's legislation is remarkably free of what can be called *canones vagantes*. Two such provisions are appended to copies of the textus receptus, in MSS Pj and Pb, concerning respectively payment of tithes to priests and clerical celibacy. Both are issues on which Pope Urban legislated at Melfi, and those earlier statements could have been reaffirmed at Piacenza.[163] Another such 'vagrant' decree also has been linked with Piacenza, i.e., a canon prescribing a common life for those who obtain ecclesiastical benefices. This ruling was first discussed by Joseph Walter in 1935, on the basis of its appearance in MS 1291 of the Archives hospitalières at the Archives communales, Strasbourg. That early thirteenth-century book derived from the house of regular canons of St.-Arbogast in Strasbourg, and contains the *Rule of St. Augustine*, part of a commentary by Hugh of St. Victor on that *Rule*, and other items pertaining to regular canons.[164] The text in question appears on fol. 8v, between the *Rule* and Hugh's commentary, and is given in full below. (Walter omitted the inscription and the lines after *Prosperi instituta*.)[165]

> Urbanus papa ii. De communi vita clericorum novum quid nequaquam indicimus, set eos qui ecclesie beneficiis potiuntur propriis abrenunciare ad exemplum primitive ecclesie in qua nemo aliquid suum esse dicebat sub communione una vivere precipimus, secundum sanctorum patrum scilicet Urbani pape decreta Augustini et Prosperi instituta. Qui enim de sorte Domini sunt vel quia ipse Dominus sors eorum est et pars, vel quia ipsi pars Domini sunt tales se exhibere debent ut possideant Dominum et possideantur a Domino.

De communi vita was also printed in 1948 by Charles Dereine, from a fourteenth-century manuscript at Utrecht, Bibliotheek der Rijksuniversiteit, MS 111, a book that contains various items dealing with regular canons, including on fol. 96r *De communi vita*, inscribed *Item in Placentino concilio Urbani II*.[166] Three years later Dereine reprinted the text, adding the information that it also occurred in MS 1291 from Strasbourg, but without indicating the difference in the inscriptions of the

---

[163] Somerville–Kuttner, *Pope Urban* 253–54.

[164] Joseph Walter, 'Das Regelbuch des Augustinerchorherrenstifts St. Arbogast bei Strassburg', *Archiv für Elsässische Kirchengeschichte* 10 (1935) 391–414; see especially 397–99, where Walter gave a partial description of the manuscript's contents. See L.H. Cottineau, *Répertoire topo-bibliographique des abbayes et prieurés* 2 (Mâcon 1939) 3094.

[165] This information is based on Walter and on notes, together with a transcription, made in situ by Stephan Kuttner, probably in 1967. The codex is misbound; fol. 8 marks the end of a quire; and the beginning of Hugh's commentary is now missing. Walter wrote that 'two canons' ('zwei Canones') of Urban II are found on fol. 8v; but *De communi vita* is followed by an unknown excerpt that lacks an inscription and begins *Nemo ad hoc debet fieri clericus*, breaking off at the bottom of fol. 8v.

[166] Cf. Dereine, 'Le problème de la vie commune chez les canonistes, d'Anselme de Lucques à Gratien', *Studi Gregoriani* 3 (1948) 298. See the description of MS 111 in *Catalogus codicum manu scriptorum bibliothecae Universitatis Rheno-Trajectinae* (Utrecht 1877–1908) 1. 8, and 2. 32, which does not mention *De communi vita*.

two versions.[167] Subsequently other scholars occasionally alluded to *De communi vita*, Giovanni Miccoli and Andrea Tilatti for example, accepted it as a regulation from Piacenza, while Horst Fuhrmann and Johannes Laudage were cautious on the matter.[168] Another copy of the provision, inscribed *Urbanus II in Placentino concilio.*, was discovered by Linda Fowler-Magerl on fol. 90r of the twelfth-century canonical collection in Cologne, Historisches Archiv, MS W.Kl. fol. 199, among a series of texts attributed to Urban II dealing with regular canons, including at fol. 87v *Mandamus et mandantes* (= Gratian C. 19, q. 3, c. 2), inscribed *Urbanus II in Placentino concilio.*[169]

Both *De communi vita* and *Mandamus* fall outside the textus receptus of Piacenza, but that does not prove that their attribution to the council is incorrect. The former contains echoes of JL 5761, a fragment from Urban II dealing with regular canons, but that resonance equally does not make the decree's authenticity suspect. More suspicious perhaps is the fact that the end of *De communi vita* repeats part of a letter of St. Jerome that turns up often in the canonical tradition, e.g., in Gratian, C.12, q.1, c.5, and elsewhere (cf. Friedberg's apparatus).[170] The possibility that *De communi vita* and/or *Mandamus* were promulgated at Piacenza will be considered in a future study devoted to various texts, some of cloudy pedigree, that are ascribed to Urban II (see also the Postscript, n. 8).

---

[167] Id., 'L'élaboration du statut canonique des chanoines réguliers spécialement sous Urbain II', *Revue d'histoire ecclésiastique* 46 (1951) 551, and 557–58. Dereine (598) speculated that the Utrecht manuscript was a copy of an earlier work from Marbach.

[168] Giovanni Miccoli, *Chiesa Gregoriana* (nuovo ed. a cura Andrea Tilatti) (Italia sacra 60; Rome 1999) 125, n. 88; Horst Fuhrmann, *Papst Urban II. und der Stand der Regularkanoniker* (Sitzungsberichte Bayerische Akademie, 2; Munich 1984) 30, n. 78; Johannes Laudage, 'Ad exemplar primitivae ecclesiae: Kurie, Reich und Klerusreform von Urban II. bis Calix II.', in Stefan Weinfurter (ed.) (mit Mitarbeit von Hubertus Seibert), *Reformidee und Reformpolitik im spätsalisch-frühstaufischen Reich* (Quellen und Abhandlungen zur mittelrheinischen Kirchengeschichte 68; Mainz 1992) 54. Cf. Klaus Schreiner, 'Ein Herz und eine Seele: Eine urchristliche Lebensform und ihre Institutionalisierung im augustinisch geprägten Mönchtum des hohen und späten Mittelalters', in Gert Melville and Anne Müller (eds.), *Regula Sancti Augustini* (Publikationen der Akademie der Augustiner-Chorherren von Windesheim 3; Paring 2002) 16, n. 34, citing Fuhrmann and Laudage.

[169] Fowler-Magerl, *Clavis* 191–92 (cf. Kéry, *Collections* 287); the author is grateful to Dr. Fowler-Magerl for providing copies of sections of this manuscript. For *Mandamus*, see the edition by Horst Fuhrmann, 'Un papa tra religiosità personale e politica ecclesiastica: Urbano II (1088–99) ed il rapimento di un monaco benedettino', *Studi Medievali*³ 27 (1986) 13–14, and repeated id., 'Das Papsttum zwischen Frömmigkeit und Politik – Urban II. (1088–1099) und die Frage der Selbstheiligung', in Ernst-Dieter Hehl, Hubertus Seibert, und Franz Staab (eds.), *Deus qui mutat tempora. Menschen und Institutionen im Wandel des Mittelalters: Festschrift für Alfons Becker* (Sigmaringen 1987) 166–67; cf. Peter Landau, 'Die "Duae leges" im kanonischen Recht des 12. Jahrhundert', in id., *Officium und Libertas christiana* (Sitzungsberichte Bayerische Akademie, Jahrgang 1991, 3; Munich 1991) 73–4.

[170] *Epistulae* 52.5, ed. Isidore Hilberg, ed. altera Conrad Smolak (Corpus scriptorum ecclesiasticorum Latinorum 54; Vienna 1996) 421.

3
The Historiography of the Canons of Piacenza

In light of the discussions in the last chapter it is possible to unravel the historiographical traditions of Piacenza's legislation.[1] A printed version of the decrees first entered the stream of early-modern conciliar scholarship in the seventeenth century, making its way finally in 1775 to Mansi's *Amplissima collectio*.[2] A little more than a century later Ludwig Weiland offered another edition, together with information on about twenty manuscripts where these texts were found.[3] Weiland's presentation supersedes Mansi, but also prompts questions. Notwithstanding the list of manuscripts and an apparatus of variants accompanying the edition, little is offered about either the codices cited or the context in which the decrees occur within those books. The order in which the manuscripts are listed also is not explained, beyond the observation that MSS 1–5 contain fifteen canons, and MSS 6–12 only fourteen. Weiland knew Bernold of Constance's *Chronicon* and the *Gesta Romanae ecclesiae contra Hildebrandum* (his MS 10), and had interesting things to say about Bernold (discussed in Chapter 2). No comment is provided, however, about the *Gesta*, nor is anything said about the 1099 Council of Rome's repetition of a significant portion of Piacenza's decrees.

Chapter 2 showed that Piacenza exists in many more manuscripts than were known to Weiland; but how did he use what he knew to construct the text that has stood for more than a century as the standard account of this legislation? The answer is not obvious. His MS 4 was a paper manuscript cited according to an old shelfmark in the Barberini Library, XVI.67. It is in fact BAV, Barb. lat. 860, the book designated ΦVa in the previous chapter (cf. Chapter 2 *Survival*, *Polycarpus* Supplement). Weiland wrote that Philippe Labbe and Gabriel Cossart used this book and that Mansi noted its variant readings, 'whose editions we followed' ('quorum editiones secuti sumus').[4] The presence in Barb. lat. 860 of more texts than elsewhere led Weiland to write that the 'the Barberini codex is distinguished by the tenth preface of the

---

[1] An early version of this chapter appears as 'The Presentation of the Canons of Piacenza (March, 1095): An Overview, Baronius to Mansi', *Festschrift für Walter Brandmüller* (= AHC 27/28 [1995–96]) 193–205. For medieval secular chronicles and annals pertaining to Piacenza see Emilio Nasalli Rocca+, 'Agli albori della storiografia Piacentina', *Storiografia e storia: Studi in onore di Eugenio Duprè Theseider* (Rome 1974) 66, n. 4, and 70, and Racine, *Plaisance à la fin du XIIIème siècle* (see in Chapter 1, n. 25) 1. xxviii ff. The author has not found the canons in any of those sources. Poggiali, *Memorie* 25–32, for example, has a discussion of the synod based on other early-modern printed sources.
[2] Piacenza is in vol. 20 (Venice 1775) 801–16.
[3] Weiland's work is discussed in this chapter and at other points throughout the study.
[4] Labbe–Cossart 10. 500–505.

Mass, which directly follows c. 15, and the vagrant c. (16) on investiture' ('excellit Barberinianus notitia de decima missae praefatione, quae immediate sequitur caput 15, et canone (16) extravagante de investitura'.) It thus could readily be concluded that this early-modern book was a, if not *the*, key to the printings of Piacenza in both Labbe–Cossart and Mansi, and was in addition pivotal for Weiland.

But caution is advisable. Proceeding to Weiland's MS 9, a reader finds no shelfmark provided for a book described as 'a certain Vatican codex that the editions of Holstenius, *Collectio Romana bipartita* II.170, and Labbe-Cossart used' ('codex quidam Vaticanus, quem adhibuerunt editiones Holstenii Collectio Romana bipartita II, 170 ac Labbei et Cossartii'). These citations to Lukas Holste's *Collectio Romana bipartita* (1662), and again to Labbe–Cossart, complicate the question of how the text printed by those two French editors was derived, and by implication does the same for Weiland's edition, acknowledged as being based on Labbe–Cossart.[5] An assessment of Weiland's work thus appears to depend on Holste's edition, on understanding the use made of that edition by Labbe–Cossart, and on determining the importance of the Barberini codex.

As in other similar cases, sorting out the roots of Weiland's text can begin with Cardinal Cesare Baronius' *Annales ecclesiastici*.[6] Baronius' presentation of Piacenza focused on Bernold of Constance, whose account was repeated in full, although the erudite librarian of the Biblioteca apostolica knew more about the synod than what was found in the *Chronicon*.[7] He wrote that fifteen of its canons were contained in Book seven of the *decreta* of Anselm of Lucca, but that it was unnecessary to copy them because they agreed with what had been recounted already (Bernold). A few lines from Donizo's metrical life of Countess Mathilda of Tuscany completed the account.

The information from Baronius – with no accompanying list of conciliar canons – passed through the conciliar collections of the first half of the seventeenth century with no changes.[8] Only with the appearance of Holste's *Collectio* was a substantive addition made. Holste began with a statment of self-justification that contains what could be a jab at Baronius.[9]

---

[5] *Collectio Romana bipartita* (2 vols., Rome 1662), for Piacenza see 2. 169–76. For Holste, who was Vatican Librarian from 1653 to his death in 1661, see Suzanne Wemple, 'The Codex Holstenianus in Toledo: a Collection of Ninth, Tenth and Eleventh Century Capitularies', *Manuscripta* 13 (1969) 90–95, Stephan Kuttner, 'The Council of Carthage 535: A Supplementary Note', ZRG Kan. Abt. 73 (1987) 347–50, and Roger Aubert, *Dictionnaire d'histoire et de géographie ecclésiatiques* 24 (1993) 875–80 (under 'Holstenius').
[6] e.g., Somerville, *Decreta* 6–11, and 43–55, Blumenthal, *Early Councils* passim, and Somerville–Kuttner, *Pope Urban* 217–23.
[7] *Annales ecclesiastici* 11 (Rome 1605) 637–55.
[8] Binius, *Concilia* 3.2. 415–16; *Conciliorum omnium . . . collectio regia* 26 (Paris 1644) 659–62.
[9] *Collectio Romana bipartita 2.170*: 'Cardinalis Baronius anno MXCV. ubi synodi Placentinae historiam ex Bertholdo Constantiense narravit subjungit ejusdem concilii quindecim canones contineri in codice scripto Anselmi Lucensis libro VII. decretorum. Qua in re eum memoria vel potius amanuensium oscitantia fefellit. Neque enim canones illos Placentinos in suam collectionem referre potuit Anselmus, qui novennio ante decesserat: nec Vaticani codices citato libro VII. vel alibi eosdem agnoscunt. Tum vero XIV. tantum capitula statutorum libri probatissimi bibliothecae

At the year 1095, where he narrated a history of the Council of Piacenza from Bernold of Constance, Cardinal Baronius adds that fifteen canons of the same council are contained in a manuscript of the *decreta* of Anselm of Lucca, in Book 7. In this matter memory, or rather the carelessness of his copyists, failed him. For Anselm, who died nine years earlier, was unable to cite those Piacenzan canons in his collection, nor is there a trace of them in Vatican manuscripts [of Anselm] in the afore-mentioned Book 7 or elsewhere. Moreover, the most reliable [manuscript] books of the Vatican Library reveal only fourteen *capitula*, while the papers of Baronius show fifteen, the seventh incorrectly divided into two. I thought in passing that this warning ought to be given, lest perhaps the authority of such a man would cause doubt about our edition.

Baronius no doubt knew the dates of Anselm of Lucca as well as Holste did, and he had not said, as Holste implied, that Anselm himself referred to canons of Piacenza in his compilation but only that they occurred there in one manuscript.[10] Moreover, as will be seen, Holste was wrong in asserting that these decrees were found in no Vatican manuscript of Anselm. But the point behind this questionable critique of Baronius was to set the stage for Holste's edition. A preamble, preceding the heading *INCIPIVNT ACTA SYNODI*, was followed by the words *CAPITVLA STATVTORUM* and fourteen numbered canons (cc. 1–14 of the textus receptus), concluding with *Explicit synodus Placentina Vrbani Papae II*. No source for the text was indicated, although such information was given here and there for other works in the *Collectio bipartita*.[11] This silence about the manuscript standing behind the editio princeps persisted in the work of the later editors who reprinted Holste's canons, namely, Labbe–Cossart, Hardouin, Coleti, and Mansi. Even Weiland, as indicated already, said only that Holste's work was based on a 'codex quidam Vaticanus', with no shelfmark provided.[12]

The last contribution which Philippe Labbe (+March 1671), made to the *Sacrosancta concilia*, which would be completed by Gabriel Cossart, was the entry in vol. 10 for Piacenza.[13] The debt to Holste was freely acknowledged, and after reprinting Baronius' comments the edition from the *Collectio bipartita* was given, with some editorial comment added and with textual variants in the margin. One

---

Vaticanae referunt; ubi Baronii schedae septimo in duo male divulso XV. exhibent: quod obiter monendum existimavi, ne forte tanti viri auctoritas nostrae editionis fidem ambiguam reddat.' Holste's reference to Baronius' *schedae* possibly indicated Rome, Biblioteca Vallicelliana, MS C. 24, on which see below.

[10] Cf. the remark of Dom Thierry Ruinart on Baronius and the canons in Anselm of Lucca, *Beati Urbani papae II. Vita*, PL 151. 143: '... id intelligendum est de additionibus ad hanc collectionem factis; quippe cum Anselmus novennio ante illam synodum ad caelos abierit'; and also see Antonio Pagi's commentary in *Annales ecclesiastici* 18 (Lucca 1746) 16.

[11] Cf. e.g., the first numbered page of vol. 2, and 2. 222. Nothing about the canons of Piacenza appears in the posthumous note at 2. 225ff.

[12] Labbe–Cossart 10. 503–4; Jean Hardouin, *Acta conciliorum* 6. 2 (Paris 1714) 1713–15; Nicolo Coleti, *Sacrosancta concilia* 12 (Venice 1730) 824–26; Mansi, *Amplissima collectio* 20. 804–7; Weiland 560.

[13] See the 'Ad lectorem praefatio' by Cossart in the volume of Apparatus, at the bottom of the first and the top of the second unnumbered pages.

such addition following immediately upon Holste's comments about Baronius supplies the cryptic information that 'In our manuscript book these two verses precede [the legislation]' ('In MS. nostro codice praefiguntur hi duo versiculi'):

> *Vrbani papae decretum pontificale*
> *Conditur hic scripto formoso denique dicto.*[14]

After printing the synodal preamble but before giving the decrees Labbe also wrote that he had seen a manuscript containing the following introduction: *Incipiunt capitula Placentini conventus de prave ordinatis & his qui ecclesias aut praebendas emerunt.*

The first of the textual variants accompanying Labbe's edition concerned the council's date and was taken 'from our manuscript and from the Barberini [manuscript]' ('ex nostro ms. & ex Barberino'), and had been sent 'a R.P. Possino. S.I.' (see n.16). Other variant readings also were taken from one or both of these sources. Following c. 14 and Holste's *Explicit,* a fifteenth decree appears containing an ellipsis in its fourth line and prefaced by an editorial note that 'In the manuscript of the most eminent cardinal Francisco Barberini c. 15 is added thus'. ('In ms. eminentissimi cardinalis Francisci Barberini subjicitur xv. canon in hunc modum'.) This c. 15, treating church benefices, does not result from Baronius' division of c. 7 (cf. Holste's earlier comments), but offers a decree unknown to Holste (although found in Gratian, D. 70, c. 2). A comment in italics follows, indicating that Piacenza authorized a tenth preface for the mass, the text of which is given in Roman type. With no accompanying notes it is impossible to know where Labbe obtained this information and what significance to attach to the two typefaces. It could be assumed that everything following c. 14 derives from the Barberini manuscript, although Labbe specifically designated that source only for c. 15.

But the puzzles do not end here. Immediately after the tenth preface is the following: *Item post alia: [Illud summopere... mulctatur.* This text is unnumbered, has an ellipsis in its last line, and contains a prohibition of lay investiture of bishoprics and abbeys. There is nothing to reveal where it was found, the significance therein of a mixture of italics and Roman type, the meaning of *Item post alia,* or the meaning of the bracket before the word *Illud.* Two short paragraphs conclude the presentation. The first contains notices from the *Chronicle* of Saint-Maixent, one about Piacenza and the other about a synod in 1093 at Bordeaux; the second refers to a letter from Bishop Ivo of Chartres addressed to Pope Urban dealing with King Philip of France's marital difficulties.[15]

The manuscripts underlying Labbe's treatment of Piacenza can be listed as follows:

---

[14] The manuscript at issue is Vat. lat. 1208 (MS V in Chapter 2, described under *Survival,* Lists of Canons, Sect. b, and discussed below). The verses are copied correctly in Labbe–Cossart 10. 503, but in Mansi, *Amplissima collectio* 20. 804, *conditur* has been distorted to *conditor.*

[15] Cf. *Chronique de Saint-Maixent,* ed. Verdon 150 and 152; the Ivonian letter in question is no. 46, PL 162. 58–59 (= ed. Jean Leclercq, *Yves de Chartres, Correspondance* [Paris 1949] 188–90).

1. The Vatican manuscript whence Holste derived the editio princeps, which was not further identified and which Labbe probably never saw.

2. The book designated as 'noster ms.', from which variant readings were taken to supplement Holste's edition, is BAV, Vat. lat. 1208 or a copy of the same – see n. 14.

3a. BAV, MS Barb. lat. 860 (*olim* XVI. 67), i.e., ΦVa in Chapter 2 (*Survival, Polycarpus* Supplement), is the Barberini manuscript that also supplied variant readings and from which c. 15 was drawn. An underlying medieval source for that book is not indicated, although it probably was BAV, MS Reg. lat. 1026, i.e., ΦVr in the previous chapter or a copy of it (see Survival, ibid.). A note at the top of 68r by Labbe's Jesuit confrere Pierre Poussines acknowledged Holste's edition, and indicated that both c. 15, unknown to Holste, and some textual variants can be added from the Barberini book. The full group of texts printed by Labbe after c. 14 appears in MS 860, and Poussines seemingly copied them and dispatched everything to Paris.[16]

3b. MS 860 was compiled in the sixteenth and early seventeeth centuries, but turns out to be the source of confusion about the decree against lay investiture – *Item post alia: Illud summopere . . .* – that Labbe printed from the notes sent by Poussines. On 71r, after a list of decrees of Piacenza, Antonio d'Aquino copied some additional items, the first of which is the text in question.[17] It is called *c. 16*, although the list of decrees on the previous pages was unnumbered. *Item post alia* is an enigmatic inscription, but Labbe and later editors who followed him, including Weiland, seem to have interpreted it to mean 'After other decrees *of Piacenza*', and numbering as *c. 16* sealed that interpretation. This decrees, printed at the end of accounts of Piacenza, thus created a canon from this synod on the volatile issue of lay investiture, but the true identity of the decree will be revealed in the discussion that follows.

4a. Although only indirectly, another early-modern manuscript also comes into play in Labbe's presentation of Piacenza. Rome, Biblioteca Vallicelliana, MS C.24 (= Vc), is a well-known sixteenth-/seventeenth-century book that was used by Baronius, and comprises notes and papers from the erudite Spanish humanist and canonist Antonio Agustín, from members of the post-Tridentine commissions of 'Correctores Romani' who were preparing a new edition of Gratian's *Decretum*, and from other scholars of that age.[18] This was Weiland's MS 12, although his use of it was not straight forward, as will be discussed at the end of this chapter. Legislation from Piacenza is transcribed in

---

[16] For Poussines, see C. Sommervogel, S.J., *Bibliothèque de la Compagnie de Jésus, Bibliographie* 6 (Brussels/Paris 1895) 1123–34.

[17] For d'Aquino, see the comments about MS ΦVa in Chapter 2, *Survival, Polycarpus* Supplement. The other texts that he copied on 71r repeat Piacenza cc. 1–2, inscribed *Ex alio Codice veteri MS*.

[18] For this manuscript and its importance, see inter al. Somerville, *Decreta* 52–3, Blumenthal, *Early Councils* passim, and Somerville–Kuttner, *Pope Urban* 193, and 215–20. For the 'Correstores' see now Sommar, *Correctores*.

four places in MS C. 24.[19] Fols. 56–57 (proper sequence is 57–56) contain nearly a dozen decrees taken from a source that is not indicated, accompanied by variants and notes written in the margins in various hands. This material was re-copied at 74r-75v. At 82r the synodal preamble and the beginning of c. 1 are found, taken from MS Vat. lat. 1364 (the B recension of Anselm of Lucca's *Collectio canonum*, and MS Vm in Chapter 2 [see *Survival*, Lists of Canons, Sect. b], and cf. below). These texts in turn were re-copied on 72r. The content specifically of fols. 57–56 is as follows:

57r-v: cc. 3–13(part) (= Holste–Labbe–Mansi cc. 3–12[part]; c. 7 is here divided into cc. 7–8 [see Holste's comment on Baronius]).
56r: end of c. 13 (= 12 part); followed by cc. 15–14 (= 14–13); followed by the text *Item post alia. Illud summopere*..., numbered 'Cap. 16. forte' (= *post* tenth preface), but the decree is canceled out, with a marginal comment 'Deest in m.s. B⟨ibl⟩. V<at>.', together with a note by Antonio Agustín about the equivalence of this text to c. 8 of Urban II's Council of Melfi;[20] followed by cc. 1–2.

A detailed analysis of the relationship between MSS C.24 and Barb. lat. 860 is complex, adding little to the historiography of Piacenza, but it is clear that MS C.24 was a source for MS 860. Readings from the canons of Piacenza found on fols. 57–56 of C.24 were copied as variants into the margins of MS 860 opposite the decrees. Furthermore, and of special note in the present discussion, texts on fol. 56r of MS C.24 were transcribed on 71r of MS 860, including the canon on investiture, but now minus the marginal comment by Agustín that correctly identified its source as the Council of Melfi. A prohibition of lay investiture at Piacenza thus is shown to be rooted in an accident of early-modern scholarship. It is not inconceivable that Urban re-promulgated this decree at Piacenza, but there is no medieval evidence that he did so.[21]

4b. Through a process that has not been traced, the text *Item post alia. Illud summopere*... was first inserted into MS C.24 from the *Collectio Caesaraugustana*, where it occurs with decrees that initially were promulgated at Piacenza but were inscribed in the *Caesaraugustana* to Urban II's Council of Clermont (see Chapter 2, *Survival*, Canon Law Collections, Sect. c). This derivation is clear from the remark – 'al. Urbanus II in conc. Clarimontis' – found in the margin of MS C. 24, fol. 57r, opposite the heading identifying Piacenza as the ultimate source of this list of decrees.

---

[19] For a detailed description of MS C.24, but which can be revised at some points, see Gasparri, 'Osservazioni' 482–84, and 503–4, for Piacenza. The foliation noted follows the older numbers given in the upper-right-hand recto, which are generally used in the literature.
[20] See Stephan Kuttner, 'Antonio Agustín's edition of the Compilationes antiquae', BMCL 7 (1977) 2, and Somerville–Kuttner, *Urban* 280, n. 59. The decree conceivably was reaffirmed at Piacenza along with Urban's other earlier conciliar canons, but the evidence is uncertain. Repromulgation of Urban's decrees is treated in Chapter 2, inter al., *Enactment*, Bernold.
[21] Somerville–Kuttner, *Pope Urban* 280, n. 59 (but cf. Malve, *Inventing* 2. 613). See also Beulertz, *Verbot* 38–9, especially n. 37 (the statement that Urban would not have been likely to repeat the provision from Melfi verbatim at Piacenza seems unfounded, given the Reform papacy's well-documented practice of repeating conciliar decrees).

Considering the material assembled thus far, and continuing a search for the manuscript underlying Holste's editio princeps of Piacenza, the following points emerge. Neither Vat. lat. 1208, Barb. lat. 860, nor Vallicelliana C.24 was Holste's exemplar. The first two books were used originally for Piacenza by Labbe, and the relevant material in MS C.24, subsequently copied into MS 860, is more extensive than that offered by Holste. Furthermore, MS C. 24 divided Holste's c. 7 into two decrees. Easily eliminated also is Vat. lat. 1364, containing Anselm of Lucca's collection, which supplied one of the transcriptions in MS C.24. Holste pointedly rejected Baronius' statement that canons of Piacenza were found in any Vatican manuscript of Anselm's work, but MS 1364, or a copy of the same, undoubtedly was the book that Baronius cited, where Holste-Labbe's c. 7 is split into two decrees. The *Collectio bipartita* was published in 1662, the year after Holste's death, thus he probably never came across Vat. lat. 1364 and never realized that his critique of Baronius was flawed. Obviously, MS 1364 was not the basis for the editio princeps of Piacenza.

In a search for the source of Holste's edition two additional Vatican manuscripts also can be eliminated. Each preserves the appendix of conciliar texts from Urban II and Calixtus II that appears at the end of Book 8 in certain manuscripts of the *Polycarpus*, e.g., MSS Reg. lat. 987, and Reg. lat. 1026 (MSS ΦVp, and ΦVr in Chapter 2; see there under *Survival*, *Polycarpus* Supplement for all manuscripts containing this appendix). In all probability neither was known to Holste, as they entered the Vatican collection only at the end of the seventeenth century, and, furthermore, each also contains c. 15, lacking in the editio princeps. Piacenza is represented in various other eleventh- and early twelfth-century canon law collections found in Vatican manuscripts, but beyond those mentioned above none offers cc. 1–14 introduced by the synodal preamble, as in Holste's edition. The question remains: where did Holste find the fourteen canons of Piacenza that he printed in 1662?[22]

Paul Hinschius, in the course of his research on the Pseudo-Isidorian forgeries, seemingly was the first to point out that decrees from Piacenza were copied in another late eleventh-/ early-twelfth-century Vatican manuscript, Vat. lat. 629, MS Va in Chapter 2 (see *Survival*, Lists of Canons, Sect. b).[23] An equivalence between the canons found in this book and what Holste printed at first seems unlikely. The account in MS 629 begins with the words *INCIPIT SINODUS URBANI.II.PAPE PLACENTIE HABITA*, and gives a continuous text of the decrees with no divisions, no special heading between the preface and the canons, and no *explicit*. Only a collation with Holste's edition permits the conclusion that this is the book that lies behind the editio princeps of Piacenza. The following selective tabulation of variants proves the connection (for MSS ΦVa and Vc the marginal variants have not been considered). The sigla from Chapter 2 are used where possible.

---

[22] Another early-modern manuscript in BAV containing material on Piacenza is Vat. lat. 9866, an eighteenth-century book of papers from the Maurists, with notices on Piacenza at 329r-v, and a list of canons on 338v-39v, all drawn from printed works: see M. Vattasso and H. Carusi, *Codices Vaticani Latini (Codices 9852–10300)* (Rome 1914) 38–51.

[23] Paul Hinschius, *Decretales Pseudo-Isidorianae et Capitula Angilramni* (Leipzig 1863) li.

ΦVa = Barb. lat. 860 (d'Aquino's papers)
H = Holste's editio princeps
ΦVp = Reg. lat. 987 (*Polycarpus*)
ΦVr = Reg. lat. 1026 (*Polycarpus*)
Va = Vat. lat 629 (Holste's MS)
V = Vat. lat. 1208 (Labbe's MS)
Vm = Vat. lat. 1364 (Baronius' Anselm of Lucca)
Vc = Vallicelliana C.24 (sixteenth-/seventeenth-century miscellany)

Preamble:
Ind. III. = H Va Vm
Ind. III. Kal. Martii = V ΦVa ΦVp ΦVr

c. 1
quoque iudicio eorum et = H Va
quoque s. Spiritus iudicio et = MSS *praeter* Va

c. 3
et tum = H Va
et si tamen = ΦVa ΦVp ΦVr
et si tunc = Vc Vm
et si tum = V

c. 5
censemus = H Va
concedimus = MSS *praeter* Va

c. 6
cum majoris essent aetatis = H Va
cum iam maioris essent aetatis = MSS *praeter* Vc Va
cum maioris aetatis essent = Vc

c. 7
praepositurae locum = H Vc Va
prepositurae vel officii locum = MSS *praeter* Vc Va

c. 12
ut demus amplius = H Va
ut addatur apostolis = ΦVa
ut addatur amplius = V ΦVp ΦVr Vm
om. Vc

Holste had no qualms about dividing the text found in his source into numbered sections, changing the introductory inscription before the preamble, and inventing both an inscription to stand between the preamble and the canons and an *explicit*. Thus disguised, the editio princeps entered the stream of early-modern conciliar collections and its source escaped detection for over three hundred years. Passage through the works of Hardouin and Coleti introduced little if anything that was new, but changes of typefaces and sigla etc. blurred some of the editorial information that had been laid out relatively clearly in Labbe–Cossart. By the time the decrees of Piacenza reached Mansi's *Amplissima collectio* the different contributions of earlier editors were difficult to isolate without side-by-side comparisons of the printings. Variant readings in Mansi are indicated by both asterisks and letters, the former referring to marginalia, largely from Labbe, the latter to a new set of readings at the bottom of the page, 'ex cod. Vindobonensi'. Some, but not all of Hardouin's comments are preserved, indicated by 'H'.

To the accumulated presentation of Piacenza, Mansi appended two 'Additiones'. The first contains several new items and is introduced with the comment that 'some of the canons of this council are extant but the full "acta" are not, as everyone easily sees from what was collected by Labbe'. ('Concilii hujus canones quidam extant, acta integra non extant, ut ex iis quae apud Labbeum congesta sunt, facile omnes intelligunt'.)[24] Passages follow from Gerhoch of Reichersberg's *Liber de simoniacis* and the Annalista Saxo (see Chapter 2, *Survival*, Narrative Sources, Sects. c-d). Next are texts of JL 5561 and JL 5290 that Mansi found in Lucca, Biblioteca Capitolare Feliniana 124 – MS Lu in Chapter 2 (*Survival*, Lists of Canons, Sect. b). He also knew the canons of Piacenza found in Lu, which he called the 'vulgatos hujus concilii canones', that is, the same set as in Holste's edition. Mansi believed that the supplements to Burchard of Worms' *Decretum* that appear in Lu dated from the time of Piacenza. Not knowing the attribution of JL 5290 to Gregory VII, but with an eye on the treatment of fast days in Piacenza c. 14, he postulated a connection between that canon and the extended treatment of Ember Days in JL 5290.[25]

Mansi's second supplement contains two items found in a manuscript from Vienna ('MS. Vindobonensis codex'), whence he had taken variant readings for the Holste–Labbe canons. Two lengthy texts from that book, found following what Mansi termed the 'vulgati Placentini canones', are identical to cc. 1, 3–5, 6–7,

---

[24] Mansi, *Amplissima collection* 20. 809, first published by Mansi in his *Supplementum* to Labbe–Cossart and Coleti: *Sanctorum conciliorum et decretorum collectio nova* 2 (Lucca 1748) 131 ff.

[25] Mansi, *Amplissima collectio* 20. 811–12: 'Denique in MS. codice bibliothecae cathedralis Lucensis, in quo Burchardi decreta, & ad illa anonymi cujusdam additamenta quaedam extant sub hoc ipso concilii Placentini tempore scripta, post vulgatos hujus concilii canones, hoc, quod subdo, additamentum legitur, quod occasione postremi canonis hujus concilii scriptum, vel forte etiam in eodem concilio coram patribus lectum suspicor.' See the discussion of c. 14 in the commentary in Chapter 5.

9–10, 8, and 11–13, from Gregory VII's Roman synod of November, 1078.[26] Mansi, of course, knew this (although stopped short of saying it for the first set), but saw parallels between parts of that first series and c. 15 of Piacenza (printed initially by Labbe from Barb. lat. 860), 'although there are verbal differences' ('licet in verbis discrepat'). Other than scribal carelessness, Mansi wondered why anyone would append a copy of these Gregorian canons to decrees from Piacenza unless Urban renewed them in 1095. The Viennese manuscript to which Mansi somehow had access is today Österreichische Nationalbibliothek, lat. 2153 (Iur. can. 38), MS W in Chapter 2 (*Survival*, Lists of Canons, Sect. d). It is impossible to prove that Urban II did not reissue this legislation at Piacenza, but more probably, given the layout of MS W, these are texts for which a scribe neglected to provide a new inscription after copying the canons of Piacenza.

The presentation of the canons of the Council of Piacenza from Baronius to Mansi, and then to Weiland at the end of the nineteenth century, represents a grand accretion of scholarship from different centuries, sources, and editions. Weiland knew about more manuscripts containing the decrees than did his predecessors, but in constructing an edition he appears to have worked basically from the printings of Labbe–Cossart and Mansi (see his comment in the second paragraph of this chapter). To those texts, based on Holste's editio princeps from MS Vat. lat 629, he added, from MS Barb. lat. 860, Piacenza c. 15, the notice on the tenth preface, and the bogus 'c. (16)' on lay investiture (labeled a 'canon extravagans'; see ibid.). Weiland also arranged his manuscripts according to the number of canons that they contained, offered some variant readings, and touched up in places the Labbe–Cossart–Mansi printing (for example, filling in the lacuna in c. 15). Little of this was explained, nonetheless the result has stood for more than a century as the best available treatment of the legislation from Piacenza, excluding imponderables that could not be assessed from the information given, such as the status of 'c.(16)'.

One final issue can be considered. As noted above, Weiland's MS 12 is Valliacelliana MS C. 24, although he did not use the book for decrees of Piacenza, the existence of which he only mentioned in a footnote.[27] Instead he wrote that 'cc. 1–14 were edited from here by Pflugk-Harttung . . . as cc. 10–16 of the Lateran Council of 1110'.[28] These texts are found on fols. 46r-47v of MS C.24, re-copied on fols. 26r-7r. A note in the margin at both points indicated that they were copied by Francesco Torres from a 'codex antiquus' for a fellow member—Miguel Tomás Taxaquet (Michael Thomasius)—of the 'Correctores Romani'.[29] It is possible but not demonstrable that Pope Paschal II reissued the canons of Piacenza in his

---

[26] See Caspar, *Register* 402–6.
[27] Weiland 561, n. 1.
[28] Weiland 560: '. . . ex quo capita 1–14 edita sunt tamquam capita 10–16 concilii Lateranensis anni 1110 a viro d. Pflugk-Harttung "Acta pontificum Romanorum inedita" II,197 nr.238.' The reference is to Pflugk-Harttung, *Acta* 197–98.
[29] For Thomasius and Torres see Somerville, *Decreta* 50; for the former also see Somerville–Kuttner, *Pope Urban* 216. For MS C.24, see above in this chapter. For Thomasius and Torres see now Sommar, *Correctores*, passim.

Lateran Council of 1110. After admitting the possibility, however, Weiland did not include the texts from MS C.24 in his edition.[30] Uta-Renate Blumenthal was likewise cautious, noting the importance of the legislation from Piacenza in general for Pope Paschal, and also the fact that c. 14 from Piacenza on the Ember Days appears occasionally in the canonical tradition inscribed to Paschal.[31] Yet since neither Torres' manuscript nor any other medieval exemplar has come to light as evidence for a re-promulgation of the rulings from Piacenza in 1110, the matter can be tabled.[32]

---

[30] Weiland 568.
[31] Blumenthal, *Early Councils* 113–14.
[32] For another lost manuscript that once had been in the hands of the 'Correctores Romani', see Chapter 6, Lateran Council.

4

The Transmission of the Canons of Piacenza
(with an Edition)

INTRODUCTION

The last two chapters assembled what is known about the survival of the decrees from Piacenza, and outlined their historiography, from Baronius to Weiland. In this chapter that information now will be analyzed in order to study the different forms in which this legislation is preserved. The general uniformity of the *textus receptus* has been noted in the earlier discussions. Yet notwithstanding a good deal of formal similarity, Piacenza's canons survive in at least four versions, and their transmission reveals a more variegated picture than previously has been assumed for the *fortuna* of this pivotal legislation.

None of the surviving renditions of decrees from any of Urban II's councils appears to stem directly from the papal chancery.[1] The provisions survive in private copies dispersed throughout Europe, and even the quotations of Piacenza c. 8 and part of c. 9 in JL 5694 are not preserved in an original papal letter but in a twelfth-century copy.[2] The presence in the *Gesta Romanae aecclesiae contra Hildebrandum* of the synodal preamble and cc. 1–12 of the *textus receptus* might be deemed a guarantee of sorts for the content of those texts. Yet, aside from the fact that the autograph of the *Gesta* is lost, this collection of 'anti-Gregorian' treatises conveys a private point of view formulated by disaffected cardinals. The degree to which these polemics utilized material from Urban II's chancery is unknown. Anyone wishing to consult a rendition of the *textus receptus* of Piacenza's canons that was transcribed at a time and place close to the synod can choose from several copies preserved in Italian manuscripts of the early twelfth century, for example, Lucca, Biblioteca Capitolare Feliniana 124 (MS Lu), BAV, Vat. lat. 1364 (MS Vm), or indeed Holste's manuscript, Vat. lat 629 (MS Va). It is possible even to examine a twelfth-century version that probably comes from Piacenza itself: Milan, Biblioteca Ambrosiana, M.79 sup. (MS Mip). Notwithstanding proximity in space and time, however, no special claims can be made for the pedigree of the texts in these books.

The need for a new edition of these canons is clear when considering Weiland's edition of 1893. His work was essentially a distillation of information assembled by earlier editors in which only two manuscripts, Vat. lat. 629, and the early-modern

---

[1] See Somerville–Kuttner, *Pope Urban* 228, and 302. The following discussion is in part modeled on the treatment of the decrees of Melfi discussed ibid. 228 ff. See also in Chapter 1, n. 32.

[2] Cf. Chapter 2, *Survival*, JL 5694.

Barb. lat 860, played predominant roles. He listed nineteen manuscripts containing the legislation, and offered some comments about and collations from fifteen of them. Yet Chapter 2 showed that many more copies of the canons are known, and attention thus must be given to how these exemplars relate to one another. That goes beyond Weiland's presentation, which also ignored the transmission of Piacenza in the canon law tradition, even in Gratian's *Decretum*.

THE *POLYCARPUS* SUPPLEMENT (Φ), JL 5694 [IP 5.248–49, NO. 14], AND THE *GESTA ROMANAE AECCLESIAE*

In laying the groundwork for a new edition of the canons of Piacenza, the starting point must be an assessment of the versions of the legislation that, arguably, could be deemed to be close to what was promulgated by Pope Urban's chancery. The version deriving from the conciliar supplement to the *Polycarpus* (= Φ) is the longest account, including the synodal preamble, cc. 1–15, and the notice on the tenth preface for the mass. The variants among the three manuscripts that contain this text, – ΦPa, ΦVp, and ΦVr – are generally minor; and as was seen of Φ's accounts of decrees from Clermont and Melfi, Φ Pa and ΦVp provide essentially the same text, whereas ΦVr contains some unique readings.[3] Aside from its length, however, it was argued in dealing with Melfi that Φ's version deserves special consideration because it can be linked in certain ways with records from the papal chancery. The details of that argument will not be repeated here but four points can be summarized, with a fifth added specifically regarding Piacenza.

1. The format and the detail found in the records in Φ are distinctive.
2. Gabriel Cossart (1671) knew of a now lost copy of the medieval Roman Church's official tax register, the *Liber censuum*, which included some of those same synodal texts.
3. The canons of Clermont are quoted repeatedly by twelfth-century popes only in this form.
4. Ivo of Chartres cited c. 1 from Urban II's Council of Troia according to this version, inscribed by Ivo *Ex registro Urbani II*.[4]
5. The texts of Piacenza in MSS Lh and Sta (see below in Transmission, section a) are very close to Φ, despite lacking the liturgical notice after c. 15. Those two early twelfth-century manuscripts also preserve what may be a chancery memorandum about the meeting at Cremona in April 1095, soon after the council, between Urban II and King Conrad. The very close agreement between the canons accompanying that document and Φ could represent another link between Φ and records derived from the papal chancery.

---

[3] For Melfi, see Somerville–Kuttner, *Pope Urban* 247, and for Clermont, Somerville, *Decreta* 120–21 (where the sigla for the manuscripts are different from those given here and for Melfi).
[4] Somerville–Kuttner, *Pope Urban* 233–34; see also Blumenthal, 'Conciliar Canons' 371.

A decision thus was made to use Φ as the basic account in editing the decrees of Melfi, and notwithstanding more manuscripts at hand, for Piacenza too there seems no compelling reason to prefer for that purpose another version to Φ. Yet despite whatever authority adheres to Φ, the Council of Melfi demonstrated that this account is an edited, incomplete rendition of the legislation, in which c. 4 without question, perhaps the last line of c. 16, and also some of the notices accompanying the decrees, are missing.[5] Likewise, despite its length and detail, Φ's treatment of Piacenza also is incomplete. The discussion to follow will analyze that transmission in comparison with two other excerpts of Piacenza's decrees – the *Gesta*, and Urban's letter to Bishop Bernard of Bologna (JL 5694 [IP 5. 248–49, no. 14]). Neither of these survives in a chancery text, but for comparison purposes both can be considered documents of some authority, that is a twelfth-century copy of a papal letter of Pope Urban, and a treatise from a disgruntled Roman cardinal, well-informed about Piacenza.

The *Gesta*, treated in detail in the first part of Chapter 2, include cc. 1–12; Urban's letter, quoting c. 8 and part of c. 9, was edited in the same chapter (under *Survival*, JL 5694). Consider c. 8, which in Φ reads thus: *Ordinationes, que a Guiberto heresiarca facte sunt postquam ab apostolice memorie papa Gregorio et a Romana ecclesia est dampnatus, irritas esse iudicamus.* ('We judge to be illegal the ordinations that were made by the heresiarch Guibert after he was damned by Pope Gregory of apostolic memory and by the Roman Church'.) After the words *est dampnatus*, both the letter to Bologna and the *Gesta* add *queque etiam a pseudoepiscopis per eum postea ordinatis perpetrate sunt* ('and also those perpetrated by the pseudobishops afterward ordained through him').

Agreement between a letter of Pope Urban and an anti-Urban cardinal about this nearly lost portion of c. 8 might seem surprising. Yet this segment of c. 8 also appears in the re-promulgation of the decree at the Council of Rome in 1099.[6] Little or no doubt is possible, therefore, that the words *queque-perpetrate sunt* formed part of c. 8 as Urban II promulgated it at Piacenza, and, accordingly, that the pontiff condemned the ordinations made by those whom Wibert of Ravenna had promoted after Gregory VII excommunicated him. But omission of those crucial words throughout the textus receptus, the editing done in several accounts of cc. 8–9 (cf. the apparatus criticus), and the virtual neglect of c. 8 in a number of canon law collections all suggest uneasiness about the issue of schismatic orders in general and about Piacenza's synodal judgment on Wibertine ordinations in particular.[7] It is impossible to identify the earliest exemplar containing Piacenza's textus receptus, and equally impossible to know when the dossier of texts that

---

[5] Somerville–Kuttner, *Pope Urban* 253–58, and 273–78.

[6] Mansi, *Amplissima collectio* 20. 963; Rome will be treated below in Chapter 6. Piacenza c. 8 is not included among the Clermont/Piacenza decrees found in the *Collectio Caesaraugustana* (see Chapter 2, *Survival*, Canon Law Collections, Sect. c).

[7] See Chapter 2, *Survival*, Canon Law Collections, in general for the canonical tradition. For the significant gaps in cc. 8–9 where *homoioteleuton* might be at work see, e.g., the comments below under Canon Law Collections, Sect. b, the apparatus to the edition at the end of the chapter, and the commentary on cc. 8–9 in Chapter 5. *Homoioteleuton* would not be an explanation for the absence of *queque-perpetrate sunt* in c. 8 of the textus receptus.

comprises Φ was assembled. Φ, as it now stands, cannot antedate spring 1123 because legislation from Calixtus II's Lateran Council of that year was the last entry. Wibert of Ravenna died in 1100, and although a series of successors appeared in the first years of the twelfth century little steam remained in the old schism.[8] Perhaps after 1100 Piacenza's *queque-perpetrate sunt* in c. 8 represented an obsolete shot left over from Urban II's battles with the antipope.

Seaching in JL 5694 and the *Gesta* for other signs of the 'original' texts from Piacenza yields interesting if not earth-shattering results. The one line of c. 9 that JL 5694 quotes agrees exactly with both Φ and the better manuscript of the *Gesta* (MS Bg; MS Hg has one small variant – see Chapter 2, *Survival*, JL 5694. Comparing the *Gesta* and Φ for the shared portion of the textus receptus, that is the preamble and cc. 1–12, reveals that the former is not wildly idiosyncratic in its readings, although significant variants occur against Φ.

> Preamble: line 3 Turbano; line 12 comprobata] approbata.
> Canon 2: nullasque] et nullas.
> Canon 3: non simoniace ordinati sunt] consecrari passi sunt.
> Canon 4: immo execrari *om.*
> Canon 5: ecclesiarum beneficia] ex partes Bg; esse] ministrare.
> Canon 6: magna] maxima; ibi eos; contenti] contempti; apostolice *om.*
> Canon 10: vita] canonica *add.*; et scientia *om.*
> Canon 11: Amodo vero quicumque] Qui vero posthac (post haec Hg).
> Canon 12: magnaque] nimiaque.

Some of these differences might be only the result of unintended scribal changes, others may have been intentional, with polemical import. The *Gesta's* signature deprecation at the beginning of the preamble – *Turbano* for *Urbano* – is an obvious case of planned distortion; suppression of Urban's demeaning *immo execrari* in c. 4 probably also was a conscious adjustment on the part of the *Gesta*. But in other cases the matter is unclear. The wording at the beginning of c. 3 in the *Gesta* can open the door to rejection of all ordinations by simoniacs, whether or not involving simony, and thus obliterating the nuance of Pope Urban's decree, but was that an intentional change? Likewise, altering *contenti* to *contempti* toward the end of c. 6 could easily be due to a lax copyist, but perhaps there is more to it. The substitution, finally, of *nimiaque* for *magnaque* in the opening line of c. 12 can be taken as another jab at Piacenza's dispensatory tendencies, but that cannot be proven.[9]

---

[8] See the entries post JL 6627.
[9] Cf. the critique in the *Gesta* of what is taken to be arbitrary mercy in the canons of Piacenza: *Gesta Romanae ecclesiae*, ed. Francke, MGH Lib. de lite 2. 410: see Stoller, 'Councils' 319–20. Other sections of the *Gesta* also may or may not indicate statements of policy. For example, near the end of c. 5, line 4, *ibidem eos ministrare* appears for Φ's *ibidem eos esse* (but cf. in c. 6, line 4, *eos ibi ministrare* in Φ and *ibi eos ministrare* in the *Gesta*); the possibly sarcastic use in the *Gesta* of *maxima*, with *misericordia*, replaces *magna* of Φ, in c. 6; again in c. 6, at the end, the *Gesta* omit *apostolice*; in c. 10 at the end *canonica* is added after *vita* in the *Gesta* and *et scientia* is omitted. At the beginning of c. 11, MS Bg of the *Gesta* offers *Qui vero posthac* (*post haec* in MS Hg) as opposed to *Amodo vero quicumque* in Φ, which is a significantly different reading but does not amount to a change in meaning. None of the substantive divergences between Φ and the *Gesta* is duplicated in the *Collectio Caesaraugustana* or at the

Inspite of some distinctive readings, therefore, this comparison shows that the *Gesta* do not deviate consistently in a marked way from Φ. And at points of significant difference, notwithstanding the case of c. 8, Φ's text seems preferable, taking the *Collectio Caesaraugustana* and the Council of Rome in 1099 as controls. This is what might be expected in a polemical work from schismatics who sought credibility for their account. No reason exists, however, to give priority to the version of Piacenza's legislation in the *Gesta*. Φ offers a fuller text, with a pedigree that by and large seems superior.

From this discussion, together with the analysis of the *Gesta* (in Chapter 2 *Enactment, Gesta*), it can be concluded that dissemination of the decrees of Piacenza began when the papal chancery made available a full text of the canons. That document seems not to have survived, and for reasons that can only be guessed such a comprehensive account was edited, resulting in the renditions of the textus receptus that are now at hand. Φ is a version that is more complete and seems closer than others to what Pope Urban's chancery disseminated, although, as the discussion above about *queque-perpetrate sunt* revealed, what survives is not at every point what Urban promulgated. The *Gesta* charged the pope with confecting and disseminating a reworked set of canons *post synodum*. It is impossible to know what truth, if any, lies behind that claim, and if the pontiff actually called for such a revision why it was done. The events of the Council of Piacenza and its immediate aftermath can only be retrieved in shadowy fashion, with more questions than answers.

TRANSMISSION BEYOND Φ AND THE *GESTA*

The preceding section analyzed Piacenza's decrees in Φ and the *Gesta* as special cases that, mutatis mutandis, arguably stand close to the records of Urban II's chancery. Moving beyond those two sources involves using Φ as a basic text and collating the canons in other versions. Doing so reveals some textual patterns among the texts and brings to light a forest of variants that defies great systematization. In comparison with the Council of Clermont, Piacenza has been credited with a straightforward legislative tradition.[10] But the reality is that a wide and surprising range of textual differences emerges within what is essentially a stable core, represented most often by twelve, fourteen, or fifteen provisions. Yet within the texts of individual decrees variants abound, perhaps indicating that the lists of decrees were transcribed more than once, and in the process words were dropped or altered, consciously or unconsciously. That means that different forms of the textus receptus produce different 'canons of Piacenza' – lists that might mean different things to different people.

Council of Rome, and most of the *Gesta's* readings shared by the *Caesaraugusrana* and/or Rome are minor and defy analysis.

[10] Somerville, *Decreta* 7, n. 16.

Weiland's procedure of arranging his manuscripts according to the number of decrees therein was noted in Chapters 2 and 3, and is a feasible way to deal with a long list of exemplars.[11] The sigla of the twenty-eight manuscripts that were described in Chapter 2 will be repeated for ease of reference.

Preamble + cc. 1–15 (= 15+ group)
B = Brussels, Bibliothèque royale Albert Ier, 495–505 (cat. 2494)
Lh = London, BL, Harley 3001
Mid = Milan, Biblioteca Ambrosiana, A.46 inf., fols. 151r-v
O = Oxford, Bodleian Library, Canon. Pat. Lat. 39 (S.C. 19025)
Pm = Paris, BNF, lat. 3187
Sta = Stuttgart, Württembergische Landesbibliothek, Cod. theol. et phil. 4°254
Mub = Munich, Bayerische Staatsbibliothek, clm - 5129
Pb = Paris, BNF, Baluze 7, fol. 244r

Preamble + cc.1–14 (= 14+ group)
C = St.-Claude, Bibliothèque municipale, 17 (3)
E = El Escorial, Real Biblioteca de San Lorenzo, a.I.6
Fc = Florence, Biblioteca Medicea Laurenziana, S.Croce 23, dext. 5
Lu = Lucca, Biblioteca Capitolare Feliniana 124
Mic = Milan, Biblioteca Ambrosiana, H.48 sup.
Mip = _____ M.79 sup.
Pj = Paris, BNF, lat. 18083[12]
Os = Oxford, Bodleian Library, Selden supra 90
V = Città del Vaticano, BAV, Vat. lat. 1208
Va = _____ Vat. lat. 629
Vm = _____ Vat. lat. 1364
Y = New Haven, Yale University, Beinecke Rare Book and Manuscript Library, Marston 158

Preamble + varia decreta
F = Florence, Biblioteca Medicea Laurenziana, Plut. xviii.14
Li = Lincoln, Cathedral Library, 192

Lacking the preamble, cc.1–14 (= 14− group)
G = Göttweig, Stiftsbibliothek, 85 (8)
Mup = Munich, Bayerische Staatsbibliothek, clm. 11316
Muw = _____ clm. 22011
Stb = Stuttgart, Württembergische Landesbibliothek, Cod. theol. et phil. 2°210
VB = Vyssí Brod (Hohenfurt), Klásterni knihovna, CXIX
W = Vienna, Österreichische Nationalbibliothek, lat. 2153 (Iur. can. 38)

---

[11] See Chapter 2, *Survival*, immediately before *Polycarpus* Supplement.
[12] Pj is slotted into the alphabetical sequence here although in Chapter 2, *Survival*, Lists of Canons, Sect. b, it is placed at the end of this section because it offers material found nowhere else.

a) 15+

The decrees of Piacenza in the '15+' group contain the fullest account after Φ of the textus receptus.[13] As noted above in *Polycarpus* Supplement, the southern German MSS Lh and Sta are close to Φ, and they preserve, inter al., the distinctive reading *ecclesiarum beneficia* in c. 5, line 2, rather than *ecclesiarum partes* (note that *beneficia* appears both in the *Coll. Caesaraugustana* and in the Council of Rome). Neither Lh nor Sta was copied from the other, but could derive from a common source (see the descriptions in Chapter 2, *Survival*, Lists of Canons, Sect. a). The other 15+ texts exhibit little consistency, diverging from Φ, Lh and Sta, and from each other.[14]

b) 15+/14+

The inconsistencies within Piacenza's transmission are exemplified by considering a distinctive reading in the preamble. Three of the texts in the 15+ category, MSS Mid, O, and Pm, at line 1–2, lack the words *Kalendis Martii*. This lacuna occurs at a point of textual disturbance, as the critical apparatus shows. Those three manuscripts share this absence with most of the witnesses that contain the preamble and cc. 1–14, that is, MSS C E Fc Lu Mic, Mip, Os, Va, Vm, and Y – MS Pj, where the text of the preface begins only in line 4, and MS V, which will be discussed below, are the exceptions. The incomplete MSS F and Li, both of which include the preamble, also omit *Kalendis Martii*, and in addition F drops *indictione iii*, thereby eliminating all information about the date of the council other than the year.

A large group of manuscripts, therefore, including three 15+ exemplars (Mid, O, Pm), are linked through the absence of *Kalendis Martii* in the synodal prologue. But whereas MSS O and Pm in line 27 read *partes* for *beneficia*, as do most of the 14+ accounts, *beneficia* in Mid prevents a neat link between absence of *Kal. Mart.* and *partes*. Such a smooth connection is also called into question by MS Mub (on which more below), which reads *partes*, and lacks *Kal. Martii* but replaces it by

---

[13] The incomplete texts in MS Mub (Gerhoch of Reichersberg) and MS Pb (Baluze), are included here because they are witnesses for c. 15 (cf. Chapter 2, *Survival*, Lists of Canons, Sect. a, and Narrative Sources, Sect. c).

[14] MS B, for example, although retaining *ecclesiarum beneficia*, has unique readings, e.g., *probata* for Φ's *approbata* in line 12 of the preface (others including Lh and Sta read *comprobata*); omission of *postquam-sunt* in the troublesome c. 8, probably by *homoioteleuton* (cf. the commentary in Chapter 5); *vero-fiant* at the end of c. 14 is replaced by *in epdomada plena ante equinoctium, quartum in epdomada plena ante nativitatem Domini*. B has two gaps in c. 15, *Sanctorum-sentientes* (line 1), and *perpetuo-ea* (line 3–5) where *homoioteleuton* probably was at work. Yet B stands closer to Lh and Sta and thus to Φ than Mid, Mub, O, and Pm. B shares a few readings with Mid and Mub, and Mid and Mub have readings in common with O and Pm, yet a pattern of textual congruence akin to that between Lh and Sta is missing, and the relationships among Mid, Mub, O, and Pm per se and of any of these exemplars and Lh, Sta, and B, is opaque. Mid, for example, retains *ecclesiarum beneficia*, whereas Mub, O, and Pm have *ecclesiarum partes*; Mub, which lacks cc. 8–14, preserves a number of unique and distinctive readings, the most idiosyncratic of which is in the prologue, replacing *tam Galliarum quam et Longobardie et Tuscie* with the more global *et clericis fere iiii milibus ex diversis provintiis Baiorie, Alemannie, Francie, Saxonie, Burgundie, Galatie, Langobardie, Tuscie*. Pm omits both *et assensu totius concilii approbata* in the prologue, and the last sentence of c. 15.

mense Martio. Regarding the two incomplete accounts that transmit the preface minus *Kal. Mart.* – MSS F and Li – F breaks off in the midst of c. 4, while Li reads *partes*, fitting in, therefore, with the large number of texts containing *partes* and lacking *Kal. Mart.*

Most of the shared variants between the 15+ and the 14+ groups amount to word changes (*eis* for *eisdem*, or *fiat* for *fiant*), omission of words not required for sense (elimination of *iam* or *in*), or inversions of two or three words – that is, readings that could have arisen independently of a formal source when the accounts were copied.[15] A search for patterns thus yields little that is clear. Even a distinctive omission in MSS Mic (14+), and Pm (15+), (i.e., *et-approbata* in the prologue), might be due to *homoioteleuton* rather than to an ecclesiological statement.[16] In one instance, however, a textual pattern is discernible: MSS Mid and Vm clearly share a common ancestor, for they include several distinctive readings found nowhere else.[17] Yet given the discrepancy between the number of canons – 15 (Mid) versus 14 (Vm) – plus the fact that the decrees are numbered in Vm, these two exemplars would not have been copied directly from the same source and the relationship between them is difficult to assess.[18] Soundings within the 14+ group, finally, reveal incidental convergence of the sort indicated above.[19] MSS C and Os share the omission in c. 12 of the words *aliquid severitati ut addatur amplius caritati.* at the end, but have little else in common. MSS Fc and Pj diverge at several points, but uniquely offer in c. 8 *diiudicamus* for *iudicamus* at the end, and in c. 9 conclude with *excommunicatos* for *dampnatos*, as well as other less significant variants (for example in c. 5, line 4, the omission of *eos*).

c) 14– and MS Mub (Munich, clm. 5129)

The discussion thus far reveals some patterns of transmission and hints of others, yet the picture is uneven. A limitation of the procedure of classifying lists of canons solely by how many items they include comes to the fore, however, with MS Mub. Mub contains the preamble, cc. 1–7, and c. 15, and although incomplete was placed in the 15+ category given the presence of c. 15. The book is, nevertheless, anomalous, and despite the prologue and c. 15, is akin to a series of manuscripts that lack them both,

---

[15] O has a number of such readings in common with MSS Fc, Mip, Pj, Va, and Y. Pm shares differences of the same sort and also has *celebremus* and *initium* in c. 14, line 2, in common with MSS C and Os. These latter two variants perhaps are more substantive, although it is easy to see how Φ's *celebrentur* and *initio* could become *celebremus* and *initium* in transcription.

[16] A word can be said here about MS E, which transmits the 14+ series in a fourteenth-century book, the latest of the known medieval accounts of the textus receptus and the only one to survive in Spain (although it is not clear that it was written there). E and Mic share a significant lacuna at the end of c. 12, at a point of some disturbance in the text. The reading *digni habeantur* at the end of c. 11 is found in L and Stb, and also in MSS E and Mic, yet E and Mic share little else.

[17] MSS Mid and Vm both have *beneficia*, and share unique readings: *ab incarnatione Domini* in the prologue; also in the prologue, after *Urbano*, *iil secundo* is added; in c. 2 *umquam* is omitted; etc.

[18] MS Mid separates the decrees with ¶ signs, and MS Vm numbers the canons.

[19] Some readings appear promising but lead nowhere, e.g., the heading *Decretum beati* (*domini* Mic; om. Y) *Urbani pape* (*pape Urbani* Mic), occurs in MSS F Mic and Y, but they do not share a consistent set of variants (MSS Mic and Y are both connected with Cistercian houses).

that is the so-called 14— group consisting of MSS G, Mup, Muw, Stb, VB, and W.[20] MS Mub and the 14— texts share the following distinctive readings.

- In c. 2, after *pecunia*, MS Mub, along with G, Mup, Stb, and W, adds the words *lingua aut obsequio*.
- In c. 5 Mub, all 14— texts (and others as has been noted) read *ecclesiarum partes*.
- In c. 7, after *permittantur* in l. 3, Mub and all 14— exemplars, add *nec promoveri prohibeantur*.[21]

Notwithstanding a connection to the 15+ texts, MS Mub shares a common ancestor with the 14— version of the textus receptus. Both Mub and those six codices probably were written in the Empire north of the Alps, although an origin for MS W in northern Italy is possible. The following examples show the coherence of the 14— group.

- In place of the long synodal preamble, in MSS G, Muw, Stb, VB, and W (and also in MS V to be discussed below, a distinctive introduction appears (variants aside): *Capitula Placentini concilii de prave ordinatis et prebendas aut ecclesias ementibus*. Variants allow MSS G, Stb, and W to be grouped together, on the one hand, and MSS Muw and VB, on the other. MS Mup offers an abbreviated inscription, *Capitula Placentini concilii*.
- In c. 9 MSS G, Mup, Stb, and W replace *nisi probare valuerint se cum ordinarentur eos nescisse dampnatos.* with *facte sunt irritas esse* (*omnino* add. Stb) *iudicamus*. The even briefer *irritas esse iudicamus/iudicavimus.* appears in Muw and VB.
- MSS G, Mup, Muw, Stb, VB, and W all omit in c. 10 the words *cum-redierint*.
- Again in c. 10, at the end, after *commendat.* the following is added in MSS G, Muw, Stb, VB, and W: *et si his nostris decretis cognitis mox ab errore ad catholicam* (*om.* G W), *ecclesiam transierint, et nobis nostrisque legatis se per omnia obedire promiserint*. This is shortened in Mup to *et si his nostris decretis cognitis obedire promiserint*. Omission of *catholicam* perhaps links MSS G and W.[22]
- Within this group of texts, finally, MSS G, Mup, and W share the following readings in cc. 3–4: c. 3, line 1, *ab occulte* for *a*, and *vita laudabilis eos* at the end, in G and Mup (*vita* omitted in W); c. 4, *scienter-simoniacis*] *a publice simoniacis scienter se*.

In conclusion, MS Mub reiterates the complexity of the diffusion of Piacenza's decrees. With a mixture of the synodal prologue, a series of 14— readings, in addition to c. 15, that book suggests the possibility of a fuller version of the textus receptus transmitted in the Empire than is evident through the '14-' group alone. For further consideration of such possibilities, see the discussion below on Gerhoch.

---

[20] This set of manuscripts was described in Chapter 2, *Survival*, Lists of Canons, Sect. d).
[21] Other instances of agreement between Mub and these texts include, e.g., *huiusmodi* for *eiusmodi*, and *permittimus* for *patimur*, although neither of these readings occurs in VB.
[22] See Blumenthal, *Rarly Councils* 34, n. 34, for this line.

d) MS V (Vat. lat. 1208)

MS V further illustrates the vagaries of Piacenza's transmission. This book was placed in the 14+ group, yet, as with MS Mub, it offers a set of puzzles. The manuscript is a copy of an earlier book and includes a variety of texts, with Piacenza followed immediately, out of chronological order, by the canons of Melfi, 1089.[23] MS V is not among the best witnesses for Melfi's legislation, and has an odd numbering arrangement for the Piacenza–Melfi combo, in that the canons are enumerated together as cc. 1–15 ([1]-4 for Piacenza, and 5 ff. for Melfi).[24]

This codex comprises the only 14+ text that includes the council's full, formal dating information at the beginning of the preamble, that is, a date according to year, month, and indiction. Furthermore, V has the same reading as Φ, that is *beneficia* in c. 5 line 2. These factors, plus a good amount of agreement between MS V and Φ in general link it to MSS B, Lh, and Sta of the 15+ group (although other readings, some of them unique, deviate).[25] V includes other oddities as well, but their import is not always clear. For example, together with the *Gesta*, MS V has a reversal of two elements of the date in the preface: *Kalendis Martii indictione iii* in place of Φ's *indictione iii Kalendis Martii*, although this particular shared reading probably is coincidental and other variants do not tie MS V to the *Gesta*. What cannot be coincidental, however, is the appearance of the same short introduction before c. 1 that appears at the front of the 14– group. But what MS V gives, on the one hand, is taken back on the other, for the codex does not share other significant readings with the 14– list.

Any attempt to explain this curious mixture of features must be speculative. Does MS V incorporate material from an early form of the textus receptus, perhaps predating Φ? That might account for its resemblance to MSS Lh, Sta, and B of the 15+ group. Perhaps the brief introduction before c. 1 was originally placed by the papal chancery between the preamble and c. 1, but early in the text's history, maybe because it seemed to be redundant, was dropped by ancestors of the 15+/14+ exemplars. Concomitantly, for whatever reason, an ancestor of the 14– group might have eliminated the longer prologue – perhaps deemed too 'papal' in some quarters in the Empire – but retained the shorter opening.

e) Summary

The 14– version of the textus receptus presents decrees that can be placed within one manuscript family and within one geographical area. The 15+ and the 14+ series, on the other hand, reveal considerable textual jumbling, and although some links are discernible, patterns can be difficult to locate. Scribal errors and changes are plentiful, some of which could have been made as corrections based on other

---

[23] See in Chapter 2, *Survival*, Lists of Canons, Sect. b.
[24] Somerville–Kuttner, *Pope Urban* 192–93.
[25] These include in the prologue *probata* for *prolata*, at the beginning of c. 3 *autem* for *tamen*, in c. 6, line 7 *maiores* for *sacros*, and in c. 13 *baptisterio* for *baptismo*.

accounts and thus produce 'horizontal' transmissions among the copies.[26] The fact that none of the known medieval versions of Piacenza's legislation stems directly from any other indicates that a substantial number of manuscripts, which may or may not have helped to clarify the fortuna of these canons, are lost.[27]

CANON LAW COLLECTIONS

Yet notwithstanding imponderables about the major forms in which the decrees circulated, the Council of Piacenza's enduring legacy throughout the Middle Ages and beyond is its contribution to the Church's canon law. In Chapter 2, *Survival, Canon Law Collections*, the canon law books where legislation from Piacenza is found were described. Making use of those descriptions, the sections to follow here, together with the critical apparatus to the edition, focus on transmission of the textus receptus or parts of it in canonical collections. Some questions remain, but the main lines of the story seem clear, showing, inter alia, that in certain instances a significant divergence occurred between what was enacted in March 1095, and what was handed down in the twelfth-century canonical tradition. The headings used in Chapter 2 will again be employed here.

a) Variae collectiones

T = Turin, Bibl. Naz. Universitaria D.IV.33 (Pasini 239), fols. 135v-36r; cc. 1–14.
T's version of cc. 1–14 differs little from Φ (although reading in c. 5 *partes* for *beneficia*), but has no clear connection with any other manuscript of the textus receptus.[28] Yet its numbering of the decrees is curious, as both *cap. i.-iv.* (of the council), and cc. 208–211 (in the collection's bk. 7). The former enumeration corresponds to the division in MS V, although T and V are seemingly unrelated.
L = London, BL, Add. 11440, fol. 67r-v; cc. 1–12.
This unanalyzed collection has a version of the canons of Piacenza related to the 14– group and especially to MS Stb.[29] Stb is an early twelfth-century book from

---

[26] See the discussion of 'limitations of the Stemmatic Method' in L.D. Reynolds and N.G. Wilson, *Scribes & Scholars*, 3rd. edn. (Oxford 1991) 214.
[27] 'More manuscripts' are not always the answer to solving textual problems: cf., e.g., the many traditions for the decrees of Clermont, 1095 (Somerville, *Decreta* passim), and NB the observations in COD 210, about the traditions of the canons of Lateran III. Recall the comments in Chapter 2, *Enactment*, Gesta, for the *Gesta*'s claim that Pope Urban had new ways of circulating the decrees of Piacenza.
[28] T offers a few readings found nowhere else, e.g., omission of *si tunc* in c. 3, l. 3, omission of *omnino* in c. 4, the reading *duxerint* for *egerint* in c. 7, l. 2 and the addition of *ordinationes* after *separatis* in c. 10, l. 2.
[29] MS L's link to the 14– manuscripts is not simple. On the one hand, L has important readings missing from all exemplars of that group, most importantly the omission at the end of c. 12 of the phrase *ut-caritati*. (an omission also in the *Polycarpus*, the *Seven Books*, *Three Books*, and Gratian 2). Yet, on the other hand, L's tie to 14– texts is demonstrable through the following shared variants: c. 2 *lingua aut obsequio* added after *pecunia* in l. 2; c. 10, l. 3–4, the omission of *cum-redierint*, and the added sentence at the end of the decree. The specific relationship between L and Stb is shown by readings

the monastery of Zwiefalten in the diocese of Constance. While Stb is not the formal source for Piacenza in L, those two manuscripts drew on a common tradition that also influenced the Annalista Saxo and Gerhoch of Reichersberg, as will be discussed below.

b) Italian Collections

The copies of Piacenza in MSS Vp and Fv could both depend on an exemplar that remains undetected, but more likely is Fv's indirect dependence on Vp, given Fv's incorporation into the body of the *Panormia* of the same set of decrees that is found in the margin of Vp.

Vp = BAV, Vat. lat. 1360, fol. 38v; cc. 5–7, 9.

Fv = Florence, Biblioteca Nazionale Centrale, Conv. sopp. G.1.836, fols. 43v-4r; cc. 5–7, 9.

For the collections cited below the following abbreviations again are used: *Polycarpus* (Poly.), *Collection in Seven Books* (7L), *Collection in Three Books* (3L]) – *Collection in Nine Books* (9L) is derivative from 3L – and the two versions of Gratian's *Decretum* (Grat. 1 & Grat. 2).

Piacenza cc. 1–7

Aside from the special case of the 'appendix' (Φ) that emerges in certain manuscripts of Poly., decrees from Piacenza were incorporated within the body of Poly. and of the other collections listed. These works all were composed in Italy in the first half of the twelfth century and are interrelated in ways that remain to be analyzed thoroughly, for example Poly. was a source for 7L, 3L, and Gratian 1, while 3L was a source for 9L, Gratian 1, and also Gratian 2.[30] Yet Poly. lacks cc. 1–7 and thus it cannot be the route by which those decrees entered other collections.

The version of cc. 1–7 that is contained in the other Italian compilations noted above does not in general deviate greatly from Φ. There are differences – e.g., all read *partes* rather than *beneficia* in c. 5, line 2 – but not a great number of significant variants. In searching for lines of transmission, 7L seemingly can be put in a separate category. This compilation was probably assembled at Rome in the second decade of the twelfth century, and there seems to be no evidence of dependence one way or another between 7L, 3L, 9L, and either recension of Gratian. But the apparatus

---

appearing only in those two exemplars: c. 3 omission of *eos* in line 2; c. 4 *ordinationem* for *consecrationem*; in line 1 of c. 8 omission of *facte sunt*; cc. 8–9 omission of *irritas-autem*; c. 9 near the beginning, omission of *eas que*, *his* for *eis*, and the reading *facte sunt irritas esse omnino iudicamus* at the conclusion of the canon; and the added sentence at the end of c. 10, *et his nostris decretis cognitis mox ab errore ad catholicam ecclesiam transierint, et nobis nostrisque legatis se per omnia obedire promiserint.*, which, aside from L's lack of the word *si* after *et* at the beginning, is identical to the reading in MS Stb. The reading *digni habeantur* in c. 11 is found in L and Stb, and also in MSS E and Mic.

[30] For brief descriptions of these collections and bibliography, see Chapter 2, *Survival*, JL 5694. For Poly. as a sources of 7L, 3L, and Gratian 1 see, inter al., Fowler-Magerl, *Clavis* 232, Motta, *Coll. can. 3L* xxxvii, and Winroth, *Making* passim; for 3L as a source for 9L and Gratian 1, see Fowler-Magerl, *Clavis* 235–36, Fred Paxton, 'La Cause 13 de Gratien et la composition du Décret', *Revue de droit canonique* 51 (2001) 238–39, and Winroth, *Making* passim; and for 3L as a source of Gratian 2 see ibid. 17, and Motta, *Coll. can. 3L* xlii–xliv.

criticus points to a link between cc. 1–7 in 3L, 9L, and Gratian, on the one hand, and MS Va of the textus receptus, on the other, although the pattern is uneven and item by item the shared variants are not overwhelming in quality.[31] 3L was compiled between the second decade of the twelfth century and c.1140, perhaps at Pistoia.[32] Piacenza cc. 1–7 as found in 3L thus are possibly related to MS Va, which might have been copied at the monastery of San Antimo near Montalcino in the diocese of Chiusi.

Piacenza cc. 8 ff.

Piacenza cc. 8–14 as transmitted in Poly, 7L, 3L, and Gratian 2 deviate significantly from MS Va, and per se offer a uniform and unique set of readings that seems to appear first in Poly.[33] In the collections under discussion here, nearly all of c. 8, and parts of cc. 9 and 12, are eliminated, testimony either to the volatility of the issue of Wibertine ordinations, or perhaps to *homoioteleuton*, as will be discussed in the commentary in Chapter 5. But accidental or purposeful, the importance of Piacenza's readings at this point is considerable for the Church in the twelfth century. What can be called the Poly.–Gratian 2 rendition of these lines due to inclusion in the *Decretum Gratiani* thus was assured a long life, even if it did not constitute what Urban II promulgated in 1095.

3L provided a prime, but not the only, source for decrees of Piacenza in Gratian 2. Included also, in D. 70 of the *Decretum Gratiani*, is c. 15 and a shortened form of Φ's concluding notice on the tenth preface of the mass. Forty years ago Jacqueline. Rambaud speculated, with an eye on c. 15, that Gratian 2 knew a collection like Φ.[34] If that is so, and if the collection in question contained the range of conciliar resources from Urban II and Calixtus II found in Φ, Gratian used them selectively. For instance, Φ was not employed as his source for canons from Melfi, most of his decrees from Piacenza were derived from 3L, and no canons from Calixtus' Council of Toulouse appear in the *Decretum*.[35]

While much has been discovered in recent years about Gratian's sources, much too remains opaque. It seems clear, for example, that both Gratian 1 and 2 used texts from Burchard of Worms' *Decretum*, yet Burchard's vast depository of canons

---

[31] See, e.g., c. 1, absence of *sancti Spiritus*; c. 2, line 1, absence of *vel* (1); c. 3, line 3, absence of *si*; c. 5, line 6, *inveniantur*; c. 6, line 1, absence of *iam*, and line 5, *eis*.

[32] For 3L and Pistoia, see Giuseppe Motta, 'Osservazioni intorno alla Collezione Canonica in tre libri (MSS C 135 Archivio Capitolare di Pistoia e Vat. lat. 3831)', *Proceedings of the Fifth International Congress of Medieval Canon Law*, ed. Stephan Kuttner and Kenneth Pennington (Monumenta iuris canonici, Subsidia 6; Vatican City 1980) 61, and idem, *Coll. can. 3L* xix–xliv; cf. Detlev Jasper, 'Eine neue Handschrift des Liber de honore ecclesiae des Placidus von Nonantola', *Deutsches Archiv* 48 (1992) 548.

[33] In c. 10, line 5, MS Va contains the same relatively insignificant reading as Poly., 7L, 3L, and Grat. 2, i.e., the omission of *tamen*. But otherwise those collections present texts with editorial adjustments that are found neither in Va nor anywhere else. It is unknown whether not that editing was accomplished by Cardinal Gregory and his collaborators or already existed in Poly.'s formal source.

[34] Le Bras, *L'âge classique* 56–57. See Blumenthal, 'De prava constitutione' 147, and n. 39.

[35] See Somerville–Kuttner, *Pope Urban* 198–99, for Gratian and Melfi.

was a formal source for only a handful of texts.[36] Did Gratian have access to a complete exemplar of Burchard yet cite it in a very limited manner, or did he find Burchardian canons in supplements to one of his other sources? It is impossible to say. But employing Φ or something akin to Φ selectively seems not to be inconsistent with what is known about the methodology of the author[s] of the *Decretum Gratiani*. Other than in Φ and Gratian 2, no twelfth-century trace has been discovered of the notice about the tenth preface for the mass having been instituted at Piacenza. Φ or something like Φ can be cautiously suggested, therefore, as Gratian's source for both, a possibility that might prompt further investigation of the other eleventh- and twelfth-century papal councils represented both in Φ and in Gratian.

c) *Collectio Caesaraugustana* – cc. 1–7, c. 12 partim, and c. 13

The *Caesaraugustana* was discussed in Chapter 2, *Survival*, Canon Law Collections, Section c. Those comments will not be repeated, but the Clermont/Piacenza canons from this work will be collated and variants listed in a separate apparatus in the edition.

ANNALISTA SAXO AND GERHOCH OF REICHERSBERG

a) Annalista Saxo – cc. 8–12

The *Annalista* included Piacenza cc. 8–12 in his work, and although offering a few unique readings used a version of the 14– account of the provisions, which is not surprising for a historian working in eastern Germany. Specifically, a source similar to MS Stb and to the canon law collection found in MS L was utilized as, inter alia, the distinctive readings at the end of c. 10 show. The ways in which the work of the Annalista and MSS Stb and L are linked requires further study, for example the absence in both MS L and the Annalista of any decrees after c. 12 might be incidental or might suggest an underlying textual ancestor in which cc. 13ff. were absent.[37]

b) Gerhoch of Reichersberg, *Libellus de simoniacis* – c. 15 partim, followed by cc. 1–4.

The other twelfth-century narrative source, also from Germany, that includes legislation from Piacenza, Gerhoch of Reichersberg's *Libellus* on simoniacs, reveals a more complicated picture. MSS Lh and Sta showed that a 15+ account of the textus receptus circulated north of the Alps in the Empire (see above in sect. iii.a). Gerhoch provided further evidence that c. 15 was known in that region, for he

---

[36] Peter Landau, 'Burchard de Worms et Gratien: à propos des sources immédiates de Gratien', *Revue de droit canonique* 48 (1998) 233–45.
[37] The *Gesta* also conclude with c. 12, but no other connection has emerged between that account, the Annalista, and/or MS L.

inserted part of that decree into his *Libellus*, followed by cc. 1–4.[38] Sequential oddity aside, the resulting texts diverge very little from Φ, but the variants that emerge point to the 14– group and to MS L, as in the case of the Annalista Saxo.[39]

It is impossible to specify the avenue whereby Gerhoch had access to texts from Piacenza or how many of the canons he knew.[40] It would seem unlikely that he used multiple lists containing these decrees in composing the *Libellus*, and his texts probably were obtained from one rendition of the canons, although its length is impossible to determine. In this regard, notice should be taken of MS Mub, which contains Piacenza's synodal preamble in addition to cc. 1–7, and c. 15 (see Transmission beyond Φ, Sect. c, above in this chapter). This late twelfth-century book derives either from Beuerberg or from Reichersberg, and contains a copy of Gerhoch's *Opusculum de aedificio Dei*, to which the texts of Piacenza have been appended. This exemplar strengthens the possibility that somewhere behind Gerhoch's text would lie an account comprised of the entire textus receptus containing at least some readings distinctive to the 14– versions. That mixture perhaps is implied not only by MS Mub but also in line 2 of c. 3, where *eos* is omitted by Gerhoch, in two 15+ manuscripts (B and Mid), and also in two of the 14– group (Stb and VB). The existence of such a tradition is mainly suppositional, of course, and the absence of the word *eos* in these books could be coincidental.[41] But circulation in twelfth-century Germany of both 15+ and 14– versions of the textus receptus is indisputable, and Gerhoch's text and MS Mub suggest that at some point within forty years of the synod these texts were blended in ways that no longer are clearly discernible.

EDITION AND TRANSLATION

The preceding sections have described the textual interrelation of the known accounts of Piacenza's legislation, and it remains to edit the canons. The need for a new text and the rationale for structuring it around Φ was delineated in the Introduction, and the Sect. titled *Polycarpus* Supplement above. The edition will be based on a transcription of ΦPa, edited for capitalization and punctuation and with spelling unified. No compelling arguments exist for preferring any other version of Φ over Φ Pa (Paris,

---

[38] Gerhoch appears to offer the only instance where the sequence of the decrees is altered: see in Chapter 2, n. 8.
[39] See the distinctive reading in c. 4, l. 2, i.e., *ordinationem* for *consecrationem*, found in Gerhoch, in the canon law book MS L, and in MS Stb of the 14- group.
[40] All of the decrees that Gerhoch cited are also found in Gratian 2, and it is well known that he used that collection: see Classen, *Gerhoch* 276, n. 19, and 463. But Gratian 2 must be dated after 1139 because of the presence therein of legislation from Innocent II's Lateran Council of that year, and thus cannot be a source for the *Libellus*, composed in 1135. This is confirmed by comparing the texts of Piacenza cc. 1–4 and 15 in Gerhoch and in Gratian.
[41] Cf. also in c. 2, l. 3, *et nullas* for *nullasque*, found in Gerhoch and in a variety of other accounts including 14- manuscripts and MSS B and Mid.

BNF, lat. 3881, fols. 182v-83r), and the reasons for that particular choice have been given elsewhere and need not be repeated.[42] Φ Pa was, moreover, the basic manuscript used in editing the acts of the Councils of Melfi, Benevento, Troia, and Clermont. Adding now Piacenza, this manuscript constitutes the basis for modern editions of five of Urban II's six synods where a significant block of legislation survives (adding, as the sixth, Rome, 1099).

A word is in order about the numbering of the decrees. The provisions are not numbered in Φ and the numbers assigned here are editorial, following for convenience the enumeration in Weiland's edition. Decrees of eleventh- and twelfth-century synods often are not numbered in manuscripts, and divisions for the same set of legislation can vary. No information is at hand to indicate how the texts were divided in Urban's Register, and the Register of Gregory VII provides no reliable help on the matter because chancery procedures in the 1090s were different from what was done in Gregory's years.[43] The account of Piacenza is divided by ¶ signs more or less consistently among manscripts of Φ, but that does not necessarily show how divisions occurred in the papal Register. Nor, to consider another prominent version of the textus receptus, can it be assumed that the textual blocks offered by the disaffected cardinals in the *Gesta* match the appearance of the decrees in Urban's Register.

After printing the transcription of MS Φ Pa, textual variants for other manuscripts of the textus receptus are given in an apparatus criticus. As was done for the canons of Melfi, Troia, Benevento, and Clermont, this apparatus proceeds canon by canon. When the same variant exists in multiple, collated manuscript Φ is listed first, with others exemplars given alphabetically based on the sigla of the codices. Spelling variants, dittography, and textual corrections found in isolation in one manuscript are usually not noted in the apparatus (although they often are for MS Hg of the *Gesta* – see in Chapter 2, *Survival*, Narrative Sources, Sect. a). The form *-ti* will be given instead of *-ci*; *v* serves for the consonant and *u* for the vowel; *i* is used for both consonant and vowel; editorial insertions are placed within pointed brackets, e.g., U<rbanus>.

Following the critical apparatus for the textus receptus, additional variants are noted in a group of subsequent apparatus, that is for the *Gesta*, for the relevant canonical collections (*Coll[ectiones] can[onicae]*) – with the *Coll. Caesaraugustana* treated separately – and, as applicable, for JL 5694, the Annalista Saxo, and Gerhoch of Reichersberg. The order followed for *Coll. can.* is the sequence in which the collections were treated in Canon Law Collections, Sects. a-b above, i.e., MSS T, L, Vp, Fv, followed by Poly., 7L, 3L, 9L, and Grat.1 and Grat.2. As was done in *Decreta Claromontensia*, and *Pope Urban II, the Collectio Britannica, and the Council of Melfi (1089)*, editorial notes within the apparatus are in simple Latin:

---

[42] Cf. in Chapter 2, *Survival*, Polycarpus Supplement, a discussion based on Somerville–Kuttner, *Pope Urban*, 247, with reference to other sections of that study and to Somerville, *Decreta*.

[43] See Caspar, *Register* passim (e.g., 368 ff., and 400–1 ff.) For chancerial reorganization by John of Gaëta early in Urban II's reign, see Somerville–Kuttner, *Pope Urban* 239–40.

corr.= correctio
dext.= dextra etc.
eras.= erasum etc.
in marg.= in margine
lin.= linea

litt.= litterae
om.= omisit
rep.= repetitum etc.
sin.= sinistra etc.
sup.= super

The list below contains the sigla and folio/page references for the manuscripts used in the edition: copies of the textus receptus, the *Gesta*, canon law collections, and so on.

ΦPa = Paris, BNF, lat. 3881, fols. 182v-83r
ΦVa = Città del Vaticano, BAV, Reg. lat. 399, fol. 71v-r
ΦVp = Città del Vaticano, BAV, Reg. lat. 987, fols. 165r-66r
ΦVr = Città del Vaticano, BAV, Reg. lat. 1026, fols. 209v-10r
B = Brussels, Bibl. royale Albert Ier, 495–503, fols. 17v-18r
C = St.-Claude 17(3), fols. 283v-84r
E = Escorial, a. I. 6, fols. cxxi(r)
F = Florence, Bibl. Laurenz., plut. xviii.14 (cc. 1–4 part), fol. 114v
Fc = Florence, Bibl.Laurenz., S. Croce 23, dext. 5, fols. 182v-84r
Fv = Florence, Bibl. naz., Conv. sopp. G. 1. 836 (cc. 5–8), fols. 43v-44r
G = Gottweig 85(8), fols. 1v-2r
L = London, BL, Add. 11440 (cc. 1–12 part), fols. 67r-v
Lh = London, BL, Harley 3001, fols. 80v-81r
Li = Lincoln 191, fols. 110v-11r
Lu = Lucca, Bibl. Capitolare Feliniana 124, fol. 196r
Mic = Milan, Bibl. Amb., H.48 sup., fols. 162v- 63v
Mid = Milan, Bibl. Amb., A.46 inf., fols. 151r-v
Mip = Milan, Bibl. Amb., M.79 sup., fols. 248v-49r
Mub = Munich, clm. 5129, fols. 85v-86r
Mup = Munich, clm. 11316, fols. 115–16r
Muw = Munich, clm. 22011, fol. 1r
O = Oxford, Bodl., Canon. pat. Lat. 39, fols. 86r-v
Os = Oxford, Bodl., Selden supra 90, fols. 24v-25r
Pb = Paris, BNF, Baluze 7, fol. 244r
Pj = Paris, BNF lat. 18083, fols. 149v-50v
Pm = Paris, BNF lat. 3187, fols. 123r-24r
Sta = Stuttgart, Württemb. Landesbibl., theol. et phil. 4°254, fols. 123r-25r
Stb = Stuttgart, Württemb. Landesbibl., theol. et phil. 2°210, fols. 134r-35r
T = Turin, Bibl. Naz. Universitaria, D.IV.33, fols. 135v-36r
V = BAV, Vat. lat. 1208. fols. 127r-28r
Va = BAV, Vat. lat.629, fols. 269v-70r
Vm = BAV, Vat. lat.1364, fols. 189v-90v
Vp = BAV, Vat. lat.1360, fol. 38v
VB = Vyssí Brod CXIX, fols. 30r-v
W = Vienna, Österreich. Nationalbibl., lat. 2153, fols. 67v-69r
Y = New Haven, Yale University., Beinecke Lib., Marston MS 158, fol. 1r

Gesta Romanae aecclesiae contra Hildebrandum
Bg = Brussels, Bibl. roy., 11196–97, fol. 8r
Hg = Hannover, XI.671, fols. 124v-25v
Agreement of both MSS not designated with sigla

Canonical Collections [Coll. can.]
Polycarpus [Poly.], Coll. in Three Books [3L], Seven Books [7L], Nine Books [9L], and Gratian (Grat.). Agreement among copies of collections is noted in the critical apparatus by abbreviated title of the collection without manuscript designation, e.g., Poly.; agreement of Grat.1 and Grat.2 indicated by Grat.

POLYCARPUS
Poly.m = Madrid, Bibl. nacional, lat. 7127, fols. 336r, 354v, 442v
Poly.p = Paris, BNF, lat. 3881, fols. 56r, 78r, 170v-71r

7L
7Lv = BAV, Vat. lat 1346, fols. 88r, 109v, 188r
7Lw = Vienna, ÖNB 2186, fols. 152r-v, 196v

3L
3Lp = Pistoia, Bibl. capitolare 135 (109), fols. 37v-38v, 177v, 186r
3Lv = BAV, Vat. lat. 3831, fols. 34v-33r, 103v-4r, 106v-7r

9L
9L = BAV, Arch. S. Pietro C. 118, fols. 31r, 91r, 92v

GRATIAN 1
Grat.1a = Admont, Stiftsbibl. 23, fols. 104v, 107v
Grat.1b = Barcelona, Archivo de la Corona de Aragón, Ripoll 78, fols. 109vb-110ra, 115vb-16ra
Grat.1f = Florence, Bibl. nazionale centrale, Conv. sopp. A.1.402, fols. 23ra, 25rb
Grat.1p = Paris, BNF, nal 1761, fols. 95ra, 101vb-2ra
Grat.1s = St. Gallen, Stiftsbibl. 673, pp. 40–41

GRATIAN 2
Grat.2 (= Friedberg, *Decretum Gratiani*) 1.3.5, 1.1.108, 9.1.5, 76.4, 70.2; see in Chapter 2, p. 46.

Coll. Caesaraugustana
Pc1 = Paris, BNF, lat. 3875, fols. 21v-22r
S = Salamanca, Bibl. Universitaria, 2644, fols. 23r-v
Pc2 = Paris, BNF, lat 3876, fol. 17v

JL 5694
ed. supra, Chapter 2, *Survival*, Canon Law Collections

Annalista Saxo
ed. Nass

Gerhoch of **Reicherberg**
ed. Sackur; Klagenfurt, Studienbibl. MS 10, fol. 94r-v

EDITION

    Anno Dominice incarnationis mxcv, indictione iii, Kalendis
Martii, celebrata est Placentie synodus presidente domno
Urbano papa cum episcopis et abbatibus tam Galliarum quam
et Longobardie et Tuscie. Facta est autem magna consultatio
5 de his, qui ecclesias vel prebendas emerant, sed et de his,
qui in schismate Guibertino fuerant ordinati. Et primo
quidem ac tertio die in campo concilium sedit, tantus enim
convenerat populus ut nulla eos ecclesia caperet, exemplo
quidem Moysi Deuteronomium commendantis et Domini nostri
10 Ihesu Christi docentis in loco campestri. Septimo tandem
die post tractationem diutinam hec sunt capitula prolata et
assensu totius concilii approbata.

ante 1–12] Decretum beati (domini Mic; *om.* Y) Urbani pape (pape Urbani Mic). F Mic Y; Concilium Urbani pape Placentiae factum. Fc; Urbani pape in concilio Placentino de simoniacis. Li; Incipiunt decreta domni Urbani pape promulgata in synodo Placentina. O; Placentinum concilium. Os; Urbani pape decretum pontificale, conditur hic scripto formoso denique dicto. V; Incipit sinodus Urbani II pape Placentie habita. Va; Incipiunt capitula Placentine synodi que celebrata est a domno papa Urbano secundo. Vm   *1–4* Anno-Tuscie. *om.* Pj   *1* Dominice incarnationis] Domini ΦVb; incarnationis Dominice E   ab incarnatione Domini Mid Vm   mileximo triceximo v Mic indictione iii *om.* ΦVb   *1–2* indictione-Martii *om.* F   Kalendis Martii indictione iii V   Kalendis Martii *om.* C E Fc Li Lu Mic Mid Mip O Os Pm Va Vm Y; mense Martio Mub   *2* synodus Placentie B Mid Vm   *3* Urbano] U. ΦPa ΦVp ΦVr Lh; *add. sup. lin.* Sta; ii *add.* Mid; secundo *add.* Vm   et *om.* B   tam] et *add.* Li   *3–4* tam-Tuscie.] et clericis fere iiiimi milibus ex diversis provintiis Baiorie, Alemannie, Francie, Saxonie, Burgundie, Galatie, Langobardie, Tuscie. Mub   *4* et (1) *om.* B C E Fc Mic V Vm   Facta] In hac synodo *add. ante* Mub   est *om.* Va   autem *om.* ΦVb   concertatio magna ΦVr   *5–11* sed-diutinam *om.* ΦVb   *5* qui-his *om.* ΦVr   sed *om.* Mub   et *om.* F   *6* chismate C; sismate F Vm; scimate Pj   Wibertino B Mic Os V; Wilbertino(?) C; Wipertino Lh Sta; Guitbertino (ti *sup. lin.*) Li; Wigbertino Mub   ordinati fuerant B E V; ordinati sunt Mub   Et *om.* Lh Sta   *6–7* Et-die] Ac primo quidem die ac tertio sedit concilium Mub   *7* quidem die ac tertio Mic   tertia Fc V Vm   die *om.* Os   consilium V; consciulium Mib   *8* caperit ecclesia B Mub   *10* Christi *om.* Vm   docentis-campestri.] in loco campestri dicentis. Mic   loco *om.* V   capestri ΦPa   tandem] autem ΦVr V; tantem *ante corr.* O   *11* post] ob F   tradicionem Y diutinam] diuturnam ΦVr; divinam Mic V   capitula sunt Mub prolata] probata V   *11–12* et-approbata. *om.* Mic Pm   *12* a sensu ΦVr   totius] *om.* B; us *sup. lin.* M; *sup. lin.* Pj   probata B; comprobata ΦVb C E F Fc Lh Li Lu Mid Mip Mub O Os Pj Sta V Va Vm Y

Gesta: ante 1–12] ¶Incipiunt decreta Turbani, in quibus ea que sunt legitima dampnavit et que sunt heretica confirmavit. ¶Cum hec post concilium Placentinum noctu occulte

scriberentur, factus est casus stellarum, qualis non fuit ab initio, ut exprimeretur quantum nefas committeretur. *sine signis* ¶ Hg   *1–2* Kalendis (Calendas Hg) Martii indictione tercia   *3* Turbano   *4* et(1) *om.* Tus Hg   facta *iterat* Hg   *6* Ginibertino Hg   *9* quidem] nimirum   Deutronomium   *11* transactionem Hg   diutina Bg *12*   conprobata

<1> Ea, que a sanctis patribus de simoniacis statuta sunt, nos quoque sancti Spiritus iudicio et apostolica auctoritate firmamus.

ante 1–2] ¶ B; Capitulum i. C Vm; Capitula (Incipiunt *add. ante verbum* Capitula Muw V VB) Placentini concilii (consilii V) de prave ordinatis et (et] item Stb; his qui *add. ante verbum* et Muw V VB) prebendas aut ecclesias (aecclesias aut prebendas V) ementibus. (emerunt. Muw V VB) G Muw Stb V VB W (prebendas-ementibus. *scripta in lin. praeced. ante verbum* Capitula Stb); Capitula Placentini concilii. Mup; Primum capitulum. *in marg. sin.* Mub   *1* sunt] et *add.* Lh Sta   *1–2* Spiritus sancti B   sancti Spiritus iudicio] iudicio eorum Va

Gesta: ante 1–2] 1 *in marg. sin.* Hg   *1* que] sunt *add.* statuta *rep.* Hg   sunt *om.*

Coll. can.: ante 1–2] Ex concilio eiusdem pape <apud> Placentiam capitulum i. (*in marg. sin.* ccviii) T;[44] Urbanus in Placentino concilio. L; Urbanus papa ii. ex synodo Placentie habita. 7L; Ex decreto Urbani pape qui fuit Hostiensis episcopus. 3L; Ex decretis ur (*sic*) Urbani pape. 9L; Idem. Grat.2   *1* <E>a 9L   a *om.* L   *1–2* sancti Spiritus *om.* 3L 9L Grat.2

Coll. Caesaraug.: ante 1–2] Urbanus in concilio Clarimontis. Pc1 (*nonnullae litt. eras. post verbum* Urbanus); Urbanus papa in concilio Clarimontis. S; Urbanus ii in concilio Clarimontis. Pc2

Gerhoch: ante 1–2] In eadem synodo contra symoniacos ita dictum est.

<2> Quicquid igitur vel in sacris ordinibus vel in ecclesiasticis rebus vel data vel promissa pecunia adquisitum est, nos irritum esse nullasque umquam vires obtinere censemus.

ante 1–3] ¶ E Mid; ii. Vm   *1* igitur *om.* Pj   vel(1)] *sup. lin.* Fc; *om.* Va   vel(2) *sup. lin.* Stb   in(2) *om.* F Pj   vel(2)-rebus *om.* ΦVb   rebus ecclesiasticis Mup   vel(3) *om.* G Mup Stb W   *verbum eras. post* vel(3) Mip   *2* pecunia] peccunia F Fc Li Mid Pj Vm; lingua aut obsequio *add.* G Mub Mup Stb W   nullasque] nulla ΦVb; et nullas B C Li Mic Mid Mub Muw Pj V Va Vm VB; nullas F Fc G Lh Lu Mip Mup O Os Pm Sta Stb W Y   umquam *om.* Mid Vm

Gesta: 1 vel(3)] et Hg   *2* nullasque] et nullas   *3* censemus.] ¶Error generalis. *add.*

Coll. can.: 1 vel(1) *om.* 3L 9L Grat.2   *2* pecunia] lingua aut obsequio *add.* L   nullasque] et (*sup. lin.* 7Lv) nullas T L 7L 3L 9L Grat.2

Coll. Caesaraug.: 1 vel(1) *om.*   vel(3) *om.*   *2* peccunia S   umquam *om.*

Gerhoch: 1 vel(3) *om.*   *2* pecunia] obsequio aut lingua *add.*   nullasque] et nullas vires umquam

---

[44] For the marginal numbers in T, see the description of the manuscript in Chapter 2, *Survival, Canon Law Collections*, Sect. a.

<3> Siqui tamen a simoniacis non simoniace ordinati sunt,
siquidem probare potuerint se cum ordinarentur eos nescisse
simoniacos, et si tunc pro catholicis habebantur in
ecclesia, talium ordinationes misericorditer sustinemus si
5 tamen laudabilis eos vita commendat.

c. <3> om. ΦVb; ante 1–5] ¶ B Lh; ii.¶ E; iii. Vm   1 Si ΦVr   tamen] tantum Φ Vp; autem V   a] ab occulte G Mup W   ordinati] ordineti Mic; ti sup. lin. Sta   2 approbare G Mid Mup   se] seu E; om. V   eos om. B Mid Stb VB   2–3 nescisse eos esse simonicos Vm   3 si om. Va   tunc] tamen ΦVp ΦVr B; cum C E Os; tum Y   habebant Li   4–5 sustinemus. transportatum post verbum commendat E   5 laudabilis Mic Mub V   eos] om. C E Pm Os; eius Fc   vita laudabilis eos G Mup   vita om. W   commendet. ΦVp

Gesta: ante 1–5] 2 in marg. sin. Hg   1 non simoniace ordinati sunt] consecrari passi sunt   2 nescisse] nesciuisse post corr. Hg   3 tunc] tum Bg; suum ante corr. Hg   5 commendat.] Error generalis. add. Bg; (Error generalis.) add. Hg

Coll. can.: ante 1–5] De quibus Urbanus papa ait. (om. Grat.1s)[45] (C. cviii. add. Grat.2) De his qui non simoniace a simoniacis ordinantur. Grat.   1 Si L; Siquis Grat.1bp ante corr. Grat.1f   tamen] om. Grat.1abfp Grat.2; inquit Grat.1s ordinantur Grat.1s   2 probari Grat.1s   cum se Grat.1p   eos om. L   nescisse eos Grat.   3 simoniacos] esse (sup. lin. Grat.1a) add. Grat.   si om. 3L 9L Grat.   si tunc om. T tunc] tum 3L   habentur L; habeantur Grat.1s   4 ordines L   sustinemus misericorditer Grat.2   4–5 si-commendat. om. 9L   5 eos laudabilis Grat.   eos om. T

Coll. Caesaraug.: 1 ordinati (a sup. lin.) Pc1   5 vita eos S Pc2   commendet Pc2

Gerhoch: 1 tamen sup. lin.   2 eos om.

<4> Qui vero scienter se a simoniacis consecrari immo execrari passi sunt,
eorum consecrationem omnino irritam esse decernimus.

ante 1–2] iii.¶ E; ¶ Mid; iiii. Vm   1 se scienter F Mic V   scienter-simoniacis] a symoniacis scienter se E; simoniacis se scienter Fc; a publice simoniacis (simmoniacis G) scienter se G Mup W; a symoniacis <se sci>enter Pj   consecrari] consecrare Lh Sta; ordinari Li   immo] vel potius Lh Sta   1–2 Qui-omnino in marg. dext. Mip   immo execrari om. G Mup   2 exsecrari Pj Pm; exseciri V   consecra...fin. huius canon. et reliqui canones om. F; consecratione M; consec<rati>onem Pj; ordinationem Stb omnino om. Lh Sta   decernimus.] censemus. G Mup W; cernimus. M; determinamus. Pj; decernere iudicamus. Stb

Gesta: ante 1–2] 3 in marg. sin. Hg   1 se om.   immo execrari om.   eorum om.   2 confessionem ante corr. Hg   decrevimus. Hg   decernimus.] Error generalis. add. Bg; (Error generalis.) add. Hg

Coll. can.: 1 se scienter L   passi sunt] permiserint Grat.   2 ordinationem L   omnino om. T   irrita 9L

Coll. Caesaraug.: 1 execrari] permiserint vel add. Pc1 Pc2   passi sunt om. S[46]

Gerhoch: 2 ordinationem

---

[45] See Larrainzar 'Borrador' 653.
[46] The situation here is curious. The word *execrari* ends about two thirds of the way across the line, and *eorum* begins the following line although there was plenty of space for it after *execrari*. Perhaps the scribe was puzzled about what he saw at this point in the exemplar that he was copying, and left a space to be filled later, but which never was.

92 *Somerville*

<5> Quicumque sane cupiditate parentum cum adhuc parvuli
essent ecclesias vel ecclesiarum beneficia per pecunias
adepti sunt, postquam eas omnino dimiserint, si canonice in
eis vivere voluerint, pro misericordia ibidem eos esse con-
5   cedimus, neque pro hoc facto a sacris ordinibus removemus si alias
digni inveniuntur.

ante 1–6] ¶ B Mid; iiii.¶ E; v. Vm   *1* sane] pro *add.* Fc parentum] parente Pj; *om.* Va   cum adhuc *sup. lin.* Mip   parvuli] pueri Mub; <p>arv<uli>(?) Pj; parvi Mic   *2* esset ΦVp vel] aut Stb   beneficia] partes C E Fc G Li Lu Mic Mip Mub Mup Muw O Os Pj Pm Stb Va VB W Y   peccunias Li Mid; pecuniam Mub   *3* eas] *om.* Pj; eos Muw Pm; eas *fortasse* Va   omnino *om.* E   in *om.* Os Pm   *3–4* in eis *om.* C Mic Mub   *4* pro misericordia] per omnia Os   eos ibidem G Lh Mup Sta   eos] *om.* Fc Pj   esse eos ΦVr   esse] *om.* Mic; permanere Mub   *4–5* censemus Va   *5* hoc *om.* Os   facto] eos *add.* Mub   ordinibus] eos *add.* B Mic   *5–6* neque-inveniuntur. *om.* ΦVr   *6* dignum Pm   inveniuntur.] inveniantur. E Fc Mic Mip O Pj Va Y; *ante corr.* B

Gesta: *ante 1–6*] 4 *in marg. sin.* Hg   *2* ecclesiarum beneficia] ex partes Bg; ex partes *correc. ad* episcopatus *sup. lin.* Hg   *3* eas] eos   *4* esse] ministrare   *6* inveniuntur.] Error generalis. *add.* Bg; (Error generalis.) *add.* Hg

Coll. can.: *cc.* <5>-<7> *et* <9> *add.* Vp Fv; *ante 1–6*] Urbanus. Vp Fv; Eiusdem. 3L 9L; Quod vero v loco queritur, an liceat ei esse in ecclesia vel fungi ordinatione, quam paterna pecunia est assecutus, auctoritate diffinitur Urbani, qui scribens de simoniacis ait inter cetera. (ait inter cetera] inter cetera dixit. Grat. 1s; Quicumque *add. post verbum* cetera. Grat.1f; C. i. *add.* Grat.2) De parvulis, qui cupiditate parentum ecclesias emunt (ement *ante corr.* Grat.1b). (De-emunt. *om.* Grat.1s) Grat.   *1* sine Vp   ad huc *in marg. dext.* 7Lv   *2* beneficia] partes T L Vp Fv 7L 3L 9L Grat.   pecunium T; peccunias Vp   *3* eas] eos 7L; *om.* Vp Fv 3Lv 9L   *3–4* si-voluerint *om.* Vp Fv   *4* ibidem] bi *sup. lin.* L   eos ibidem Grat.2   eos *om.* Vp Fv 9L   *5* ordinibus] illos *add.* Grat.1abfp Grat.2   *6* inveniantur. 3L 9L Grat.1abfp Grat.2

Coll. Caesaraug.: *1* sine Pc2   *2* peccunias S   *4–5* esse concedimus eos Pc2

<6> Illi vero qui per se ipsos cum iam maioris essent etatis
nefanda cupiditate ducti eas emerunt, si in aliis ecclesiis
canonice vivere voluerint, servatis propriis ordinibus, pro
magna misericordia eos ibi ministrare promittimus. Quod si
5   ad alias fortasse transferri non poterunt et in eisdem
canonice vivere promiserint, minoribus ordinibus contenti ad
sacros ordines non accedant, salva tamen in omnibus
apostolice sedis auctoritate.

cc. <6>-<12> *om.* ΦVb; *ante 1–8*] ¶ C Lh Mid Sta; v.¶ E; vi. Vm   *1* vero *om.* ΦVr   semet Muw   iam *om.* E Fc Mip O Pj Va Y maioribus Pm   etatis] cupiditatis *add.* Mip   *2* cupiditate-emerunt] eas cupiditate emerunt Mic   ducti *om.* C E Os Pm   ducti cupiditate Mid Vm   eos(?) Va   *3* canonice] catholice Li vivere canonice Mup   voluerint] *non potest legi* C   ordinibus propriis Li   *4* ibi eos B C Fc Lh Li Lu Mic Mid Mip Mub Muw O Os Pj Pm Sta Stb Va Vm VB W Y; ibe eos E   promittimus.] promittibus. *ante corr.* ΦPa; permittimus. ΦVr B C E Fc G Lh Li Lu

Mic Mid Mip Mub Mup Muw Os Pj Pm Sta Stb T V Va Vm VB W Y; concedimus.
O   *4–5* Quod si ad alias *non potest legi* Pj   si ad *om.* Os   *5* ad] se C Mic; *om.* E Mup
Pm   fortasse] forte G Mup W; *om.* Mic Mub   transferri fortasse Lu Mip O Va Y;
transire fortasse B   transferre C Mic Os Pm; *ante corr.* Fc   eisdem] se *add.* E; eis Fc Mip
O Va Y   *5–6* et-promiserint *om.* Pj   *6* vivere canonice B E   vivere] se *add. sup. lin.*
Mid   promiserint] permiserint ΦVr; voluerint V; *nonnulla verba eras. post* promiserint Mip
ordinibus] *add. in marg.* Sta   contenti ordinibus Mid Vm   ad] et C   *7* sacros] maiores
V   salvata Mip   in *om.* ΦVr   *7–8* in-sedis] apostolica V   *8* apostolice sedis] canonica B;
apostolica Mid Vm   auctoritate sedis apostolice Li

   Gesta: *ante 1–8*] *5 in marg. sin.* Hg   *2* ducti *om.*   *3* noluerint Hg   *4* magna] maxima
ibi eos   *5* alias ad *ante corr.* Hg   transferre Hg   *6* contempti   *8* apostolice *om.*
auctoritate.] Error generalis. *add.* Bg; (Error generalis.) *add.* Hg

   Coll. can.: *ante 1–8*] ¶.1. Grat.2   *1* se *om.* 3Lv   iam *om.* L Vp Fv 3L 9L Grat.
etatis essent Grat.2   *2* emerint Grat.1bp   *3* canonice *in marg. infer.* L   *4* ibi eos T
L Vp 7L 3L 9L Grat.; ibi eas *ante corr.* Fv   permittimus ministrare. L   Quod] Sed Grat.
1a   *5* fortasse ad alias 9L   fortasse] forte Grat.1s; fortassis Grat.2   transferri fortasse
7L 3L Grat.1bfp (transferre *ante corr.* Grat.1f) Vp   transferre fortasse Fv   transferre
L   poterint Grat.2   eis T Vp Fv 3L 9L Grat.   *6* vivere canonice T   ordinibus] *om.*
Vp Fv   contempti 3Lv Grat. 1b; contemti 9L

   Coll. Caesaraug.:   *1* iam *om.* Pc2   *3* una litt. eras. ante verbum* vivere Pc2   vivere
canonice Pc2 S   *4* ibi eos   si *sup. lin.* Pc2   *5* ad *om.* S   fortasse *om.* Pc2; forte
S   *6* permiserint Pc1   ordinibus *om.* Pc2

<7>   ¶Siqui tamen ante emptionem catholice ordinati sunt, cum
   ea que emerunt dimiserint et vitam canonicam egerint, in
   suis gradibus permittantur nisi forte eiusmodi ecclesia sit
   ut ibi primum locum debeant obtinere. Primum enim vel
5 singularem vel prepositure vel officii locum in emptis
   ecclesiis eos habere non patimur.

ante 1–6] vi.¶ E; ¶ *om.* Fc G Lh Li Lu Mic Mip Mub Mup Muw O Os Pj Pm Sta Stb Va
Vm VB W Y; vii Vm   *1* cum] si Va   *2* canolicalem Lh Sta; canonica(?) Mip   egerint
om. Y   *3* gradibus] *om.* ΦVp ΦVr Pj; esse *add.* Mub Stb   permittantur gradibus
Fc   permittantur] nec promoveri prohibeantur *add.* G Mub Mup Muw Stb VB W;
ordinibus *add.* Pj   nisi] et si Pj   huiusmodi G Mub Mup Stb W ecclesia eiusmodi
E   sit ecclesia Fc O Pj   *4* ut *sup. lin.* Vm locum primum B Fc Pj   obtinere.] *fin. huius
canon. et reliqui canones om.* Li   Primum] viii. *add. ante* Vm   enim] *om.* Fc Mub
Pj   vel *om.* Pm   *5* singulare Fc   vel(1) *om.* Os   vel officii *om.* Fc Lu Mip Pj Va
Y   officii] alterius *add.* Mic   *6* eos *post corr.* Mid   non patimur habere. Fc   patimur.] permittimus. G Mub Mup Muw Stb W

   Gesta: *ante 1–6*] ¶ *om.*; *6 in marg. sin.* Hg   *1* tamen *om.*   *2* emerant   *4* vel] et   *5*
singulare Hg   propositure Bg; propo *sic* Hg   *6* patimur.] Error specialis. *add.* Bg; (Error
generalis.) *add.* Hg

   Coll. can.: *ante 1–4*] ¶ *om.* T L Vp Fv 7L 3L 9L Grat.1; ¶.2. Grat.2   *1* tamen] autem
9L   ante *sup. lin.* Grat.1f   emptionem] acceptionem *ante corr.* Grat.1f   ordinati sunt
catholice Vp Fv   *2* ea] eam 3Lp   que] querunt *ante corr.* 3Lv   vita canonice Vp
Fv   egerint] duxerint T   *3* permittantur] et manere *add. sup. lin.* Grat.1a; nec

promoveri prohibeantur *add.* L nisi forte] stare si T huiusmodi L *littera eras. post verbum* sit Grat.1s 3–4 nisi-obtinere. *om.* Vp Fv 4 ut ibi] ubi T Grat.1s enim] *om.* 7L; tamen Vp Fv 5 singulare T propositum(?) T vel] et *add.* T vel officii *om.* Vp Fv 7L 3L 9L Grat. 6 eos] *om.* L habere eos Grat.1s patimur.] permittimus. L

Coll. Caesaraug.: ante 1–6 ¶ *om.* 5 propositure Pc2

<8> ¶Ordinationes, que a Guiberto heresiarc<h>a facte sunt
postquam ab apostolice memorie papa Gregorio et a Romana
ecclesia est dampnatus, [queque etiam a <p>seudoepiscopis
per eum postea ordinatis perpetrate sunt], irritas esse
5 iudicamus.

cc. <8>-<14> *om.* Mub; *ante 1–5*] ¶.vii. E; ¶ *om.* ΦVr Bg Fc G Lu Mic Mid Mip Mup Muw O Os Pj Pm Stb V Va Vm VB W Y; ii. V; viiii. Vm 1 Ordinatio...facta est ΦVr Guiberto] W. B; Guitberto C Os; Wigberto G Mup Stb VB W; Wiberto Lh Mic Sta facte sunt *om.* Stb 2–4 postquam-sunt *om.* B 2 apostolice] sedis *add.* E; beate Mup; apostolico beate VB a] *om. sed una litt. eras. ante verbum* Romana ΦVr; ab Pj Romana *om.* Pj 3 est dampnatus ecclesia ΦVr Mic dampnatus est Fc Muw Pj 3–4 queque-sunt *om.* Φ *et universi alii textus praeter Gesta et JL 5694 quae suppleverunt haec verba; Concilium Romanum Urbani II apud sanctum Petrum a.1099 quoque inclusit ea (Mansi, Amplissima coll. 20.962)* 4 irritos Fc 4-c. <9> lin.1 irritas-autem *om.* Stb 5 diiudicamus. Fc Pj

Gesta: *ante 1–5*] ¶ *om.*; 7 *in marg. sin.* Hg 3 dampnatus] queque etiam a pseudoepiscopis per eum postea ordinatis perpetrate (perfecte Hg) sunt *add.* 4 irritas] veritas *ante corr.* Hg

Coll. can.: cc. <8>-<12> *om.* 9L; c. <8> *om.* Vp Fv Poly. 7L 3L Grat.2; *ante 1–5*] capitulum ii. (*in marg. dext.* ccviiii) T;[47] 1 que] quem L; quas Vp; quoque(?) Fv Wigberto L facte sunt *om.* L 3 dampnatus] est *add. et cancell.* T 4-c. <9> lin.1 irritas-autem *om.* L

Coll. Caesaraug.: cc. <8>-<11> *om.*

JL 5694 partim: 1 Ordinationes que] De ordinationibus facte sunt] factis postquam a beatae memoriae Gregorio papa 3–5 est-iudicamus.] dampnatus est, quaeque etiam a <p>seudoepiscopis per eum postea ordinatis perpetrate sunt, Placentinae synodi generale iudicium definitum est ut irritae habeantur.

Annalista Saxo: *ante 1–5*] De ordinationibus vero eiusdem Uuicberti sepedictus Urbanus papa in Placentino concilio tale decretum promulgavit, inter cetera dicens. 1 Uuicberto facte sunt *om.* 2 papa *om.* 4-c. <9> lin.1 irritas-autem *om.*

<9> ¶Similiter autem et eas, que a ceteris heresiarchis
nominatim excommunicatis facte sunt et ab eis, qui
catholicorum adhuc viventium episcoporum sedes invaserunt,
nisi probare valuerint se cum ordinarentur eos nescisse
5 dampnatos.

c. <9> *in marg. sin.* VB; *ante 1–5*] viii.¶ E; ¶ *om.* Fc G Lh Lu Mic Mip Mup Muw O Os Pj Pm Sta V Va Vm VB W Y; x. Vm 1 Similiter] ea *add.* Va autem *om.* E G Mup

---

[47] For the marginal numbers in T, see n. 44 above.

The Transmission of the Canons of Piacenza   95

W   eas] eos *ante corr.* Mip Muw; ea Va   eas que *om.* Stb   *2* nominatim] om. Fc; nominais Y facte sunt *om.* G Mup Stb W   eis] illis Pj; his Stb; aliis Y   *3* catholicorum] et *add.* B C G Lh Lu Mid Mup Muw Os Pm Sta Stb V VB W; vel *add.* E   adhuc] ad ut *ante corr.* Mip   adhuc viventium] adviventium Fc   episcoporum *om.* O   sedes episcoporum Mid Vm   invaserunt sedes B   *4* nisi] si C Mic Os Pm   probare valuerint] probaverint Fc   valuerint] voluerint B Pj Pm; noluerint C Os   eos *om.* B E   valuerint-nescisse] noluerint eos cum ordinarentur se necisse Mic   *4–5* nisi-dampnatos.] facte sunt irritas esse (omnino *add.* Stb) iudicamus. G Mup Stb W; irritas esse iudicamus. (iudicavimus. VB) Muw VB   *5* dampnatos.] irritas esse censemus. B; excommunicatos. Fc Pj

Gesta: ante *1–5* ¶ *om.*   *1* eas] ea   *2* nominatis   *3* catholicorum] et *add.*   *4* nisi] nec Hg   *5* dampnatos.] Error generalis. *add.* Bg; (Error generalis.) *add.* Hg

Coll. can.: ante *1–5*] ¶ *om.* T L; Eiusdem. Fv; Urbanus II. Poly.; Urbanus/// *fortasse quicquid nunc obliteratum* 7Lv; Idem 7Lw; Eiusdem. 3L; Unde idem Urbanus ait: C. v. Qui nominatim excommunicati sunt, et qui aliorum sedes inuadunt, alios ordinare non possunt. Grat.2   *1* ¶ Similiter autem et eas, que a ceteris] Ordinationes ab Vp Fv Poly. 7L 3L Grat.2   eas que *om.* L   *2* factae sunt nominatim excommunicatis Grat.2   excommunicatas Vp facte sunt] *om.* L; factas Vp Fv   his L   *2–3* et-invaserunt] irritas esse iudicamus Vp Fv   *3* catholicorum] et *add.* T L episcoporum *om.* T   invaserunt] invaserint 7Lw; irritas esse iudicamus *add.* Poly. 7L 3L Grat.2   *4–5* nisi-dampnatos.] *om.* T; facte sunt irritas esse omnino iudicamus. L

JL 5694 partim: *4–5* nisi-dampnatos. *sine variationibus*

Annalista Saxo: *1* eas que *om.*   *2* facte sunt *om.*   his   *3* catholicorum] et *add.*   *4–5* nisi-dampnatos.] facte sunt irritas esse omnino iudicamus.

<10> ¶Qui vero ab episcopis, quondam quidem catholice
      ordinatis sed in hoc scismate a Romana ecclesia separatis,
      consecrati sunt, eos nimirum cum ad ecclesie unitatem
      redierint, servatis propriis ordinibus, misericorditer
5   suscipi iubemus si tamen vita eos et scientia commendat.

ante *1–5*] ix.¶ E; ¶ *om.* B Fc G Lh Lu Mic Mid Mup Muw O Os Pj Pm Sta Stb V Va Vm VB W Y; xi. Vm   *1* quondam] comdam Mip[48]   quidem] quod ΦVp; qui ΦVr Pm   *2* ordi<natis> Pj; *post* ordinatis *tres litt. eras.* (s??) Lu; sed in hoc *non potest legi* Pj   hoc *om.* Fc Mip O Y   scismate] Wibertino *add.* Mic   ab Pj   Romana *om.* Pj   separatis] separati ΦVr   *3* consecrati] conseparati E; consecuti C Pm Os   unitatem ecclesie B Pj   *3–4* cum-redierint *om.* G Mup Muw Stb VB W   *4* miscorditer ΦPa ΦVp ΦVr; m<iseri>corditer G   *5* tamen] tantum ΦVr; *om.* Va   vita *non potest legi* G   eos vita B Lh Sta   eos *om.* E Os Pj Y   et scientia eos C Fc G Lu Mic Mip Mup Muw O Pm Stb Va VB W   scientia] conscientia B Y; conscientia eos Os   commendat.] commendant. ΦVr; et si his nostris decretis cognitis obedire promiserint. *add.* Mup; et si his nostris decretis cognitis mox ab errore ad (ab-ad *non potest legi* G) catholicam (*om.* G W) ecclesiam transierint, et nobis nostrisque legatis se per omnia (per omnia *om.* Muw) obedire promiserint. (promiserint obedire. VB) G Muw Stb VB W

Gesta: ante *1–5*] ¶ *om.*; 8 *in marg. sin.* Hg   *1* quidem] (quidam) Hg   *5* vita] canonica *add.* et scientia *om.*

---

[48] The occurrence of the unusual form *comdam* for *quondam* at this point in Mip and T seems to be a coincidence; no other connection seems to link these two versions of c. <10>.

Coll. can.: ante 1–5] ¶ *om.* T L Poly. 7L 3L; ¶.1. Grat.2   *1* quondam] comdam T   quidem *om.* L   *2* hoc *om.* Poly. 7L 3L Grat.2   separatis] ordinationes *add.* T   *3* consecuti T   *3–4* cum-redierint *om.* L   *5* tamen *om.* Poly. 7L 3L Grat.2   vita *om.* T et scientia eos T Poly. 7L 3L Grat.2   commendat.] et si probare voluerint se cum ordinarentur eos nescisse dampnatos. *add.* T; et his nostris decretis cognitis mox ab errore ad catholicam ecclesiam transierint, et nobis nostrisque legatis se per omnia obedire promiserint. *add.* L

Annalista Saxo: *3–4* cum-redierint *om.*   *5* iubeatis et scientia eos   commendat.] et his nostris decretis cognitis mox ab errore (errorem *ante corr.*) ad catholicam ecclesiam transierint, et nobis nostrisque separatis (*sic*) se per omnia obedire promiserint. *add.*

<11> Amodo vero quicumque a predictis scismaticis sancteque Romane ecclesie adversariis se ordinari permiserit, nullatenus hac venia dignus habeatur.

ante 1–3] ¶ B C Mid Mip; x.¶ E; xii. Vm   *1* Ammodo Fc   vero] *sup. lin.* B   *2* adversatus ordinari se Mic   se *om.* C Fc Pm   permiserit] permiserint ΦPa ΦVp ΦVr E Mic Stb T V; *verbum non potest legi* Pj   hac] ac Fc V; h *sup. lin.* Mid   *2–3* digni habeantur E Mic Stb (habeantur *in marg.; al. man. [?]* E)

Gesta: *1* Amodo vero quicumque] Qui vero posthac (post haec Hg)   sancte

Coll. can.: ante 1–3 ¶.2. Grat.2   *1* Ammodo Poly.m   vero *om.* L   scismaticis predictis Poly.m   scismaticis *om.* T sancte T Grat.2   *2* permiserint L   ac 3Lp   *2–3* digni habeantur L

Annalista Saxo: *1* Admodo   Romane *om.*   *2* se] adver *add. et cancell.*   permiserint *2–3* digni habeantur.

<12> Quamvis autem misericordie intuitu magnaque necessitate
cogente hanc in sacris ordinibus dispensationem con-
stituerimus, nullum tamen preiudicium sacris canonibus fieri
volumus, sed optineant proprium robur, et cessante neces-
5   sitate, illud quoque cesset quod factum est pro necessitate.
Ubi enim multorum strages iacet subtrahendum est aliquid
severitati ut addatur amplius caritati.[49]

ante 1–7] ¶ Lh Sta; xiii. Vm   *1* misericordie intuitu] nomine ΦVr; *non potest legi* Pj   *2* cogente] habeatur *add.* E   dispensationem] constitutionem B   *2–3* statuerimus VB   *3* preiudicium] in *add.* Fc; Romanum iuditium Pj   canonibus] actionibus Mic; ordinibus Muw   *4* rubor Pm   *4–5* necessitate cessante Fc   *5* cesset] et *add.* G Mup   pro necessitate factum est. E Mic Vm   *6* Ibi Mip   enim *om.* ΦVr   iacet] populorum *add.* B   *6–7* Ubi-caritati. *om.* E Mic   aliquid-caritati. *om.* C Os   *7* severitate V   addatur] demus Va   amplius] *om.* B; aliquid *add.* Fc   caritati *om.* ΦVr

Gesta: *1* magnaque] nimiaque   *6* iacet] iacent   caritati.] *cc.* <13> seq. *om.*

Coll. can.: ante 1–7 ¶.3. Grat.2   *2–3* ordinibus-sacris *marg. sin.* L   *3* canonibus] ordinibus *ante corr.* T   *7* ut-caritati. *om.* L Poly. 7L 3L Grat.2   caritati.] *cc.* <13> seq. *om* L

---

[49] See the commmentary at n. 25 in the following chapter.

Coll. Caesaraug.: ante 1–7] Infra. *add.* Pc1; Et infra. *add.* Pc2 S   *2* cogente] urgente Pc1   *6–7* Ubi-caritati. *om.*

Annalista Saxo: *4* et] nam   *5* pro necessitate factum est.   *7* amplius addatur

<13> Illud quoque precipimus ut pro crismate et baptismo et sepultura nichil unquam exigatur.

ante 1–2] ¶ B Mid; xi.¶ E; Ex decretis domni Urbani pape secundi in Placentino concilio prolatis. Pb; iii. V; xiiii. Vm   *1* Illud-precipimus] Sanctorum canonum statutis sane consentientes decernimus Pb   et...et] vel...vel B   et(1) *om.* G Mup Stb W baptisma Mic; baptisterio V   *2* exiguatur. ΦVp

Coll. can.: ante 1–2] iii. *(iiii. ante corr.; marg. dext.* ccx.*)* T;[50] Urbanus papa II. Poly. 7L; Urbanus II. 3L 9L

Coll. can.: c. *<13> om.* Grat.2

Coll. Caesaraug.: ante 1–2 Item.   *1* precipimus] Sanctorum canonum statutis sane consentientes decernimus Pb   et...et] vel...vel B   et(1) *om.* G Mup Stb W   baptisma Mic; baptisterio V

<14> Statuimus etiam ut ieunia quattuor temporum hoc ordine celebrentur: primum ieiunium in initio Quadragesime, secundum in ebdomada Pentecosten, tertium vero et quartum in Septembri et Decembri more solito fiant.

ante 1–4] ¶ B Lh Mid Sta; xii.¶ E; iiii. V; xv. Vm   *1* etiam *om.* ΦVr   ut] vel Pm   *2* celebremus C E Os Pm; celebrantur Pj   initium C Os Pm   secunda Pm   *3* Pentecoste Fc Lh Lu Mip Pm Sta; Pentecostes E G Mic Mid O Pb Pj Stb Vm   vero *om.* ΦVb Fc G Mic Mip Mup Va W   *3* et(2)] vel V   *3–4* vero-fiant.] in epdomada plena ante equinoctium, quartum in epdomada plena ante nativitatem Domini. B   *4* soluto Lh   solito more Pb   fiant.] fiat. Fc Mip O Pj Va Y; celebrentur. Mic

Coll. can.: ante 1–4] iiii *(marg. dext.* ccxi.*)* T;[51] Urbanus II. Poly.; Urbanus. 3L 9L; Paschalis papa II. 7L;[52] Contra Urbanus. C. iv. De eodem. Grat.2   *1* etiam *om.* 7L   *2* initium 7L   Quadragesime *om.* 9L   *3* Pentecostes Grat.2   vero *om.* T   *4* fiat. Poly. 3L 9L Grat.2

Coll. Caesaraug.: c. *<14> om.*

c. <15> in Φ B Lh Mid Mub O Pb Pm Sta & Grat.2

<15> ¶Sanctorum canonum statutis consona sentientes, decernimus ut sine titulo facta ordinatio irrita habeatur, et in qua quislibet titulatus est in ea perpetuo perseveret. Omnino autem in duabus aliquem titulari non liceat, sed
5 unusquisque in qua titulatus est in ea tantum canonicus

---

[50] For the marginal number in T, see n. 44 above.
[51] For the marginal number in T, see n. 44 above.
[52] For this text inscribed to Pope Paschal II in 7Lw (fol. 252r), and in Cortona 43 (fols. 226v), see Chapter 2, *Survival*, Canon Law Collections, Sect. b; cf. Somerville–Zapp, "Eighth Book" 171–72.

habeatur. Licet enim episcopi dispositione unus diversis
preesse possit ecclesiis, canonicus tamen aut prebendarius
nisi unius tantum ecclesie qua conscriptus est esse non
debet. Sique tamen capelle sunt, que suis reditibus clericos
10   sustinere non possint, earum cura ac dispositio preposito
maioris ecclesie, cui capelle subdite esse videntur,
i<m>mineat, et tam de possessionibus quam et de
ecclesiasticis capellarum officiis ipse prevideat.

ante 1–13] ¶ *om.* ΦVr Lh Mid Mub O Pb Sta; Cap. xv *in marg. dext. manu recen.*
Mub   *1–10* Sanctorum-earum] Illut quoque totius concilii assensu praecipimus ut capellarum Pb   *1* Sanctorum-sentientes *om.* B   statuta Lh Sta   consona sentientes] consentientes ΦVb   *2* decernimus] etiam *add.* B; decrevimus *ante corr.* O   *3* qua] ecclesia
add. Mub   quislibet] quilibet B Mub; ecclesia *add.* O   intitulatus B Mub   est
titulatus O   est] ecclesia *add.* B   eo Mub   *3–5* perpetuo-ea *om.* B   *4* autem *om.*
Mub   aliquem in duabus titulari ecclesiis O   *5* canonice Pm   *6* ¶ *ante* Licet Mid
episcopus O   dispensatione Mub   *7* possit] debeat ΦVr   tamen] tantum ΦVp Pm;
om. ΦVr   prebendaris Pm   *8* unius] *om.* B; unis Pm   tantum unius O   ecclesie]
in *add.* B Lh Mid Mub O Pm Sta   scriptus B   *9* debeat ΦVr   *9–13* Sique-prevideat.]
Nullus clericus in duabus ecclesiis ministrare presumat. ΦVb; *om.* Pm   capelle *om.*
Mid   *10* earum] eorum *ante corr.* Lh; eorum Mid   ac] aut ΦVr   *11* esse *om.* B Lh
Mid Mub O Pb Sta   *12* immineat ΦVr   et(2) *om.* B O; *sup. lin.* Sta   *13* provideat.
ΦVr Lh Mid Mub O Pb Sta

   Grat.2: *ante 1–13* Item ex sinodo Urbani habita Placentiae.   *1* sanctientes   *3* qua]
ecclesia *add.*   quislibet] quilibet   *4* ¶.1. *ante* Omnino   *7* aut *om.*   *8* tantum *om.*
ecclesie] in *add.*   *9* ¶.1. *sic sed vere* ¶.2. *ante* Si que   *10* sustentare earum] ea   *12* et
(2) *om.*   *13* provideat.

   Gerhoch: *ante 1–2*] Placentinum concilium presidente papa Urbano celebratum dicit.
solummodo 1–2 Sanctorum-habeatur *sine variationibus*

Notitia in Φ & Grat.2

In eodem etiam concilio antiquis viiii
prefationibus decima addita est, que ita se habet.
Equum et salutare nos tibi semper et ubique gratias agere,
Domine sancte, Pater omnipotens, eterne Deus, et te in
5   veneratione beate Marie semper virginis collaudare,
benedicere, et predicare, que et unigenitum tuum sancti
Spiritus obumbratione concepit et virginitatis gloria
permanente lumen eternum mundo effudit, Ihesum Christum
Dominum nostrum.

1 consilio *post corr.* ΦVb   *3–4* salutare-Deus] sa. n. tibi s. 7 u. gra. a. d. s. p. o. e. d.
ΦVr   *7–8* concepit-effundit] c. 7. v. g. per. h. m. l. ef. ΦVr

   Grat.2: *ante 1–3* Gratian.   *3–6* nos-predicare *om.*

Post c. <14> solummodo in Pj
Siquis decimam tenuerit aut ad presbiterum non dederit de omnibus que possidentur, anathema sit, cum Dominus dicat, 'Date decimam de omnibus que POSSIDETIS DEO.'

Post c. <15> solummodo in Pb
Presbiteros et diaconos et subdiaconos concubinarum cathenis insertos a sacris ordinibus penitus abstinere censimus.

TRANSLATION

This English translation can give readers without knowledge of Latin access to the canons of Piacenza. An effort has been made to provide a smooth rendering of these texts, with apologies for inconsistencies and rough spots that remain. The two canons at the end of the textus receptus are included, although they may not derive from Piacenza.

In the year of the Lord's Incarnation 1095, in the third indiction, on March 1, a synod was celebrated at Piacenza, the lord Pope Urban presiding, with bishops and abbots of Gaul, Lombardy, and Tuscany. A thorough inquiry was made about those who bought churches and prebends, and about those who were ordained in the Wibertine schism. And on the first and the third days the council met outside in an open field, for such a crowd of people convened that no church could hold them, following the example of Moses' action in Deuteronomy, and our Lord Jesus Christ teaching in the plain. Finally, on the seventh day, after lengthy deliberation, these provisions were set forth and approved with the assent of the whole council.

<1> Those things that were stated by the holy fathers about simony we also, by the judgment of the Holy Spirit and by apostolic authority, affirm.

<2> Whatever, therefore, either in sacred orders or in ecclesiastical matters has been gotten with money either given or promised we decree to be illegal and never to have any power.

<3> We mercifully allow, however, the ordinations of those who were ordained by simoniacs but not simoniacally, if they can indeed prove that when ordained they were unaware that these [others] were simoniacs, and if a laudable life recommends them.

<4> But whoever knowingly allows themselves to be consecrated – rather, that is, execrated – by simoniacs, we decree that their consecration is totally illegal.

<5> Those who indeed by the cupidity of parents have gained churches or ecclesiastical benefices through money when they were still little boys but afterward fully relinquished them, if they wish to live there canonically we concede it, through mercy, nor do we remove them because of this from sacred orders, if otherwise they are found worthy.

<6> But those who on their own, when they now are of age, led by detestable greed bought these things, if they wish to live canonically in other churches, preserving their own orders, through great mercy we permit them to minister there. Yet if perchance they are unable to be transferred to other churches and promise to live canonically in the same churches, content with minor orders they should not advance to sacred orders, saving, nonetheless, in everything the authority of the apostolic see.

<7> Those, however, who were ordained canonically before making a purchase, when they relinquish what they bought and live a canonical life they are permitted to remain in their ranks, unless perchance the church is such that they could obtain in the first place. For we do not permit them to have in the purchased churches either the first or an unshared [or 'leading'] place, either that of a provostship or of another office.

<8> We judge to be illegal the ordinations that were made by the heresiarch Guibert after he was damned by Pope Gregory of apostolic memory and by the Roman Church, and also those perpetrated by the pseudobishops afterward ordained through him.

<9> Similarly for those [ordinations] that were made by the other heresiarchs who have been named specically as excommunicated, and by those who invaded the sees of catholic bishops who are still alive, unless they can prove that when they were ordained they were ignorant of the fact that those men were damned.

<10> We order in fact that those who were consecrated by bishops formerly ordained catholic but separated from the Roman church by this schism, when they return to the unity of the church they should be received mercifully, retaining their own orders.

<11> From now on whoever permits himself to be ordained by the afore-said schismatics, the adversaries of the Roman Church, should in no way be worthy of this pardon.

<12> Although because of mercy and compelled by great necessity we established this dispensation in sacred orders, we do not wish thus to establish a precedent for the sacred canons. But let them maintain their proper rigor, and with necessity ceasing, what was done on account of necessity should cease. For when many are imperiled something should be subtracted from severity so that charity might increase.

<13> We also order this, that nothing ever should be exacted for chrism, baptism, and burial.

<14> We also establish that the Ember Days should be celebrated in this order. The first fast should be made at the beginning of Lent, the second in the week of Pentecost, but the third and fourth should be made in September and December in the accustomed manner.

<15> Thinking in harmony with the statutes of the holy canons, we decree that an ordination made without a 'title' should be illegal, and in whichever church anyone at all is 'entitled' he should persevere in it perpetually. It is totally forbidden for anyone 'to be entitled' in two churches, but everyone should be a canon only in that one in which he is 'entitled'. For although by the decision of a bishop one person is able to reside in diverse churches, he ought not to be, nevertheless, a

canon or a prebendary except of the one church only in which he is registered. If, however, chapels exist that are unable to sustain clerics by their own revenues, their care and disposition should devolve on the *prepositus* of the major church to which the chapels are regarded to be subordinate, and he should look out for both the possessions and the ecclesiastical offices of the chapels.

Notice
Also in the same council a tenth preface was added to the nine ancient prefaces, which goes like this. It is proper and salutary that we always and everywhere give thanks to you, holy Lord, Father almighty, eternal God, and to praise, bless, and proclaim you in the veneration of Blessed Mary, ever virgin, who both conceived your only begotten Son through the overshadowing of the Holy Spirit, and, with the glory of virginity enduring, poured forth the Eternal Light to the world, Jesus Christ our Lord.

Post c. <14> only in MS Pj
If anyone retains a tithe, or does not give [a tithe] to a priest from everything possessed, let him be anathema, since the Lord says, 'Give a tithe to God from all that you possess'. (Cf. Luke 18:12)

Post c. <15> only in MS Pb
We decree that priests, deacons, and subdeacons bound up in the chains of concubines should totally abstain from [the exercise of] sacred orders.

5

Commentary on the Canons

INTRODUCTION

From the eleventh/twelfth-century textus receptus, including the diatribe of 1098 by the schismatic cardinals, to the early-modern printings, Weiland's edition, and into the twentieth and even the twenty-first centuries, the canons of Piacenza have been repeatedly presented, paraphrased, and analyzed.[1] The oft-noted textual uniformity among copies is both striking and deceptive. Leaving aside Bernold of Constance's idiosyncratic account, all renditions of the decrees per se share much the same format and include large sections of essentially identical text. But there are differences of other sorts: the presence or absence of the introductory synodal preamble; a varying number of canons in different manuscripts; and textual variants throughout.[2] The absence of an official chancery version of Piacenza's acta removes an obvious control over these vagaries. Although an argument was offered in the previous chapter for the priority of Φ, little is certain about the source and pedigree of the decrees found in Φ, the *Gesta*, and elsewhere.

Attempting, therefore, to write a commentary on Piacenza's legislation akin to what was provided for the Council of Melfi is complicated.[3] In the first place, the many manuscripts of a textus receptus make it easy to overlook discrepancies among different forms of the standard text. Additionally, use of the textus receptus by prominent authors such as the Annalista Saxo, Gerhoch of Reichersberg, and Gratian inadvertently lends a kind of authority to their particular version, notwithstanding uncertainty about its pedigrees. A commentator thus must make choices among competing renditions of an account that is often remarkably uniform, remaining alert to differences, sometimes small ones, that will reveal distinct versions of the account. In 1893, concluding the introduction to his new edition of the canons of Piacenza, Weiland wrote that he was confident he had included enough textual detail that 'the differences among the codices and recentions of the

---

[1] For the cardinals' *Gesta Romanae aecclesiae contra Hildebrandum* see Chapter 2, *Enactment, Gesta*; for Piacenza in the canonical tradition see Survival Canon law, and at the end of the Conclusion; for the synod's early-modern historiography see Chapter 3; for selected modern analyses see, inter al., Hefele–Leclercq, *Histoire* 391–95; Fliche, *Réforme* 262–68; Becker, *Papst Urban* 1. 157–59; Ziese, *Wibert* 225–26, Picasso, 'Tradizione canonistica', and Gresser, *Konzilien* 298–300.

[2] Bernold's invaluable but idiosyncratic witnesses for Piacenza was discussed in Chapter 2, *Enactment*, Bernold.

[3] For the commentary on Melfi, see Somerville–Kuttner, *Pope Urban* 264–98.

"breviarium" will be sufficiently evident in our apparatus criticus'.[4] A similar plea can be offered here. Chapter 2–4 have delineated the manuscripts and mapped out the versions of the textus receptus. The present chapter now aims to provide a framework for discussing the content of the decrees.

What do these canons stipulate? It depends which version is being considered, and the question can be answered in various ways depending on where an investigator is looking – at a version with or without the prologue, a version that includes the prologue and twelve, or fourteen, or fifteen items, or a version with or without the concluding liturgical notice about the tenth preface for the mass. Writing in 1965 about issues that were central at Piacenza, John Gilchrist remarked on the large secondary literature on simony and the sacrament of orders.[5] The ensuing forty-plus years have added substantially to that list, but the analysis to follow will not be focused on detailed bibliography. It strives instead to describe the content of the decrees from Piacenza and to situate them within the context of Urban II's pontificate and especially the framework of his councils. The 15+ version of the legislation, from Φ, will serve as the basis for that discussion. The reasons for this choice have been delineated in the previous chapter when discussing Φ and need not be repeated here (see Chapter 4, *Polycarpus* Supplement).

COMMENTARY

Preamble
Piacenza opens with a formal synodal prologue of the type found at the beginning of Pope Urban's councils of Melfi, Benevento, Troia, and Clermont–*Anno Dominice incarnationis mxcv*...[6] The introduction for Piacenza is longer than that for these other councils, and, in fact, no other council during the period between 1049 and 1123 starts with anything as detailed. It is unknown what accounts for the shorter preface found at the beginning of the 14- series of decrees (all examples that derive from German territory [see Chapter 4, Transmission beyond Φ, Sect. c]). The preamble states that the council 'was celebrated' (*celebrata est*) at Piacenza on the kalends of March, which would indicate a formal, ceremonial opening on March 1. The canons were said to have been approved unanimously on the seventh day of the assembly, i.e., March 7, after lengthy discussion, although it is not stated

---

[4] Weiland 561: 'discrepantias codicum seu recensionum Breviarii ex apparatu nostro critico satis elucere confisi'. His 'Breviarium' is equivalent to what is termed in this study the textus receptus.
[5] See Gilchrist, "'Simoniaca'" 209, n. 1, for a good survey of the literature up to the 1960s. Melve, *Inventing*, esp. Ch. 1, provides an update.
[6] See Somerville–Kuttner, *Pope Urban* 252, and 302–4, for Melfi, Benevento, and Troia; and for an analysis of the form of these prefaces, ibid. 235ff., and 264ff.; for Clermont see Somerville, *Decreta* 121. It is unclear what can be made of the variations among these synodal openings, e.g., in attendance information, or about what occurred on specific days. The decrees that survive for the Council of Rome in 1099 do not commence with a formal protocol: see at the end of Chapter 6.

that this was in fact the last day of the gathering.[7] Many manuscripts of this preamble show signs of textual disturbance at the beginning, and one well-attested series of readings omits the synod's opening date but not March 7 as the date for approval of the legislation.[8]

The preamble states that the council was attended by bishops and abbots from France, Lombardy, and Tuscany, and because no building could contain the throng on hand the sessions had to be held out of doors.[9] The presence of churchmen representing a wide geographical range was obviously important for papal prestige, and also probably for Urban's conception of a general council.[10] Parallels then are adduced with Moses' speech in Deuteronomy in which he proclaimed the Jewish law, and Christ preaching the Sermon on the Plain (Deuteronomy 5:1 ff.; Luke 6:17 ff.) Bernold of Constance, who had access to a version of the textus receptus, expanded these precedents also to include Christ's Sermon on the Mount.[11] This is obviously very elite company for Pope Urban, and indicates the importance that the pope and his advisers attached to the set of decrees so introduced.[12]

cc. 1–12

This series of a dozen rulings condemning simony and dealing with orders conferred by both simoniacs and the schismatics (the followers of Wibert of Ravenna), was the heart of Piacenza's program.[13] At Melfi in 1089 Pope Urban promulgated a condemnation of simony in c. 1, an elaborate text that formed part of the reform papacy's long onslaught against ecclesiastical venality.[14] Detailed guidelines for handling orders generated by the schism had been anticipated for several years, as the pope's letters to Bishops Gebhard and Pibo show (see below, and in Chapter 1, Background). Piacenza's cc. 1–12 maintained and sharpened a distinction between simoniacal and schismatic orders, and were careful formulations with various nuances. In spite of Urban's improved political fortunes, these decrees did not announce a program of reform that was more sweeping and more rigorous than

---

[7] See Chapter 1, and also Chapter 2, *Enactment, Gesta*, for an attack by the author of the *Gesta* on the idea that the decrees were promulgated officially at the last session of the assembly.

[8] See the apparatus criticus to the edition at the end of Chapter 4. MSS Mic and Pm omit the last line of the preamble, *et assensu totius concilii approbata.*, but neither has other variants which would distinguish it.

[9] For attendance see Chapter 1, Attendance.

[10] See the discussion of this question ibid.

[11] Bernold, *Chronicon*, ed. Pertz 462 / ed. Robinson 518.

[12] A concerted search for other texts c.1100 that use these Biblical passages and images has not been done, but cf. Gratian, C. 26, q. 5, c. 14, near the end (citing what is noted as Augustine's *De civitate Dei*, but in reality is from Rabanus Maurus).

[13] The comments to follow are much indebted to Becker, *Papst Urban* 1. 157 ff. Gilchrist, "'Simoniaca'" 222, noted the ambiguity of the terms *ordinare/ordinatio* in the late eleventh century, which 'was open to a variety of meanings, which can only but not always be determined from the context'.

[14] Somerville–Kuttner, *Pope Urban* 252 ff. Conciliar decrees of Pope Nicholas II in particular contain formulations that anticipate both Urban II condemnations of simony and the possibility of dispensation: cf., for example, JL 4431a (ed. Weiland 550–51).

what the pontiff already had set forth during the early years of his reign.[15] In all probability there was, for example, no new canon enacted against lay investiture, but was the prohibition found in Melfi c. 8 re-enacted? This issue remains somewhat murky.[16] What was undoubtedly new at Piacenza, however, was the level of detail in many of the regulations, and the effort to enact statements putting an end to the Wibertine schism at a point when Urban II's reign was at its peak.[17]

Canons 1–7 contain a detailed rejection of all simoniacal transactions, with special emphasis on ordination. The terms are set forth in uncompromising fashion in c. 2 regarding anything gained through money either given or promised for sacred orders or other ecclesiastical things. Whatever thus is acquired is gained illegally and never can have any force.[18] Following this unambiguous condemnation, the decrees make allowances for special circumstances, such as cases where the ordinand was not a simoniac and was ignorant of the fact that the person performing the ordination was, and cases where parents bought benefices for *parvuli*. The words *irritum* and *irritam* are employed in cc. 2 and 4 to characterize ordinations by simoniacs. These terms are well known in the late eleventh century, but seem not to appear in Urban II's rulings prior to Piacenza and certainly are not found in the synodal acts of Melfi, Benevento, and Troia. Gilchrist has shown that generally in this period, in debates about orders the meaning of the adjectives *irritus -a -um* was 'unlawful'.[19] What is at issue is 'the lawfulness of a sacrament', or, conversely, its illegality, as determined by ecclesiastical authority, in this case Pope Urban.[20] It is in this sense that sacred orders and ecclesiastical appointments stained by simony are said to be powerless (*nullasque umquam vires obtinere*). But along with that emphasis on legality, these canons at times exhibit a tempered quality. In c. 5 the pope allows those whose parents purchased churches for them to remain, *pro misericordia*, in ecclesiastical orders but with benefices relinquished. Similarly in c. 6, Urban explains a series of rules, in this case *pro magna misericordia*, that allow those who purchased churches themselves to remain in orders.

With cc. 8–12 the decrees move in a different, but not unrelated, direction.[21] These canons treat the rejection of schismatic orders, specifically those of the Wibertines. This series of regulations might seem more stringent than cc. 1–7,

---

[15] Cf., e.g., Fliche, *Réforme* 267, and Robinson, *Papacy* 128.

[16] If at Piacenza Urban's earlier decrees were reissued in toto Melfi c. 8 would have been included: see Chapter 2, *Enactment, Gesta* and Bernold, for a discussion of the possibility that Piacenza repeated the canons from the pope's earlier councils. For the investiture decree that appears as c. 15 in earlier printings of the canons of Piacenza see the discussion in Chapter 3 on BAV MS Barb. lat. 860 and Bibl. Vallicelliana MS C.24.

[17] Becker, *Papst Urban* 1. 156, calls Piacenza the 'Höhepunkt' of Urban's pontificate.

[18] For the unusual formulation *nullas vires obtinere*, cf. Gratian, C. 2, q. 6, dictum post c. 41, and C. 9, q. 1, dictum ante c. 1. Those comments on Gratian's part could have been inspired by Piacenza, c. 2.

[19] Gilchrist, '"Simoniaca"' 222–25, but see 223, n. 87, for cases where the word meant 'invalid'. See Somerville, 'Gregory VII' 47–8, for a discussion of the choice of *irritas* in c. (5) (11) of Gregory VII's Lateran Synod of November, 1078 (see Caspar, *Register* 403–4; *irritas* also is used in c. 14 of the Lenten Synod of 1078).

[20] Gilchrist, '"Simoniaca"' 225.

[21] For a complicated analysis of theological implications of the canons of Piacenza, especially cc. 8–12, see Fliche, *Réforme* 266–67; cf. Robinson, *Authority* 48, and also 174, where these decrees are said to have declared that the ordinations of the Wibertines were 'invalid (*irritae*)'.

but they are based on earlier Gregorian policies and constitute a synodal reply on the question of Wibertine ordinations that had troubled prelates such as Gebhard of Constance and Pibo of Toul at the beginning of Urban's pontificate.[22] From a practical viewpoint the pope could not countenance a rival who had designs on the headship of the Church and was prepared to institute his own clergy. But even while attempting to suppress the Wibertine hierarchy, Piacenza offered possibilities for dispensation. In c. 9 schismatic ordinations were to be tolerated if the ordinand could prove that he was unaware that the person ordaining had been condemned.[23] Canon 10 used the word *misericorditer* to characterize its permission for reintegration into Urban's obedience of morally worthy clerics who had been ordained by schismatic bishops once catholic.

With cc. 11–12 the framework shifts from the past and present to the future. Canon 11 removes the possiblity of this lenience for those who henceforth permit themselves to be ordained by schismatics. Canon 12 is a sort of valedictory that sums up both the mood and the content of cc. 8–12. The talk again is of *misericordia* governing the pope's actions, mercy that is 'compelled by great necessity' *(magnaque necessitate cogente)*. The concessions that have been granted do not derogate from the authority of the canons, which remain in force.[24] Canon 12 ends with statements that combine ideas from Pope Innocent I (JK 303), and St. Augustine (Ep. 185.45).[25] When necessity ceases, what was done because of that urgency is no longer necessary, but when a profound catastrophe threatens, the balance between severity and charity ought to be tilted toward the latter. To put the point in another way, Pope Urban might agree with the maxim that *Necessitas non habet legem*.[26] Yet after the recent defeats suffered by Henry IV in northern Italy, and with Urban's efforts to consolidate his supporters at Rome and in the north, the pressures about what was once necessary could yield to a rule of canon law. The decrees of Piacenza are less about a return to rigor per se than about careful measures for handling simoniacal and schismatic orders, and especially for wrapping up the Wibertine schism by disenfranchising its hierarchy.[27]

---

[22] Indeed, as early as his Lenten Synod of 1078 Pope Gregory VII decreed (Caspar, *Register* 372, c. [14]): *Ordinationes vero illorum, qui ab excommunicatis sunt ordinati, sanctorum patrum sequentes vestigia irritas fieri censemus.*

[23] The proviso about ignorance on the part of an ordinand is often ignored by modern commentators on this canon. Cf. the Ordinary Gloss to Gratian's *Decretum* on this canon, at C. 9, q. 1, c. 5, ¶ *Nisi probare*, and ¶ *Nescisse*, for commentary on that portion of the text.

[24] Cf. JL 5740 (= IP 6.1. 334, no. 3), and see Somerville–Kuttner, *Pope Urban* 153.

[25] See Kuttner, 'Urban' 69 ff. (where the refence in n. 54 to Augustine's letter should be 'ep.185': *S. Aureli Augustini . . . Epistulae*, ed. Al. Goldbacher, 4 (Corpus scriptorum ecclesiasticorm Latinorum 57; Vienna 1911) 39–40. Kuttner, 'Urban' 70, n. 54, also noted the similarity between the Augustinian ending of Piacenza c. 12 and the famous *Prologue* attributed to Bishop Ivo of Chartres. See also the use made of this Augustinian text by Pope Paschal II at the Council of Guastalla in 1106: Blumenthal, *Early Councils* 52–53, and especially 52, n. 1.

[26] See Franck Roumy, 'L'origines et la diffusion de l'adage canonique *Necessitas non habet legem* (VIIIe–XIIIe s.)', in Wolfgang P. Müller and Mary E. Sommar (eds.), *Medieval Church Law and the Origins of the Western Legal Tradition: A Tribute to Kenneth Pennington* (Washington DC 2006) 301–19.

[27] Robinson, *Henry* 291, states specifically that Urban's intention at Piacenza was 'to dismantle the obedience of Clement III'.

Canons 11–12 function as a kind of coda to cc. 8–10. This can be seen in different ways, but most clearly in the topical progression from c. 10 through 11–12. Canons 11–12 are concerned much less with schismatic ordinations than with Urban's views about the boundaries for mercifully integrating the schismatics into his obedience. In addition to the promulgated decrees, attention can be given to statements that appear at the end of c. 10 in several manuscripts connected to the 14- group of canons (deriving from the Empire): ... *commendat, et si his nostris decretis cognitis mox ab errore ad catholicam ecclesiam transierint, et nobis nostrisque legatis se per omnia obedire promiserint.* ('if, having recognized these decrees of ours, they then return from error to the catholic Church and promise that they will obey us and our legates in all things.')[28] A boundary was reached with c. 10, it seems. The schism was being legislated out of existence and the rehabilitation of Wibertine clergy was now a canonical reality. Concessions for reasons of expediency had been mercifully possible, but the doorway to mercy on these fundamental matters was being closed - cf. the word *Amodo* ('From now on') at the beginning of c. 11.

The intellectual framework of cc. 11–12 is less taken up with canonical issues arising from schismatic ordinations than with Urban's views about integrating with mercy the schismatics into his obedience. As such cc. 11–12 specifically, and in a general sense cc. 1–12 as a whole, could be seen as the 'legislative enactment of the legal principles announced in Ivo of Chartres' *Prologue.*'[29] The origin of this important treatise is unclear, but it appears at the beginning of a group of canon law collections attributed to Bishop Ivo that probably were assembled in the 1090s.[30] As noted already (at n. 25), the Augustinian language cited at the end of c. 12 is also quoted in the *Prologue*. This does not prove that Urban II used that long treatise about canonical hermeneutics. It does demonstrate, however, the importance of concepts such as mercy and dispensation, and of the process for tailoring the Church's law to circumstances.[31] Urban's texts, especially in the early years of his pontificate, repeatedly use and develop those ideas, and *Prologue* and pontiff are sharing concepts that were in the air at the time.[32]

---

[28] The vagaries of the text can be found in the apparatus. For Piacenza cc. 11–12, see also Alfons Becker, 'Rechtsprinzipien und Verfahrensregeln im Päpstlichen Gerichtswesen zur Zeit Urbans II.', in Winfried Dotzauer et al. (eds.), *Landesgeschichte und Reichsgeschichte: Festschrift für Alois Gerlich zum 70. Geburtstag* (Geschichtliche Landeskunde 42; Stuttgart 1995) 64; for c. 12, see Laudage, 'Ritual' 303.

[29] This phrase is owed to Edward Reno III, Columbia University. For the *Prologue*, see Robert Somerville and Bruce C. Brasington, *Prefaces to Canon Law Books in Latin Christianity, Selected Translations, 500–1245* (New Haven 1998) 111ff., and 132 ff., and the editions, translations, and comments by Jean Werckmeister, *Yves de Chartres, le Prologue* (Sources canoniques 1; Paris 1997), and Bruce C. Brasington, *Ways of Mercy: The Prologue of Ivo of Chartres* (Vita regularis 2; Münster 2004).

[30] The literature on these works is vast but for a recent introduction, see Brett, 'Creeping', and the references in the previous note.

[31] Cf. Becker, *Papst Urban* 1. 158–59. Traditions of papal dispensation are, of course, not an invention of the late eleventh century: see Kuttner, 'Urban' 61 ff.

[32] See the texts in the *Collectio Britannica*: Somerville–Kuttner, *Pope Urban* 41ff., and esp. CB 30 (ibid. 104 ff; JL 5383 = IP 3. 119, no. 2, and 320, no. 6); CB 33 (ibid. 120 ff.; JL 5386, IP 6.1. 53, no. 124 [cited by Becker, *Urban* 1. 158]). Cf. also JL 5760; for this famous text see Somerville, 'Inspired Law'. Ivo of Chartres' close association with Urban II is well known, e.g., the pope consecrated him as bishop in late 1090: see the works of Brasington and Werckmeister cited in n. 29.

Yet the attack against Piacenza's legislation by the schismatic cardinals in the *Gesta* shows that not everyone was persuaded about the utility and the correctness of these developments, considered by Urban's enemies to be opportunistic tampering with the tradition.[33] The *Gesta*'s version of Piacenza in general displays a curious blend of truth and diatribe. Included, on the one hand, is the only witness for the full text of c. <8> other than JL 5394, yet, on the other hand, the *Gesta* contain some distinctive readings that support the cardinals' partisanship. This is so even though by the time these tracts were composed in 1098 Urban's account of Piacenza's decrees surely was fixed.[34] Cardinal Beno, or whoever composed the pamphlet, railed against Urban II for what was deemed Piacenza's serious disregard of traditional canonical norms and for dangerous innovations. Urban's decrees, which the schismatics subjected to a ritual burning at their council in August, 1098, were characterized as having 'damned those things that are legitimate and confirmed those that are heretical'.[35] Aside from specifics about what was considered the pope's lenient treatment of simoniacs, or his recognition of baptism performed by schismatics, the arguments of Urban's opponents seem intended, as Ziese and Stoller note, 'to embarrass the pope with the apparent contradictions of his own decrees, to reveal the supposedly pure doctrine of the Gregorians to be in fact riddled with inconsistencies'.[36] At the end of several canons of Piacenza the rendition in the *Gesta*, which cover cc. 1–12, adds the words *Error generalis* or in one case *Error specialis* (c. 7 of the textus receptus; c. vi according to Weiland's numbering).[37] The source of those two seemingly rare terms is unclear, but they encapsulate the disgruntlement on the part of cardinals who opposed Pope Urban about both Piacenza and his new exegetical techniques.[38]

As was discussed at the beginning of this chapter, the history that emerges from the 15+ version of cc. 1–12 is only one of the possible histories that can be derived from the canons. Even without anything approaching the confusion surrounding the canons of Clermont, questions can arise within different versions of Piacenza's texts. The following examples deal with a set of non-trivial issues, and are chosen to illustrate the complications of coming to grips with 'the canons of Piacenza'.

---

[33] See the discussion in Stoller, 'Councils' 319–20.

[34] See Chapt. 4, *Polycarpus* Supplement, for distinctive readings in the *Gesta*'s account. For solidification of the canonical transmission for these decrees by the time of the Council of Clermont, see, Chapt. 2, *Enactment, Gesta*, at the end.

[35] *Gesta Romanae aecclesiae*, ed. Francke, MGH Lib. de lite 2. 408: *Incipiunt decreta Turbani, in quibus ea quae sunt legitima dampnavit et quae sunt heretica confirmavit*. For the schismatic synod, see inter al. Stoller, 'Councils' 315–21, and Gresser, *Synoden* 317–21.

[36] Stoller, 'Councils' 320, who notes 'the capricious manner' in which the Wibertine cardinals thought that Urban conducted his office; cf. Ziese, *Wibert* 246–48.

[37] *Gesta Romanae aecclesiae*, ed. Francke, MGH Lib. de lite 2. 208–9; cf. Becker, *Papst Urban* 1. 159, and Gresser, *Synoden* 302, n. 227.

[38] The author has yet to find another contemporary occurrence of these terms; they do not turn up in the PL database, in Friedberg's edition of Gratian, nor do they seem to have a basis in Roman law, at least not according to Adolf Berger, *Encyclopedic Dictionary of Roman Law* (Transactions of the American Philosophical Society, NS 43.2; Philadelphia 1953).

1. Canon 1, *Ea, que a sanctis patribus de simoniacis statuta sunt, nos quoque sancti Spiritus iudicio et apostolica auctoritate firmamus*. ('Those things that were stated by the holy fathers about simony we also, by the judgment of the Holy Spirit and by apostolic authority, affirm.') A papal conciliar text determining something *sancti Spiritus iudicio* seems unusual in the late eleventh century, but the wording is found, other than at Piacenza, in Gregory VII's Lenten synod of 1076, and at Urban II's Council of Benevento, c. <2>.[39] Not all of those texts are concerned with eradicating simony, an abuse particularly against the Spirit. A small amount of textual disturbance occurs at this point in Piacenza c. 1, removing the words *sancti Spiritus* and thus altering the meaning. Most noteworthy in this regard is the tradition deriving from the *Collection in Three Books* which then came into Gratian 2, a reading attested in early-modern editions of the *Decretum* (the passage from C. 1, q. 3, c. 5, does not occur in Gratian 1).[40] In the *Editio Romana* of the *Decretum Gratiani*, however, published at Rome in 1582, the Spirit has been restored to the canon as the basis, along with papal authority, for the conciliar judgment.[41] Is the removal of *sancti Spiriti* at this point a theological statement on the part of the compiler of 3L, and did Gratian simply follow his source (3L), or did he consciously agree?[42] Or, on the other hand, is the absence of those words in 3L and in Gratian 2 merely the result of a scribal slip? There is no way to know.

2. Canon 5, *Quicumque sane cupiditate parentum cum adhuc parvuli essent ecclesias vel ecclesiarum beneficia per pecunias adepti sunt....* ('Those who indeed by the cupidity of parents have gained churches or ecclesiastical benefices through money when they were still little boys....') This passage was discussed in Chapter 4, at several points. A widespread variant tradition replaces Φ's *beneficia* with *partes*. The basic sense of the decree at this point is seemingly clear, but the nuances of these two words are not necessarily so. Gratian's version, at C. 1, q. 5, c. 1, reads *partes*, and the word was accorded a comment in the Ordinary Gloss to Gratian, perhaps indicating that at the end of the twelfth and the beginning of the thirteenth century, when that gloss was being solidified, clarification about the word was needed: *Partes.] id est praebendas....* That is to say, *ecclesiarum partes* means ecclesiastical livings, e.g., 'benefices', or *partes* ('shares' of a church's revenues).

3. Canons 6–7 continued the treatment of simonical appointments. Canon 7 specified that if clerics ordained *catholice* gained positions through simony but later

---

[39] Caspar, *Register* 268 (Reg. 3.10a), for 1076, and Somerville–Kuttner, *Pope Urban* 303, for Benevento. Cf. JL 4887, JL 4962, JL 5091, and JL 5107. This result is surely incomplete. For a useful general reference about simony, see John Gilchrist, *New Catholic Encyclopedia*, 2nd edn., (2003) 13. 135–36.

[40] The author is grateful to librarians at Columbia University – in the Rare Book and Manuscript Library, in the Burke Library, and in the Diamond Law Library – for facilitating access to Columbia's rich collections of early-modern printed books. The following printings of Gratian's *Decretum* prior to the publication of the *Editio Romana* have been examined: Mainz 1472 (Goff G365); Basel 1481 (Goff G370); Basel 1493 (Goff G384); Paris 1506; and Lyons 1541. For the content of Gratian 1, see Winroth, *Making*, Appendix 197–227. For 3L see Chapt. 4, Canon Law Collections, Sect. b.

[41] The author has consulted Friedberg's edition and the first and several subsequent printings of the *Editio Romana*: Rome 1582; Venice 1584; Venice 1595; Venice 1604; Lyons 1606.

[42] Cf. the reading of MS Va, where reference to the Holy Spirit also is lacking but where the context is handled differently from 3L; see the apparatus criticus for the edition in Chap. 4.

relinquished them, if living a *vita canonica* they can retain their ranks, although unable to advance to the prime positions in a church. The wording seems to a modern investigator opaque, although the text by and large is well attested: *Primum enim vel singularem vel prepositure vel officii locum in emptis ecclesiis eos habere non patimur.* ('For we do not permit them to have in the purchased churches either the first or an unshared [or 'leading'] place, either that of a provostship or of another of fice.') The general sense of these troublesome lines, however, is clear, and they point to an effort to retain repentant simoniacs in their churches, but in subordinant positions. In several canonical collections, including 3L and Gratian (C. 1, q. 5, c. 1), the words *vel officii* were dropped, nor were they restored in the *Editio Romana* of the *Decretum Gratiani*. They fell out of c. 7 early in the twelfth century, but why, whether by design or by accident, is unknown. Did an early twelfth-century writer conclude that *vel officii* was redundant and/or unclear? Or did those words fall out of the text by a copyist's error? There is no way to know. What is clear, of course, is that the absence of *vel officii* in Gratian defined how the canon was read from the mid-twelfth century onward. Whatever Pope Urban II meant in the last lines of c. 7, the form in which the text was most widely available from the mid-twelfth century onward presented a truncated and, from Urban's perspective no doubt, an incomplete rendition.

4. The most interesting of these example involves cc. 8–9, that is, decrees that deal with Wibertine orders. Piacenza's treatment of simoniacs and schismatics differed, and the volatility surrounding particularly the latter is well known.[43] Problems involved with cc. 8–9 have been noted earlier. In Chapter 2, *Survival*, for example, JL 5694 presents a nearly lost segment in the second part of c. 8: the condemnation of ordinations by bishops created by Wibert after his excommunication by Gregory VII. The critical apparatus for cc. 8–9, especially in the canonical tradition, tells a striking and even somewhat enigmatic story that has important implications for the transmission of Piacenza's legislation. Canon 8 began with the words *Ordinationes, que a Guiberto*, condemned Wibertine ordinations, and, notwithstanding the complications surrounding the text's survival, also condemned ordinations performed by those labelled 'pseudobishops'—the bishops consecrated by Wibert after his excommunication. All of the ordinations thus covered in c. 8 are 'illegal' (*irritas*). Canon 9 opens with the words *Similiter autem et eas, que a ceters*, and delineated additional condemnations and qualification. But six important witnesses in the canon law tradition–Vp, Fv, Poly., 7L, 3L, and Grat.2 (see Chapter 4, Canon Law Collections, Sect. b, for the specifics) jump from c. 8, *que a [Guiberto heresiarca]* in line 1, to c. 9, line 1, *a [ceteris] heresiarchis*, thereby eliminating the bulk of c. 8. The substance dropped from c. 8 included naming Wibert as a heresiarch, the anathema against him by Gregory VII and the Roman Church, and the second portion of c. 8 that survives only very precariously.

---

[43] A glance through the volumes of the *Libelli de lite* readily shows this; see, for example, Melve, *Inventing* 88.

One of two conclusions can be drawn. On the one hand, perhaps serious reservations arose in some quarters about the manner in which Pope Urban was striving to liquidate the schism, and someone thus deleted the missing lines in an effort to soften the strictures against the Wibertine ordinations. This construct suggests but cannot prove that apprehension about the substance of a large part of line 3–4 of c. 8 prompted their suppression. On the other hand, rather than substantive canonical reasons, it is possible to propose *homoioteleuton* as the cause of the jump in Vp, Fv, Poly., 7L, 3L, and Grat. 2, from early in c. 8 to c. 9. Either explanation is possibly true and there is no way to know which is correct.[44]

Two further comments can be offered. MS T, the Turin *Collection in Seven Books*, which perhaps is an Italian compilation, does not have the noted lacuna in cc. 8–9, nor does MS L, which comes from northern France or the Low Countries (see, for both books, Chapter 2, *Survival*, Canon Law Collections, Sect. a, and Chapter 4, Canon Law Collections, Sect. a). The fact that these two manuscripts contain the full 'textus receptus' version of cc. 8–9 shows that cuts in those decrees were not universal among canonical collections that transmit Piacenza. But MSS Vp and Fv include the gap in cc. 8–9 (see Chapter 2, *Survival*, Canon Law Collections, Sect. b, and Chapter 4, Canon Law Collections, Sect. b). These books contain the *Panormia* with nearly identical blocks of decrees of Piacenza (cc. 5–9) inserted as additions into bk. 3. A relationship between MSS Vp and Fv and the works listed in the previous paragraph is thus implicit, although the details of that relationship is a matter for further investigation.

cc. 13–15

Canons 1–12, with their treatment of simoniacs and schismatics, are at the heart of Piacenza's legislation, but cc. 13–14 also are well attested and thus an important part of the council's fortuna.[45] Canon 15 appears less frequently, but gains special prominence because of its inclusion in Gratian 2.[46] Neither c. 14 nor c. 15 is listed among the decrees of Piacenza that were re-promulgated at Urban II's last council, at St. Peter's in April 1099 (see the following chapter).

c. 13 Canon 13 is the shortest of Piacenza's decrees. Its subject breaks the topical sequence of the previous set of five rulings which were concerned with schismatics. Disregarding the situation of c. 8, the last line of c. 12 and the full text of c. 13 are the only portions of the textus receptus not found in the *Decretum Gratiani* (although c. 13 is found in the *Collection in Three Books*, i.e., Gratian 2's source for cc. 1–7, 9–12, and probably c. 14). This absence of c. 13 perhaps is

---

[44] MS B, which has been classed with the 15+ texts, presents a somewhat idiosyncratic version of the canons, including textual disturbance in cc. 8–9: see Chapter 4, n. 14, for a significant omission in c. 8, probably due to *homoioteleuton*. No correlation presents itself between MS B and the gap within cc. 8–9 in the canonical tradition.

[45] Becker, *Papst Urban* 1. 157–58, in his main discussion of Piacenza, does not deal with provisions after c. 12.

[46] Gossman, *Urban* 121, did not find c. 15 in any of the collections that he analyzed, but it occurs apart from the textus receptus occasionally in canonical books that he did not treat: see Chapter 2, n. 150. Cf. the description of the 15+ manuscripts listed ibid., *Survival*, List of Canons, Sect.iii.a, some of which include canon law texts; cf. also Chapter 4, *Transmission*, Sects. a-b.

explained by the fact that prohibitions against payment for ecclesiastical services is well covered by Gratian elsewhere.

The question of paying for ecclesiastical services relates c. 13 to the elaborate discussion of simony in cc. 1–7. Free access to baptism, anointing, and Christian burial is a venerable tenet of canon law. A decree attributed to the Council of Tribur in 895 that appeared in several legal works, such as Burchard of Worms' *Decretum*, the *Decretum Ivonis*, and Gratian 2, labeled such exactions simoniacal and prohibited clerics from seeking anything for ordination, chrism, baptism, balsam, burial, and communion.[47] At the Council of Mantua in 1064 Pope Alexander II forbade Bishop Rainald of Como to exact an annual payment (*annualem pecuniam*) for chrism.[48] The Register of Gregory VII does not include a similar prohibition, although the Gregorian initiatives against simony are well known (cf. the sweeping condemnation from the autumn Lateran Council of 1078).[49] In addition to c. 13 of Piacenza, the selling of ministrations was condemned at the Council of Clermont six months later.[50] Repetition at Clermont of the decrees from Piacenza would thus account for versions of this ruling among Clermont's legislative traditions.[51]

c. 14   The reform papacy's concern about *puritas ecclesiae* is a cornerstone of its reforming program, and decrees such as Piacenza cc. 1–7 against simony are prime exhibits for that concern. The reformers' liturgical regulations have been accorded less attention. Canon 14 defines the four major fasts of the year, that is the Ember Days. They were discussed recently by Uta Blumethal and Detlev Jasper in a study of Pope Gregory VII's text *Licet nova consuetudo* (JL 5290), promulgated at his Lenten Synod of 1078.[52] Gregory's decree was in reaction to what was termed a 'new custom supported by no authority of the Church' (*nova consuetudo ecclesie nulla fulta auctoritate*), embodied particularly in c. 2 of the Synod of Seligenstadt in 1023.[53] The Gregorian provision cited an array of *auctoritates*, both Biblical and papal, in defining the four Ember Days. The 'spring' (*vernum*) and 'summer' (*estivum*) fasts were to be observed at the beginning of Lent and in the week of Pentecost, respectively. The 'autumnal' (*autumnale*) and the 'winter' (*hiemale*) fasts

---

[47] The text is found in Gratian 2 at C. 1, q. 1, c. 105 (= Burchard of Worms, *Decretum* 4. 101 [PL 140. 749–50]; Ivo of Chartres, *Decretum* 1. 295 [PL 161. 130]). For the 'Versio Catalaunensis' (Châlons-sur-Marne MS 32), of the acts of Tribur, where this text appears as c. 26, see Hartmut Hoffmann and Rudolf Pokorny, *Das Dekret des Bischofs Burchard von Worms* (MGH Hilfsmittel 12; Munich 1991) 69ff., and 267, with reference back to Emil Seckel, 'Zu den Acten der Triburer Synode 895', *Neues Archiv* 18 (1893) 395–401.

[48] JL 4558 (= IP 6.1. 400, no. 7); see Franz-Josef Schmale, 'Synoden Papst Alexanders II. (1061–1073): Anzahl, Termine, Entscheidungen', AHC 11 (1979) 319–21. Cf. JL 4657 (= IP 3. 233, no. 9), and see Schmale, op. cit. 328–29.

[49] Caspar, *Register* 403–4 (Reg. VI. 5b, c.[5] [11]).

[50] Somerville, *Decreta*, 144, no. 9, with nn. 7–9.

[51] This repetition often has been noted; cf. Somerville, *Decreta* 123, and also id., 'Crusade and Canons' 71–2.

[52] Blumenthal and Jasper 45–68, with bibliography, and see also Blumenthal, 'De praua constitutione' 148–49.

[53] Weiland 636.

occurred in the seventh and in the tenth months, September and December, but no additional specification was provided.[54]

JL 5290 circulated widely, although it was not included in Gratian, and two legatine synods that convened between 1078 and 1095 took over this usage.[55] Cardinal Odo of Ostia, before his election as Urban II in 1088, presided over a synod at Quedlinburg in April, 1085, that has been well studied, and this assembly issued a decree reiterating the recent papal ruling on the Ember Days of Lent and Pentecost. Nine years later another legatine council, this time organized by Bishop Gebhard of Constance in April, 1094, repeated the same provision.[56] The surviving texts from Pope Urban's early synods seem not to deal with Ember Days, but Piacenza c. 14 decreed that the fasts should be observed at the beginning of Lent, at Pentecost, and also in September and December 'in the accustomed manner' (*more solito*), presumably meaning that the autumnal and winter fasts were deeply rooted in tradition and thus need not be specified more exactly. This canon was diffused extensively through the textus receptus and also found a place in Gratian 2, at D. 76, c. 4.[57] Versions of legislation on Ember Days also show up at Clermont.[58]

Repeated legislation defining Ember Days might seem curious to modern minds inclined to ask what 'really is at stake' in defining these ceremonial regulations. A more detailed commentary might offer different perspectives for answering that question, but one point can be noted here. The popes of the late eleventh century and their supporters sought to base their actions on papal traditions, and the older the better. The fact that Popes Leo I, Gelasius I, and Gregory I were cited along with the Bible as sanctioning Ember Days at the beginning of Lent and at Pentecost constituted a powerful incentive in the minds of the reformers to shun developments that arose subsequent to Antiquity.

Attention also can be drawn to a small treatise on the Ember Days that is seemingly unedited, and ascribed to Pope Urban II. The work was mentioned in Chapter 2, *Survival*, Lists of Canons, Sect. b, and occurs in Oxford, Bodleian Library, MS Selden supra 90, fols. 27v-29v, a twelfth-century composite manuscript that also contains the textus receptus of Piacenza (= MS O). The pages at issue are of unknown provenance, but possibly English. The inscription – 'Decree

---

[54] The liturgical traditions involved are noted in Blumenthal and Jasper, passim.

[55] For circulation of JL 5290, see the tabulation ibid. 60–1, where sixteen full copies of the decree and three excerpts are listed; see ibid. 56, for Gratian.

[56] See the texts from Quedlinburg in Weiland 651, c. 10, and Bernold, *Chronicon*, ed. Pertz 442–43 / ed. Robinson 451; for the assembly at Constance see ibid. 458/511. See also Blumenthal and Jasper 57–58, n. 48 and n. 51; and cf. Gresser, *Synoden* 238–45, and 287–90, for these synods.

[57] The canon is short, and collations cannot prove that *Coll. in Three Books* is Gratian's source, as was the case for cc. 1–7 and 8–12, but not for c. 15 below. See also Laudage, 'Ritual' 325.

[58] Somerville, *Decreta* 146, nos. 28–29; cf. a Clermont text (ibid. 72, c. 1), found in the *Coll. in Nine Books* (compiled probably in the diocese of Thérouanne early in the twelfth century), that lists specifics for all four fasts. See in general for the Ember Days, Bernold of Constance's *Micrologus*, PL 151. 995–1000, which dates from the last decade of the eleventh century, and thus is contemporary with Piacenza and Clermont. For the *Micrologus*, see Daniel S. Taylor, 'Der Micrologus Bernolds von Konstanz und der Codex Stuttgart, Württembergische Landesbibliothek, HB VI. 114', DA 52 (1996) 171–79, and id., 'Inventory'; cf., the editors' comments in Bernold, *De excommunicatis*, ed. Stöckly and Jasper, 6. See Chapter 4 in the critical apparatus for c. 14, for the text ascribed to Pope Paschal II.

of the lord Pope Urban II concerning the fast of the Ember Days' (literally, 'of the four times/seasons') (*Decretum domni pape Urbani secundi de ieiunio quattuor temporum*) – introduces a ruling that employs early papal and Biblical proof texts in an even more elaborate definition and gloss on the fast days than that found in JL 5270. The provision remains to be analyzed. In MS O it follows directly on an unusual form of the canons of Clermont, and this placement can suggest, very cautiously, that what is at hand is another 'membrum disiectum' stemming from the Council of Clermont, or perhaps from one of Urban II's synods after Clermont between 1096–1099.

c. 15   Canon 15 marks a significant formal shift within the textus receptus. The set of texts designated by Weiland et al. as c. 15 appears in Φ, Gratian 2, and a handful of manuscripts (the 15+ group).[59] It commences with a statement reminiscent of the beginning of the legislation from Melfi in 1089: (Piacenza) *Sanctorum canonum statutis consona sentientes, decernimus ut*...; (Melfi) *Sanctorum patrum sententiis consona sentientes, ex Dei et apostolorum eius parte precipimus ne*...[60] Rules follow on appointments to a church benefice, that is, to a *titulus*. No one should be ordained without a 'title', otherwise the ordination is *irrita*; a cleric should remain permanently in any church where he receives a 'title'; no one can be 'entitled' in two churches; a person can be a canon only in a church where he is 'entitled'; even if by episcopal dispensationn one man presides over different churches, he can hold a benefice only in the one in which he was appointed (*conscriptus*, literally 'enrolled'). Poor chapels (*capelle*) that cannot support clergy should be cared for by the ecclesiastical superior of a major church, who should supervise both the possessions and the ecclesiastical duties.[61]

Regulations of this sort are deeply rooted in the canonical tradition. The Council of Melfi, for example, promulgated decrees against absentee clerics and those who attempt to obtain multiple benefices. The word *titulus* to designate a benefice seems not to appear in the correspondence or synods of Pope Gregory VII, nor in Pope Urban's early councils, but is used at Clermont in the same way as in c. 15 (cf. the *Decretum Gratiani*, e.g., C. 21, q. 1).[62] Canon 15 is not included in the *Collection in Three Books*, and where Gratian found it remains unclear, although, as noted in Chapter 4, Canon Law Collections, Sect. b, Φ or something like Φ may well provide the answer. This probably is the case both for c. 15 and for the subsequent liturgical notice, two items that are copied in sequence in the *Decretum*, at D. 70, c. 2, and in the following *dictum* (abbreviated in Gratian; see the apparatus criticus to the edition).

---

[59] See n. 46 above. Weiland 563, at 'm)' at the beginning of his text of c. 15, mistakenly wrote 13 and 14 instead of 14 and 15 to indicate the manuscripts where the decree appears.

[60] Somerville–Kuttner, *Pope Urban* 232.

[61] The Latin term for what is termed here 'ecclesiastical superior' is *prepositus*, which at the time of Piacenza could mean a provost, prior, or simply a superior. In the canonical *Glossa ordinaria* on c. 15 (Gratian, D. 70, c. 2), the word is glossed *id est, episcop[us]*.

[62] See Somerville, *Decreta* 145, nos. 13 ff., and this usage makes sense at Clermont given the repetition there of Piacenza's decrees. In general, see Vinzenza Fuchs, *Der Ordinationstitel von seiner Entstehung bis auf Innozenz III* (Kanonistische Studien und Texte 4; Bonn 1930) 246 ff. for Urban II. A thorough search for occurrences of the word *titulus* between Urban II and Gratian has not been done.

Tenth Preface It is well established that at Piacenza Urban II added to the mass a tenth preface in honor of the Virgin Mary.[63] The notice from Piacenza describing this innovation is known in three ways: through Φ (see Chapter 2, *Survival, Polycarpus* Supplement); abbreviated in Gratian 2 (D. 70, dictum post c. 2);[64] copied apart from Φ in a few manuscripts (see Chapter 2, n. 150). Urban's action on this issue also was ascribed to his synods at Clermont and Nîmes, which makes sense given the often-noted repromulgation of conciliar acts of the time from assembly to assembly. It was, nevertheless, the *Decretum Gratiani*, and in the thirteenth century the *Rationale divinorum officiorum* of William Durandus, that accounted for the widespread diffusion of the tenth preface.[65] Enrico Mazza has explicated the background and the content of this prayer. Its roots stretch back to the early Middle Ages, and Pope Urban did not compose but rather authorized it.[66] The pontiff's reasons for so doing, at Piacenza, have been impossible to discover. Devotion to Mary was an important part of Cluniac piety, but if Cluny provided the impetus for this decision why was Piacenza chosen to formalize it, years after Odo/Urban had departed from the abbey to serve in Pope Gregory VII's chancery? Local liturgical usages in northern Italy might be a better place to seek light on the question, especially if studied in connection with other decisions of Urban on Marian devotion.[67]

---

[63] See Gerardo Posada, *Der Heilige Bruno* (Cologne 1987) 142: 'Man betrachet ihn [Bruno] als Verfasser oder zumindest als Befürworter der Präfation der allerseligsten Jungfrau, die 1095 durch das Konzil von Piacenza gebilligt wurde. Ein Beweis dafür kann nicht erbracht werden.' Posada continued, speculating that Bruno was at Piacenza and that the Preface related to the First Crusade. Cf. Giuseppe Fornasari, 'Urbano II e la riforma della chiesa nel secolo xi, ovvero la riforma nella *dispensatio*', *Cristianità ed Europa: Miscellanea di studi in onore di Luigi Prosdocimi* 1.1 (Rome 1994) 108.

[64] This text is presented in the *Decretum* as a 'dictum' (thus printed in italics).

[65] See Somerville, 'French Councils' 63–4, and also id., *Decreta* 130; information given there about the tenth preface can now be expanded. For Durandus see *Rationale* 4.33.36 (Antwerp 1570) 151r.

[66] Enrico Mazza, 'Il prefazio della Vergine Maria istituito da Urbano II', *Concilio di Piacenza* 71–87 (cf. id., *Marianum* 57 [1995] 269–89). Cf. Bernard Capelle, 'Les origines de la préface romaine de la Vierge', *Revue d'histoire ecclésiastique* 38 (1942) 46–58 (repr. *Travaux Liturgiques* 3 [Louvain 1967]), and Joseph A. Jungmann, S.J., *The Mass of the Roman Rite: its Origins and Development (Missarum sollemnia)*, trans. Francis A. Brunner, C.SS.R (New York 1955; org. 1949) 2. 120 (see n. 32).

[67] Cf. (+)Henri Barré, 'Un "Statut" d'Urbain II', *Marianum* 32 (1970) 1–14, Somerville, *Decreta* 127–30, and Candidus Mesini, O.F.M., 'De auctore et loco compositionis praefationis B.M.V', *Antonianum* 10 (1935) 59–72, esp. 70–72. See also John Boe, *Beneventanum Troporum Corpus* 2. 3 (Recent Researches in the Music of the Middle Ages and Early Renaissance 25; Madison 1996) 21, n. 39, who notes that Urban's 'decree' from Piacenza on the tenth preface was 'generally observed' (a reference that I owe to Anne Clark).

6

Legislation from the Councils of Urban II between Piacenza and Rome (April 1099)

INTRODUCTION

The six councils of Urban II that were held after Piacenza will be discussed in this last chapter, with attention particularly devoted to the conciliar legislation. Between Piacenza and spring 1099 Pope Urban celebrated synods at Clermont (November 1095), Tours (March 1096), Nîmes (July 1096), the Lateran (in 1097, probably no later than Easter), Bari (October 1098), and St. Peter's in Rome (April 1099).[1] He thus continued the tradition of frequent papal councils established by the reforming popes from Leo IX's day onward, and which was to be maintained in the following decades by Popes Paschal II and Calixtus II.

1095 was the only year during which Urban II presided over multiple synods, these being the two large gatherings that met six months apart at Piacenza and at Clermont. Clermont has been studied in detail, and the chaotic array of legislation claiming to derive thence is well known. Many different records purport to be 'canons of Clermont', engendering a level of confusion that is unparalleled in papal councils of the period.[2] The contrast in that regard between Clermont and Melfi or Piacenza is striking. No fully satisfactory explanation is at hand for the matchless diversity of provisions claiming to originate at Clermont, although a solution may be embedded in the fact that Clermont reissued the decrees of Urban's earlier synods.[3] Clermont, of course, is generally remembered as 'the Crusade council',

---

[1] See Becker, *Papst Urban* passim (both volumes), and Gresser, *Synoden* passim. Useful information about Clermont and Tours is found in Jean-Hervé Foulon, 'Les relations entre la papauté réformatrice et les pays de la Loire jusqu'à la fondation de Fontevraud', in Jacques Dalarun (ed.), *Robert d'Arbrissel et la vie religieuse dans l'ouest de la France* (Disciplina monastica 1; Turnhout 2004) 47–53; JL 5654, written July 15, 1096, immediately after the Council of Nîmes, identifies the synod as the *tertia synodus* that Pope Urban held north of the Alps: see Somerville, 'French Councils' 60. For Odette Pontal, *Les conciles de la France capétienne jusqu'en 1215* (Paris 1995), see *Cahiers de civilisation médiévale* 43 (2000) 224–25.

[2] See in previous chapters (e.g., Chapter 2, *Enactment* Introduction, and Chapter 4, Transmission beyond Φ), and in this chapter, Tours; cf. Somerville, *Decreta*, passim, and various studies in id. *Papacy, Councils and Canon Law*. Material continues to emerge about 'the canons of Clermont', e.g., see id. 'Crusade and Canons' 75, and the odd combination of texts from two versions of the canons of Clermont found in Accademia Nazionale dei Lincei, MS 41.E.1 (formerly Bibl. Corsiniana, MS 1808), which was kindly called to the author's attention by Martin Brett.

[3] See Somerville, *Decreta* 123 (no. 6), and especially id. 'Crusade and Canons' 71–2.

although it is well established that the campaign to the East cannot be regarded as the assembly's prime business. That Urban was the instigator of the First Crusade is undeniable, and he promoted it in his synods after Clermont. But that gathering and indeed all of his councils were first and foremost reforming synods akin to many others between 1049 and 1123. At Clermont the pope enacted decrees, handled Church business – such as the sticky issue of the marriage of King Philip of France – adjudicated local and regional disputes, and also, probably in the final session, announced plans for the Crusade. The famous address that sparked the expedition eastward presented only one facet of the *acta Claromontensia*.

The detail at hand about Clermont and its decrees constrasts with the little that is known about Tours, Nîmes, the Lateran synod of 1097, and Bari. The Roman Council of 1099 necessitates a more elaborate discussion, as the final section of this chapter will indicate. Once it was thought that Urban II presided over a council in Limoges a month after Clermont, at Christmastime 1095. The pope was then at Limoges and promoted the Crusade there, but he did not convoke a synod.[4] A thirteenth-century text from a manuscript at Seo de Urgel has Urban holding a council at Chartres, but this too is a mistake.[5] Provincial synods in France in 1096 owe much to Clermont, yet nothing indicates that the pope was directly involved with such gatherings, although given the poor state of the sources the possibility cannot be precluded.[6] Urban referred to Clermont at different times as a *generalis synodus*, a *generale concilium*, a *plenaria synodus*, and a *plenarium concilium*.[7] Bernold of Constance called Tours a *generalis sinodus* and perhaps the pope thought so too.[8] Urban spoke of Nîmes as a *plenaria synodus*, and labelled Bari a *plenarium concilium*.[9] Bernold designated the Roman council in 1099 as a *generalis sinodus*,

---

[4] Somerville, 'French Councils' 59–60.
[5] Somerville, 'Pseudo-Council' 19–21.
[6] See Gresser, *Synoden* 310, n. 257, on provincial synods in France at the time, following Monika Minninger, *Vom Clermont bis zum Wormser Konkordat* (Forschungen zur Kaiser- und Papstgeschichte des Mittelalter, Beiheft zu J.F. Böhmer Regesta Imperii 2; Vienna 1978) 88. See the specific examples of the Council at Rouen in 1096 (Somerville, 'Crusade and Canons' 70, and *Decreta* 38, n. 91), and a gathering, probably in the Touraine, around the same time (ibid. 131). See the discussion in Hoffmann, *Gottesfriede* 126–28, esp. 222, and Marcus Bull, *Knightly Piety and the Lay Response to the First Crusade: the Limousin and Gascony, c.970-c.1130* (Oxford 1993) 63–4.

[7] JL 5636–5637 contain interesting general observations about councils, with specific references to Clermont and Tours: see Dietrich Lohrmann, *Papsturkunden in Frankreich, Neue Folge 7: Nördliche Ile-de-France und Vermandois* (Göttingen Abhandlungen, Dritte Folge 95; Göttingen 1976) 252–54 (no. 16), for a new edition of 5637. See ibid. for Clermont as a *generalis synodus*; and cf. JL 5600 for *generale concilium*, JL 5654 for *plenaria synodus*, and JL 5788 for *plenarium concilium* (where the synods of Tours and Nîmes were noted without qualifiers).

[8] Bernold, *Chronicon*, ed. Pertz 464 / ed. Robinson 527. It cannot be assumed that Tours was not classed as 'general' although not so specified in JL 5636–37 (yet see Somerville–Kuttner, *Pope Urban* 181–85, for Melfi, which probably was not regarded by Urban as 'general': cf. also in Chapter 1 Background).

[9] For Nîmes see JL 5653 (also JL 5964 of Paschal II); for Bari see JL 5716 (IP 8. 156–57, no. 151), and cf. Romuald of Salerno and Lupus Protospatarius, both of whom called Bari a *universalis synodus* (Romuald, *Chronicon*, ed. C.A. Garufi [Rerum Italicarum scriptores, nuova ed. 7.1; Città di Castello 1935] 201; Lupus, *Annales Barenses*, ed. G.H. Pertz [MGH Scriptores 5; Hannover 1844] 63). In general, for conciliar terminology at the time, see Somerville–Kuttner, *Pope Urban* 181–85, and Chapter 1 Background).

although papal sources seem not to use an adjective to modify the nouns when referring to it.[10] That omission emphasizes the fluidity of terminology about councils and synods at the end of the eleventh century, and Pope Urban, in all probability, did not view his last council any differently than those held in France or at Bari.

Conciliar legislation is the focus of the discussion that follows, but other issues pertaining to these synods also merit attention, and some of them will be noted in the pages ahead. The episodes chosen are, however, an idiosyncratic, incomplete list, selected according to this author's preferences. Fuller information can be found readily, inter al., in Jaffé, Hagenmeyen, Hefele–Leclercq, Tangl, Becker, and Gresses. A few words are needed, finally, about two issues alluded to earlier, both of which transcend Urban's pontificate: the marital problems of Philip I of France, and the Crusade. Philip's refusal to separate from his mistress, Bertrade de Montfort (the wife of a royal vassal, Count Fulk IV of Anjou), created a dilemma for the French Church and the French pope. King and consort were excommunicated at Clermont, and tension between Urban and Philip clouded the pontiff's tour in 1096 across southern France, where negotiations failed to resolve the issue.[11] And if King Philip's private life continued to occupy Urban in his later years, the same was true of the Crusade, notwithstanding a paucity of direct evidence. The papal itinerary for the first half of 1096 is well known, and recruiting sermons along the way during those months were frequent. The Crusade was also on the agenda of the councils after Clermont, although detailed information is once more hardly plentiful.[12]

COUNCIL OF TOURS, MARCH 1096

A small amount of information about the legislation from Tours is offered by Bernold of Constance, Ordericus Vitalis, and a fragment of the *Historia Andegavensis*. Bernold reported that Urban reaffirmed the statutes of his earlier synods, but given the variegated and voluminous nature of the canonical traditions from Clermont just what that meant is uncertain.[13] Ordericus is more specific, noting

---

[10] See, e.g., JL 5791, *Data Romae, apud Beatum Petrum, in concilio quod ibi celebratum fuit in pace, IIII kalendas Maii.*, or the similar formulation in JL 5800.

[11] See Somerville, *Decreta* 5, n. 10, and Bernold, *Chronicon*, ed. Robinson, 516, n. 558; and in general see Fliche, *Réforme* passim, Becker, *Papst Urban* 1. 193–201, and id. 'Voyage' 132–33. Cf. Georges Duby, *The Knight, the Lady, and the Priest* (Chicago 1993) 3–21, which deals with Philip I, but must be used with caution. See also the forthcoming monograph on the letter of Bishop Chartres by Christof Rolker.

[12] For Urban's itinerary, see the references in Somerville, 'Pseudo-Council' 18, n. 1, and 20, n. 12, and to the works listed there the following can be added: Zadoka-Rio, 'Lieux' (a reference kindly provided by Dr. Oliver Münsch). See in general for Urban preaching the Crusade after Clermont Jonathan Riley-Smith, *The First Crusade and the Idea of Crusading* (Philadelphia 1986) Ch. 2 (pp. 31ff), and more recently Becker, 'Urbain et l'Orient'. For recruitment of participants for the Crusade see also the analysis of Riley-Smith, *First Crusaders*, esp. Ch. 3 (pp. 53ff). For the Crusade and Urbans's synods after Clermont, see below.

[13] Bernold, *Chronicon*, ed. Pertz 464 / ed. Robinson 527: *suorum praeteritorum statuta concilirum... reboravit.*

that Tours confirmed what had been done at Clermont.[14] The text from Angers, describing an interesting ceremony that will be treated below, listed events that occurred on Sunday, March 23, 'after the decrees were given to (or "in") the venerable council'.[15] It is hard to make much of this statement, but perhaps it implied a pre-packaged slate of canons. If Clermont ratified Urban II's earlier assemblies, and if Tours in turn ratified Clermont, taken literally this encompassed a long catena of rulings to be (re)issued, or 'given', at the synod. The schismatic cardinals' *Gesta Romanae aecclesiae contra Hildebrandum* decried what was taken as Pope Urban's inventive duplicity in spreading a uniform canonical program from Piacenza (cf. Chapter 2, *Enactment, Gesta*). The 'canons of Clermont', on the other hand, could imply that pope and chancery had little or no control over the synod's legislative record (cf. **n.** 2). The question mark hanging over these seemingly contradictory records was pondered in Chapter 2 (see especially *Enactment, Gesta*, and Bernold). Perhaps Tours reverted to something like what might have occurred at Piacenza, that is to say a digest of legislative highlights, maybe in this case from all of Urban II's previous councils, in some manner or other assembled and distributed to participants.

Two copies of a canon ascribed to Tours survive, repeating legislation from Clermont. The text is the well-attested c. 3 of the *Polycarpus*–Cencius list of decrees (sometimes designated as the Cencius–Baluze version), a provision that condemned as simoniacal the practice whereby bishops sold benefices in churches given to monasteries (*redemptio altarium*).[16] Each of these items survives among additions to twelfth-century manuscripts that contain, inter al., Augustine's *Enchiridion*: Erlangen, Universitätsbibliothek, MS 176, fol. 50r, from the Cistercian abbey of Heilsbronn; Metz, Bibliothèque municipale, MS 1212, fol. 169r, an Italian book that also contains letters of Walter de Honnecourt.[17] The canon is inscribed thus: Erlangen 176, *Ex concilio Turonis habito. Urbanus servus servorum Dei. Quoniam quidam symoniace pravitatis ramus... quem ex eis hactenus habuerunt.*; Metz 1212, *In concilio Turonis habito. Urbanus qui et Odo dictus est. Urbanus servus servorum Dei. Quoniam quidam symonicace pravitatis ramus... quem ex eis hactenus habuerunt.*

Exactly how these two copies are related requires further investigation. They can be matched, however, with another piece of evidence about Tours, a section of a

---

[14] *History* ix. 4, ed. Chibnall, 28: *Urbanus papa... Turonis aliud consilium tenuit, et ea unde apud Clarum montem tractauerat confirmauit.*

[15] *Chroniques*, ed. Halphen and Poupardin, 238: *Unde discendens, Cenomannim venit [Urbanus papa] et inde Turonum; ibique datis venerabili concilio decretis....* The text is found printed, inter al., in Paul Marchegay et André Salmon, *Chroniques des comtes d'Angers* (Paris 1856–71) 381, and in the *Recueil* 345: see Becker, *PapstUrban* 2. 446, under March 16–22.

[16] Somerville, *Decreta* 122–23; see also 139–40, for other occurrences of that text, a list that could be expanded.

[17] Dr. Linda Fowler-Magerl kindly called Erlangen 176 to the author's attention. See Hans Fischer, *Die lateinischen Pergamenthandschriften der Universitätsbibliothek Erlangen* 1 (Erlangen 1928) 194–95. Dr. Consuelo Dutschke expressed a cautious opinion to the author that this book was written in a German hand. For Metz 1212 see Germain Morin, 'Un écrivain inconnu du XI siècle: Walter, moine de Honnecourt, puis de Vézelay', *Revue Bénédictine* 22 (1905) 165 (repr. Id. *Etudes, textes, découvertés* [Abbaye de Maredsous 1913] 466), and also P. Marot, *Catalogue général* (Quarto Series) 48 (Paris 1933) 410–11.

papal grant issued for the abbey of St.-Bertin in northern France that is dated March 23, 1096, immediately after the council.[18] Embedded therein, without a special attribution, is the same canon. Because no other conciliar decrees are included this document would not qualify as a papal *synodalis epistola* of the sort that Ordericus Vitalis mentioned, by which legislation from Clermont was sent to absent churchmen in Normandy.[19] The St.-Bertin privilege is difficult to interpret as a piece of evidence for papal conciliar practice, yet it shows at a minimum that the chancery cited recent synodal enactments in its correspondence.[20] Someday, therefore, a full dossier of canons from one of Urban's councils might turn up in a *synodalis epistola* that was sent to a bishop or a religious house. Such a discovery would go far toward clarifying the puzzling disparity, within a period of twelve months, between the canons attributed to the Councils of Piacenza and of Clermont, and the meagre legislative 'fortuna' that survies from Tours.[21]

Turning briefly away from the canons, two episodes from Tours deserve notice. Neither happened in the synod per se, but both preserve views of Pope Urban in action at the time of the gathering. A text from Marmoutier described events that occurred on Sunday, March 9, a week before the council opened. After celebrating the liturgy appropriate for the Lord's Day, as was his custom (*ex more*), the pontiff, again as was customary (*ut est consuetudinis*), addressed a crowd from a wooden platform set up for him on the banks of the Loire (which was seemingly not customary but noteworthy enough that the chronicler noted it).[22] Nothing is said about the Crusade, but why would the pope have been silent about that on this occasion, given his advocacy of the venture throughout the spring and summer of 1096? The wooden platform whence Urban spoke was not described, but might it have been moved to Marmoutier for the council?[23] It is likely that Urban presided over the synod from a dais of some sort, perhaps the same platform from which he spoke on the banks of the Loire a week earlier.[24]

---

[18] JL 5628.
[19] *History* ix. 2, ed. Chibnall, 19 ff. See the discussion about papal encyclical letters in Rudolf Schieffer, *Die Entstehung des päpstlichen Investiturverbots für den deutschen König* (MGH Schriften 8; Stuttgart 1981) 64 ff., and cf. Somerville, 'Crusade and Canons' 70 ff.
[20] See examples of the use made of Urban II's conciliar texts in twelfth-century papal correspondence noted in Somerville, *Decreta*, Appendix II.
[21] Cf. the perceptive remarks of Blumenthal, 'Conciliar Canons' 372, on recordkeeping at the time.
[22] *Textus de dedicatione ecclesiae Majoris monasterii*, in Salmon, *Recueil* 359: *Pridie siquidem, quae fuerat dies dominica, celebratis ex more missis ab eodem, adierat gradum ligneum sibi ad loquendum populo, ut est consuetudinis, in littore Ligeris praeparatum* (text also printed, inter al., by Thierry Ruinart, *Ouvrages posthumes de D. Jean Mabillon et de D. Thierri Ruinart* 3 [Paris 1724] 387–88 [reprinted in PL 151. 274], in *Recueil des historiens des Gaules et de la France* 12 [Paris 1877] 466, in MGH Scriptores 6 [Hannover 1882] 461–62, and post JL 5619).
[23] For the council's location at Marmoutier and not in the cathedral, see Hefele-Leclercq, *Histoire* 446.
[24] The use of platforms in councils remains to be investigated in detail. See, for example, Eadmer, *Historia novorum*, ed. Rule, 105–6, in the accounts of Urban's and St. Anselm's activities at the Council of Bari; cf. William of Malmesbury, *Gesta Pontificum*, ed. Winterbottom and Thomson, i. 53 (154): *Apostolicus ante corpus sancti Nicholai, constrictum, tapetibus et palliis, tribunal ascendit*, and cf. ibid. (156).

The Council of Tours had concluded its business by Sunday, March 23, a day on which a remarkable series of events took place.[25] It was the fourth Sunday of Lent, mid-Lent and Letare Sunday.[26] Pope Urban, *coronatus*, led a solemn procession from the cathedral of St. Mauritius to the abbey church of St. Martin where he celebrated mass, *more Romano*, and gave a golden rose to Count Fulk IV of Anjou.[27] Count Fulk was the jilted husband of Bertrade de Montfort, now the royal consort and, along with King Philip, under papal censure. Urban's actions thus were a slap at Philip, however much the rose was presented with the hope that Fulk would be enlisted for the Crusade.[28] The ceremony at Marmoutier also marks the first known instance of a golden rose being bestowed by a pope on someone else, although the use of the rose in papal ceremonies is attested as early as the pontificate of Pope Leo IX, a half-century earlier.[29]

COUNCIL OF NÎMES, JULY 1096

Pope Urban planned a council for the octave of the Feast of Sts. Peter and Paul (July 6) at Arles, but the assembly met instead at Nîmes.[30] This synod might deserve monographical treatment, for as with Clermont the Council of Nîmes offers a forum for a good deal of surviving local and regional ecclesiastical business. The assembly presented an occasion for papal preaching of the Crusade, and for attempts to resolve the quagmire surrounding the royal marriage.[31] As with Tours,

---

[25] See the references provided by Becker, *PapstUrban* 2. 446, under Sunday, March 23, 1096.
[26] For Laetare Sunday ses G. Cyprian Alston, *Catholic Encyclopedia* 8 (1910) 737–38. Cf. Gresser, *Synoden* 310, n. 258, at the end, which probably refers to the events of March 23.
[27] See the *Fragmentum Historiae Andegavensis*, *Chroniques*, ed. Halphen and Poupardit 238: . . . *media quadrigesima, coronatus est et cum sollempni processione ab ecclesia sancti Mauticii ad ecclesiam beati Martini deductus; ubi mihi florem aureum quem in manu grebat donavit*. For an English translation of the episode, see Riley-Smith, *First Crusaders* 59 (using the text in *Recuei* 345–45); for Fulk's probable authorship see Becker, *PapstUrban* 1. 224, n. 840. The *Chronicon Turonense magnum*, in Salmon, *Recueil* 129, recounted these events but omitted the rose, and noted that Urban *more Romano corona palmarum se coronavit* (text also printed, inter al., in *Recueil des historiens des Gaules et de la France* 12 [Paris 1877] 466, and in MGH Scriptores 26 [Hannover 1882] 461). W. Scott Jessee, *Robert the Burgundian and the Counts of Anjou, ca.1025–1098* (Washington 2000) 147, describes the ceremony in very general terms without comment. Just what kind of crown the pope wore is unclear: Elisabeth Cornides, *Rose und Schwert im päpstlichen Zeremoniell* (Wiener Dissertationen aus dem Gebiete der Geschichte 9; Vienna 1967) 72, considers the reference to *corona palmarum* an 'Abschreifehler', since such a crown is otherwise unknown, but her following comments about Fulk and the papal tiara seem confused. Riley-Smith, loc. cit., writes that Urban at the ceremony in question was 'wearing his tiara', although no text known to this author says that specifically.
[28] Becker, *PapstUrban* 1. 223–24.
[29] See Charles Burns, *Golden Rose and Blessed Sword* (Glasgow 1970) 3, and Charles Duggen, 'Golden Rose', *New Catholic Encyclopedia*, 2nd edn., 6 (2003) 335–36.
[30] See JL 5636, and 5637, for Arles. The reasons for the change are not clear but probably, at least in part, had to do with King Philip: see Gresser, *Synoden* 311. For specific details about the participants at Nîmes, see Tangl, *Teilnehmer* 182.
[31] For these marital complications see Fliche, *Réforme* 291, and Becker 'Voyage' 133; and for the Crusade see Somerville, 'Beyond Clermont'. Nîmes was cited after Urban II's time, e.g., by Paschal II (JL 5964, 6117, 6118, 6161), and by Calixtus II (JL 6702). See also references in the letters of Bishop

Nîmes reaffirmed the decrees from Clermont, and texts specifically labeled as deriving from Nîmes are found more frequently than those attributed to Tours. In 1661, moreover, a series of eighteen canons was published by Luc d'Achery and ascribed to the Council of Nîmes – provisions then reprinted by others and eventually in 1775 by Mansi.[32] The first item in this set carries an attribution specifically to Nîmes, but the others, including two well-known forgeries, lack inscriptions. The discovery of d'Achery's manuscript – Paris, BNF, MS lat. 3860, where the canons in question appear on fol. 138r-v as a supplement to Burchard of Worms' *Decretum* – shows to an overwhelming degree of probability that unattributed provisions written in various early-twelfth-century hands were later additions at the end of this book to a text from Nîmes.

Nîmes' authentic legislation occurs in nine twelfth-century manuscripts and carries the distictive incipit *In Arvernensi concilio*.[33] These opening words refer back to the Council of Clermont, and the genuine selection from Nîmes comprises c. 3, or in some versions cc. 3–4, of the *Polycarpus*–Cencius text of Clermont (see the discussion of Tours above for the content of c. 3; c. 4 stipulates cooperation between bishops and monks in appointing pastors in parishes that monks control).[34] The incipits and explicts of the major sections are as follows.

In Arvernensi concilio quesitum est de episcopis qui altaria ... compellebant. Quia quidam simoniace pravitatis ramus ... quem ex eisdem altaribus habere soliti sunt. (= Clermont, *Polycarpus*–Cencius, c. 3) *Sane quia monachorum quidam ... et sic cuique sua jura serventur.* (= Clermont, *Polycarpus*–Cencius, c. 4)

Nothing in these texts deals with the Crusade. If such canons were issued at Nîmes they remain to be discovered, although a tradition from the monastery of Fleury connects Clermont and Nîmes to an order on the part of Pope Urban commanding bishops to preach the Crusade in their dioceses.[35]

Lambert of Arras, in Giordanengo, *Arras* 376–78 (E.35), and 416 (E.94) (both with French translations); cf. Kéry, *Arras* 411.

[32] For the details see Kuttner–Somerville, 'Nîmes' (cf. Mansi, *Amplissima collectio* 20. 931–37). In at least two instances prior to Mansi, the 'Nîmes' attribution for this set of decrees was questioned, although no one could be criticized for missing them: see the remarks of Etienne Baluze in 1677 (Kuttner–Somerville, 'Nîmes' 185–86), and the description of Paris, BNF, MS lat. 3860 in the catalogue of the Bibliothèque du roi published in 1744 (cf. ibid. 187). Cf. Gresser, *Synoden* 312, who seems to have reservations about the conclusions of Kuttner and Somerville.

[33] See the references in Kuttner–Somerville, 'Nîmes' 178, n. 18 (five occurrences), 185, n. 41 (three occurrences where the folio number for Paris, BNF, MS lat. 10402 [81r], was omitted), and 186 ff. for BNF lat. 3860. New bibliography (since 1970) for some of these manuscripts now could be added, and other occurrences of the authentic canon must exist, although none appeared in a search using Fowler-Magerl, *Clavis* (a result for which the author is grateful to Steven Schoenig, S.J., of St. Louis University.)

[34] Somerville, *Decreta* 122–23.

[35] *Narratio Floriacensis de captis Antiochia et Hierosolyma et obsesso Dyrrachio*, in *Recueil* 356: *Jubet etiam omnibus episcopis, ut unusquisque in sua diocesi praedicet, praeconetur, exoret haec.* Cf. *La Chronique de Saint-Maixent*, ed. Verdon, 154: *Ubicumque fuit, precepit cruces facere hominibus et pergere Jerusalem et liberare eam a Turcis et aliis gentibus.*

In summarizing what is known about the legislation from the Councils of Tours and Nîmes the centrality of the *Polycarpus*–Cencius version of Clermont's canons is pivotal.[36] Several twelfth-century popes cited Clermont from this tradition, and the existence of these decrees in a Roman copy of the *Liber censuum* – a manuscript that remains undetected – also suggests their importance.[37] The only known canons from Tours and Nîmes are re-promulgated *Polycarpus*–Cencius items, yet the very limited survival of provisions ascribed to those two gatherings is puzzling given the fact that Clermont generated more than a dozen different canonical traditions. Where are the other decrees of Tours and Nîmes that reiterated Clermont's legislation and even, following Bernold of Constance, repeated Urban's pre-Clermont program?[38] The answer is not at hand.

LATERAN COUNCIL, 1097

The synod at the Lateran in the year 1097 is the least well known of all of Urban II's councils and has nearly vanished totally.[39] A date of January 9 sometimes has been assigned, but this resulted from assumptions based on Jaffé, rests on no historical evidence, and would have been most unusual.[40] It is unknown when in 1097 the council met.[41]

Despite his return to the city, Rome still was not fully secure for Urban II and his adherents, as demonstrated by Fulcher of Chartres' well-known description of violence at St. Peter's caused by Wibertine adherents.[42] Urban had yet to convoke a council in Rome and surely was eager to do so, especially at the Lateran, given the traditions and prominence of the church. It could be assumed, furthermore, that the pope would be sure to announce a comprehensive canonical program at his first Roman council and his first in the 'head and summit of all churches in the entire world' (*caput et verticem omnium ecclesiarum in universo orbe terrarum*), as the *Donation of Constantine* termed the Lateran.[43]

But if such a program was set forth in 1097 it has left virtually no trace. The sole item that resembles a canon is a text found printed among the 'notationes' of the

---

[36] As has been noted by various authors: for example, Gossman, *Urban* 4 (with n. 9), and 9, Somerville, *Decreta* 119–20, and 139–41, and Blumenthal, 'Conciliar Canons' 369.

[37] Somerville–Kuttner, *Pope Urban* 233; for the *Liber censuum* text see Chapter 4, *Polycarpus* Supplement.

[38] See n. 13.

[39] Tangl's view in *Teilnehmer* 183, that 'eine gewisse Stagnation' in synodal development set in after Urban's French trip seems severe given the paucity of sources at hand. Cf. Gresser, *Synoden* 314. The discussion ibid. 314–17, about canonizations late in Urban's reign must refer to the Councils of Bari and Rome and not the assembly at the Lateran.

[40] Ibid., 313, n. 273, calls it 'singulär'.

[41] But even so Gresser, ibid. 313, decides that the Lateran Council was 'Die Fastensynode des Jahres 1097'.

[42] Heinrich Hagenmeyer, *Fulcheri Carnotensis Historia Hierosolymitana (1095–1127)* (Heidelberg 1913) I.7, 165–66.

[43] *Das Constitutum Constantini (Konstantinische Schenkung) Text*, ed. Horst Fuhrmann (MGH Fontes iuris Germanici antiqui in usum scholarum 10; Hannover 1968) 84.

sixteenth-century 'Correctores Romani' of Gratian (JL 5775).[44] The provision was found added to two old copies of Gratian, after C. 13, q. 2, c. 12.[45] It seems to be part of a letter from Urban II to Bishop Gottfried of Maguelone specifying that parishioners desiring burial in a monastery should bequeath to a parish church either half of their alms, or, 'according to our dispensation promulgated in the Lateran Council' (*iuxta dispensationem nostram in Lateranensi concilio promulgatam*), a third.[46] It would be helpful, of course, to know something about the two manuscripts of the 'Correctores', but they remain to be traced.[47] Finally, it can be noted that Urban's decision was paraphrased in a privilege issued by Calixtus II that was edited by Ulysse Robert in 1891.[48]

This small amount of information offers a shaky basis for drawing conclusions about JL 5775. The fragment may convey either a judgment rendered for a specific case or part of a synodal canon. Notwithstanding its presence in two copies of Gratian that were known to the 'Correctores Romani', the text's absence from twelfth-century canon law books might suggest that it was not part of the 1097 council's general legislation. Yet that point cannot be pressed, as many synodal decrees of the time did not find their way into canonical collections. The fact that the pontiff delivered his ruling *iuxta dispensationem nostram* also does not help to determine whether he intended to formulate a general canonical statement or instead was issuing a judgment in a particular case. Ideas of dispensation abound in Urban's pronouncements, both in the conciliar decrees and in the correspondence.[49]

Excursus: Remnants in Rome, Bibl. Vallicelliana, MS C. 24, of a late Roman council of Urban II?

In 1884 Pflugk-Harttung published ten canons that carry no attribution, but to which he added the editorial conjecture that they were decrees from a synod of Urban II held between 1097 and 1099.[50] He found these texts in Vallicelliana MS C. 24, fols. 63r-64v (copied again on 94r-95r).[51] They were accompanied by a note from Michael Thomasius, a member of the commission of 'Correctores', indicating that they were taken from a codex owned by Hieronymus Parisetti, an Italian

---

[44] For the post-Tridentine commission of canon law experts known as the 'Correctores Romani' see in Chapter 3, passim.

[45] ... *in duobus antiquis exemplaribus*; the text does not appear among the *paleae* to Gratian according to Jacqueline Rambaud, in Le Bras et al., *L'âge classique* 109.

[46] Printed in the 'Notatio Correctorum' to C. 13, q. 2, c. 12, in Friedberg, *Decretum*. Bishop Gothfrid was in office 1080–1103: Pius Bonifacius Gams, *Series episcoporum ecclesiae catholicae* (Regensburg 1873–86) 579.

[47] Perhaps one of them was the book noted by Wilhelm Wiederhold in the Archives départementales de l'Hérault: *Papsturkunden in Frankreich* 7 (Nachrichten Göttingen, Beiheft 1906) 4 (repr. op. cit. [Acta Romanorum pontificum 8; Vatican City 1985]).

[48] JL 7093: Ulysse Robert, *Bullaire du Pape Calixte, 1119–1124* 2 (Paris 1891) 238 (no. 430), from a manuscript also found in the departmental archives.

[49] E.g., Council of Piacenza, c. 12 (text in Chapter 4), and Somerville–Kuttner, *Pope Urban* 104ff., for *Collectio Britannica* no. 30 (JL 5393 [IP 3.119, no. 2, and 320, no. 6]).

[50] *Acta* 167–68.

[51] For this well-known book see Chapter 3, passim.

humanist and canonist and fellow 'Corrector'. But not only did Thomasius preserve these canons, he thought (*putamus*) that they derived from a synod of Urban II.[52]

Parisetti's manuscript has not come to light, so it is impossible to know how the provisions occurred therein and whether or not the context offered a basis for attributing them to Pope Urban.[53] The decrees' formulation is consistent with what might be expected in a papal synod of the time: the use of the first person plural, 'we command' (*praecipimus*, cc. 1–2), 'we forbid' (*interdicimus*, c. 3), 'we prohibit' (*prohibemus*, c. 6), and also the invocation in c. 1 of 'the authority and command of the holy fathers and the entire holy Roman Church' (*Ex auctoritate et praecepto sanctorum patrum totiusque sanctae Romanae ecclesiae*). A *Lateranense concilium* is cited in cc. 1–2 as a point of reference, and Pflugk-Harttung speculated that the canons were issued by Pope Urban's Lateran Council of 1097.

The origin of these texts has been debated since Pflugk-Harttung printed them.[54] There is no question that some of them repeat, at times verbatim, twelfth-century canons from both Calixtus II's and Innocent II's Lateran Councils of 1123 and 1139. Furthermore, the set of decrees lacks items expected from a late synod of Urban II, especially a prohibition against lay investiture, something that was promulgated at Bari in 1098, at Rome in 1099, and presumably also at the Lateran Synod of 1097. Pflugk-Harttung's canons could, of course, include pieces of legislation from Urban II that were transcribed with later material. The question can remain open because of Michael Thomasius. Why did this learned churchman think that these canons derived from Pope Urban II? The answer, if an answer is possible, would perhaps be found in the unpublished correspondence and papers of the 'Correctores' and their collaborators.[55]

COUNCIL OF BARI, OCTOBER 1098

If the Lateran Council of 1097 is the most obscure of Urban II's councils, Bari is among the best known. After spending most of the year 1097 in Rome, Urban left the city in May 1098 and moved south, spending several months in the vicinity of Salerno and Benevento before arriving in Bari.[56] The opening of the synod probably was scheduled for October 1, but the assembly seems to have been in session October 3–10, with more than 100 bishops on hand.[57] Although the

---

[52] See Gasparri, 'Osservazioni' 483, and 485. For Parisetti, see Kuttner, 'Roman Manuscripts' 13 ff.
[53] For another lost manuscript that once had been in the hands of the 'Correctores', see at the end of Chapter 3.
[54] See the discussion in Gossman, *Urban* 11, and Hoffmann, *Gottesfriede* 222, and 225.
[55] See Kuttner, 'Roman Manuscripts' 13 ff.
[56] See Jaffé for details of the pope's itinerary. During Urban's absence from Rome supporters of Clement III, but without the antipope, met in a council in August 1098: Stoller, 'Councils', 315–21, and Gresser, *Synoden* 317–21 (cf. Chapter 5, n. 35). See ibid. 320–21, and Becker, *PapstUrban* 1. 159, for the Wibertine council proposed for Vercelli in October 1098, which may not have occurred.
[57] See Eadmer, *Historia novorum*, ed. Rule, 104, and *Life*, ed. and trans. Southern, 112, for October 1. See Gresser, *Synoden* 322, n. 319, for the date, and n. 321, for the attendance (cf. Tangl, *Teilnehmer* 184, who called Lupus Protospatarius' figure of 185 bishops at the council a 'sicherlich übertriebene

reasons for the choice of this particular city are unknown, Bari, situated in Apulia on the frontier between Latin and Greek Christianity, made possible both Latin and Greek participation at a gathering where issues important to the churches in southern Italy were to be considered. The Crusade also was on the agenda.[58]

The Council of Bari is famous for debate about the Procession of the Holy Spirit, which in the West means the doctrine of the Double Procession or of the *filioque*. The western view, which developed in the early Middle Ages, maintained that the Spirit proceeds from both the Father 'and from the Son' (*filioque*). The Greeks adhered to the older formulation that the Spirit proceeds from the Father alone, or from the Father through the Son.[59] During the synod at Bari Pope Urban, eager to integrate the Greek churches in the south of Italy into the Latin obedience, lectured about the Double Procession. Meeting opposition, he summoned an expert opinion, namely St. Anselm of Canterbury, in exile from England and travelling with the pope.[60] Eadmer of Canterbury, fellow monk, travelling companion, and biographer of his exiled archbishop, related that after Anselm marvelously explicated the Latin position, an anathema was pronounced against anyone who was opposed.[61] That unecumenical gesture might well have led the Greeks to stomp out of the council, and it can be wondered if Eadmer is accurate in his report, for which corroborating testimony is lacking.

Aside from what they could add to the theological debate and to Crusading history, the loss of the acts from Bari is a significant blow to understanding Urban II's policies near the end of his reign. In 1102 Pope Paschal II, who as a cardinal was present at Bari, recalled the *excommunicationis . . . sententia* against lay investiture of

---

Nachricht'). The gathering at Bari received attention recently, not totally but in great part due to its 900th anniversary: e.g., Nicola Bux, "Sant' Anselmo al Concilo di Bari (1098)', in Inos Biffi and Costana Marabelli (eds.), *Anselmo d'Aosta figura europea* 103–8 (Milan 1989), Gerardo Cioffari o.p., 'Sinodalità e concili a Bari nel Medioevo', in Salvatore Palese, *Le tradizioni sinodali della Chiesa di Bari* (Per la storia della Chiesa di Bari, Studi e materiali 15; Bari 1997), 7–69 (esp. 32–55), and a volume of proceedings from a conference held in 1998: Palese–Locatelli, *Bari*. For the sources of the council, see Carmelo Capizzi S.I., 'Il Concilio di Bari (1098): riflessi e silenzi nella tradizione bizantina e nella storiografia orientale', ibid. 69–90. Indicative, however, of the paucity of evidence for the council is the overwhelming attention given to discussion of the Procession of the Holy Spirit, a matter of undoubted importance at the synod yet only one of the issues treated therein.

[58] See Hagenmeyer, *Chronologie* 190–91; and more recently Becker, *PapstUrban* 2. 190 ff, id. 'Urbain et l'Orient' 141–44, and Somerville, 'Beyond Clermont', for the details, including the statement by the Crusading prince Bohemond early in the pontificate of Paschal II that Urban pledged either at Bari or at the Council of Rome in 1099 to come to the East. By the time he reached Bari at the beginning of October, 1098, Urban probably had heard of the death of his legate for the Crusade, Adhémar of Le Puy, at Antioch on August 1, and perhaps also had received the letter of September 11 from the Crusading princes urging him to come to Antioch and assume leadership of the expedition (Hagenmeyer, op. cit. 182–83).

[59] See J. Gill and B.L. Marthaler, 'Filioque', *New Catholic Encyclopedia*, 2nd edn., 5 (2003) 719–22, and in general, Henry Chadwick, *East and West: The Making of a Rift in the Church, From Apostolic Time until the Council of Florence* (Oxford 2003), and for Bari 222–27. See also Somerville–Kuttner, *Urban II* 176–80, for Urban II and Greek bishops at the Council of Melfi in 1089, nearly a decade before Bari.

[60] For Anselm at Bari see Eadmer, *Historia novorum*, ed. Rule, 104–5, and *Life*, ed. and trans. Southern, 112–13.

[61] Eadmer, *Historia novorum*, ed. Rule, 106; cf. William of Malmesbury, *Gesta Pontificum*, ed. Winterbottom and Thomson i. 53 (156), an account derivative from Eadmer.

churches issued at the council.[62] Behind Paschal's reference to this condemnation could exist a group of decrees, including a provision against lay investiture (cf. the Council of Clermont).[63] No canons specifically attributed to Bari are known, but texts surviving in canon law collections with a general attribution, e.g., *Urbanus papa*, could derive from any of Urban's councils, including Bari.[64] The four synods held at Tours, Nîmes, the Lateran, and Bari between 1096 and 1098 are the least well documented of the pontificate. It probably is an anomaly and in no way connected to papal policy that, setting aside the 1097 Lateran Council, Bari and not Tours or Nîmes is the gathering for which no specifically ascribed decree survives.

COUNCIL AT ST. PETER'S, ROME, APRIL 1099

As noted at the beginning of the previous section, the Council of Bari has in the recent past been the object of special studies. It was suggested above that Nîmes might also deserve that treatment. The same is true, maybe more so, for Pope Urban's last synod, celebrated after Easter 1099, not at the Lateran but at St. Peter's.[65] Bernold of Constance indicated that Urban circulated letters 'everywhere' (*usquequaque*) announcing the council, which convened April 24–30, in the third week after Easter, although the precise opening and closing dates are unknown.[66] Furthermore, according to Bernold, at this gathering of 150 bishops and abbots Urban confirmed both the *statuta* of his predecessors and the anathema against Wibert of Ravenna and his accomplices, stipulated that those who retain concubines should not receive communion, and also made a plea for assistance for those on the Crusade.[67] A small number of participants are named at the end of JL 5788, which was issued at St. Peter's on April 24, and Gresser identifies others.[68] Rome also provided a vivid scene of conflict between Bishop Rangerius of Lucca and Pope

---

[62] JL 5929; not listed in Jaffé are the editions of the letter in Eadmer, *Historia novorum*, ed. Rule, 139, and in *Anselmi opera*, ed. Schmitt, 4. 198–99 (no. 282). The *sententia* was presumably against both those who performed and those who received lay investiture. Cf. Eadmer's report on the condemnation at the Council of Rome in 1099 that was formulated against those who give and those who receive investiture: *The Life of St Anselm, Archbishop of Canterbury*, ed. Richard Southern (Oxford 1979) 115. See also Beulertz, *Verbot* 13 and passim.

[63] Somerville, *Decreta* 145, no. 18.

[64] See *Councils & Synods* 1.2. 650–51; cf. Brett, 'Lateran Council' 15. See also Chapter 2, p. 33.

[65] Becker, *PapstUrban* 1. 112, for the still unsettled political–religious situation at Rome in 1099. The author is grateful to Dr. Edward A. Reno III for permitting use of his work on the Council of Rome.

[66] JL 5779*; cf. the differences about dates for the council among the texts noted in Mansi, *Amplissima collectio* 20. 966B, and in *Councils & Synods* 1.2. 653, n. 4, and 6.

[67] Bernold, *Chronicon*, ed. Pertz 466 / ed. Robinson 537: *Romae domnus papa generalem sinodum CL episcoporum et abbatum et clericorum unnumerabilium in tercia epdomada post pascha collegit. In qua sinodo, confirmatis suorum antecessorum statutis, etiam sententiam anathematis super Guibertum heresiarcham et omnes eius complices iteravit. Statuit quoque ibi, ne communicare praesumerent, qui concubinas haberent, nisi prius eas omnino dimitterent. De Ierosolimitano itinere multum rogavit, ut irent et fratribus suis laborantibus succerrent.* Where Bernold got his information is a question to be considered in a full treatment of the acts of this council.

[68] Gresser, *Synoden* 328–29.

Urban, a confrontation that occurred during a public reading of the conciliar decrees and which will be considered below.

St. Anselm and Eadmer were present at Rome.[69] The council provided a touchstone for Anselm in his struggles with the English Kings William Rufus and Henry I over investiture. At the Council of Bari six months earlier Anselm must had heard a sentence condemning lay investiture. But he never mentioned it, preferring to cite the ruling from the Council of Rome in which Urban II excommunicated those conferring and those receiving investiture of churches, and those who required or performed homage for ecclesiastical benefices.[70] Anselm might have viewed the demand for homage as key in the matter, an issue for which there is no evidence at Bari.

Public opinion also may have played a role in what Anselm chose to cite or not to cite about Urban's last two synods. The archbishop, in exile from his see at Canterbury, depended on papal support that could seem less forthcoming than some of his adherents hoped. Anselm's circumstances occasioned a remarkable outburst from Bishop Rangerius of Lucca. St. Peter's was not closed to visitors during the synod, and Eadmer reported that pilgrim traffic therein created substantial amounts of noise. Pope Urban thus asked Bishop Rangerius to read the conciliar canons because, as Eadmer noted, he was endowed *sonora voce*.[71] But Rangerius suddenly interrupted his recitation and with great agitation, stamping his crozier three times on the floor, and complaining about what he took to be shabby treatment of the exiled Anselm. Nodding to him (*innuens*), the pope replied, as Eadmer related it, 'That is quite enough, Brother Rangerius, we have this matter very clearly under advisement' (*Frater Reingere, sufficit, sufficit; de hac re bonum consilium erit*).[72] To which Rangerius responded in anger, after being admonished (*monitus*) to resume reading the decrees, 'Rightly so, for otherwise it will not escape the notice of the one who judges justly' (*Et equidem expedit, nam aliter eum qui justo judicat non transibit*).[73] But the bishop of Lucca was not finished, and after presenting the canons, so that the injury to Anselm would not be taken lightly,

---

[69] The focus in this chapter is conciliar legislation, but information about synodal procedures and seating exists for Bari and Rome, especially from Eadmer: cf. Somerville, *Decreta*, ch. 2 (repr. in id. *Papacy, Councils and Canon Law*), a discussion in need of revision.

[70] Eadmer, *Historia novorum*, ed. Rule, 114; see *Anselmi opera*, ed. Schmitt, 4. 112, and 195, and 5. 341, for statements from Anselm about the excommunications at the Council of Rome. Pope Paschal II, curiously, never referred to the Council of Rome, although he was in the city in April 1099, and most likely took part in the assembly, but did refer to the condemnation at Bari (JL 5929; cf. n. 62 above): Beulertz, *Verbot* 122, n. 433. See ibid. 14–15, for the Council of Rome and investiture.

[71] Eadmer, *Historia novorum*, ed. Rule, 112–13; cf. inter al. Laudage, 'Ritual' 295, n. 19, and 328–29.

[72] How likely was it that Rangerius' outburst was spontaneous? The accounts of the papal Crusading sermon delivered at Clermont – if it can be used at all as a guide to what actually occurred in the synod – together with other sources about Urban's preaching of the Crusade suggest that the pope was not immune to theatrics on such public occasions. Perhaps Bishop Rangerius and Pope Urban engaged in a bit of theater, with Rangerius' complaint planted and offering a pretext for Urban to launch condemnations. Why such a tactic would be used is another question, and *Councils & Synods* 1.2. 652, note that 'it seems clear that [Anselm's] supporters at least were thoroughly dissatisfied with [the council's] outcome'. Cf. above for Urban's request for Anselm to address the Council of Bari about the doctrine of the Procession of the Holy Spirit. Was that a spontaneous series of events?

[73] Cf. Leviticus 19:15, and Gratian, D. 45, c. 10, citing Gregory the Great's *Moralia*.

according to Eadmer (*ne parvipenderetur injuria Anselmo illata*), Rangerius repeated his warning before sitting down.

This dramatic scene seems unparalleled in papal councils of the time. Eadmer portrays Anselm as unperturbed by the commotion, hardly aware of what was happening. But notwithstanding Bishop Rangerius' disquietude, the episode serves to direct attention to what Rangerius was reciting at the pope's behest, namely the synod's decrees. Eadmer termed them both *capitula* and *decreta*, and the rendition that was read out loud by the bishop of Lucca must have been considered an official text.[74] It is reasonable to assume that Rangerius' script contained a full record of the enacted legislation, or at least what the pope was ready to present as such. Bernold noted that the *statuta* of Urban's predecessors, as well as the anathema against Guibert and his accomplices, were reiterated at Rome. With a couple of new items added, the surviving records comprise, often verbatim, decrees from Piacenza – cc. <1>-<13> – and from Melfi – cc. <2>-<3>, and <5>-<7>.[75] These texts encompass well-known reforming statements on issues such as simony and clerical appointments, with nothing included about the Crusade or the East.[76] The distance cannot be measured between what Rangerius read and the sets of decrees that survive, all of which are private accounts that do not stem directly from Urban's chancery.[77] If Urban circulated an authorized list of the legislation, that document now is lost.

Despite the reiterations from Melfi and Piacenza in Rome's provisions, hints point to other issues treated there about which very little is known. Bishop Lambert of Arras, an eye witness, wrote that the synod was convened to deal with 'the error and heresies of the Greeks' (*pro errore et haeresibus Grecorum*), and that it enacted both reforming measures for the Latin Church and 'decrees concerning the Latin and the Greek Church' (*decreta...de Latina et Greca ecclesia*).[78] Little can be said about this tantalizing description other than that it points eastward, at least as far as Constantinople and maybe further. Lambert continued by writing that a diligent reader could find these canons and read them, although he did not bother to say where and quickly moved on to speak of the death of Urban II and his burial in St. Peter's, next to Leo the Great. Yet if what Lambert said was accurate, an early twelfth-century investigator could have put his hands on a series of provisions from the 1099 council that treated Greek–Latin issues, perhaps including matters relating to the Crusade. And if such a series of decrees ever existed and circulated, at Arras or elsewhere, it is not impossible that it may reappear some day.

---

[74] Eadmer, *Historia novorum*, ed. Rule, 112–13.
[75] Somerville–Kuttner, *Pope Urban* 253–54, for Melfi; Chapter 4, above, for Piacenza; and for Bernold's observation see *Chronicon*, ed. Pertz 466 / ed. Robinson 537.
[76] Mansi, *Amplissima collectio* 20. 961–64. Melfi c. 8, with its prohibition of lay investiture, was not included among these reiterated canons, nor was Melfi c. 4, dealing with ages for those in orders (see Somerville–Kuttner, *Urban* 271–78).
[77] *Councils & Synods* 1.2. 651, n. 5, state that at least three versions are known.
[78] *Gesta Atrebatensium*, Kéry, *Arras*, 188–89 [51]; Giordanengo, *Arras* 194 (C.54) (with a French translation) (also in *Recueil des Historiens des Gaules et de France*, nouv. éd., 14 [Paris 1877] 756). For Lambert and this text see Kéry, op. cit. 71, n. 22, and Becker, *PapstUrban* 2. 200–1.

Bishop Lambert is not the only witness to suggest that the legislation from Rome was more extensive than the surviving decrees show. The *Chronicon* of the abbey of St.-Maixent in the diocese of Tour noted a reaffirmation of the Crusade in the council, and that Pope Urban also decreed that all Christians should fast every Friday on behalf of their sins, especially those that they forgot to confess.[79] Friday abstinence was a venerable practice, although no other source known specifically ascribes it to a papal decree from Urban II. Both Gregory VII and Pope Urban early in his pontificate promulgated canons differentiating true from false penance, and a decree from the Council of Melfi stated that penance for only one sin was in vain and was required for all transgressions if forgiveness was to be gained.[80] John Cowdrey linked concern about full confession to Urban's plan at Clermont for a Crusaders' indulgence that was to apply to those who made an honest and complete confession, and took the cross out of devotion only and not for honor or money.[81] Perhaps the notice from St.-Maixent is an echo of something similar.

The surviving canons of Rome exist in a set of manuscripts that stem from northern France. The historiography surrounding these decrees must form part of a full study of the synod, but a summary can be provided here. A list of the canons appeared for the first time in 1618, in the second edition of Binius' *Concilia*. Binius' source has not been identified, but he wrote that the manuscript containing the texts had been discovered by Georges Colvener, a professor of theology at Douai (+1649), at the Augustinian abbey of Hénin-Liétard near Douai in the diocese of Arras.[82] A list of nineteen canons is presented but only the first five are numbered, and Binius conjectured that the manuscript in question was connected to Lambert of Arras.[83] His list of decrees was preceded by a heading stating that they were issued *pridie Kalendas Maii*, i.e., on April 30, but where Binius or Colvener found that information is unclear. The printed text that traversed the great tomes of conciliar scholarship from Binius to Mansi is the text of Biniu–Colvener. Some additions amplified the presentations, especially in the *Sacrosancta concilia* of Labbe and Cossart, but Binius' text is what investigators have encountered, knowingly or not, when looking for 'the canons of the Council of Rome'.[84]

The assumption that Binius made about Bishop Lambert of Arras' involvement with the synod was correct. The canons are transmitted with minor variations in a group of four early-modern manuscripts that present material associated closely

---

[79] *Chronique de Saint-Maixent*, ed. Verdon 168: *Urbanus papa... decrevit in ipsa synodo, omni sexta feria, jejunare pro peccatis suis omnibus christianis et maxime pro illis quibus non confessi sunt inmemores*.

[80] For Melfi c. 16 see Somerville–Kuttner, *Pope Urban* 257, and also 293–94, where the Gregorian precedents were discussed.

[81] H.E.J. Cowdrey, 'Pope Gregory VII and the Bearing of Arms', in Benjamin Z. Kedar, Jonathan Riley-Smith, and Rudolf Hiestand (eds.), *Montjoie: Studies in Crusade History in Honour of Hans Eberhard Mayer* (Aldershot 1997) 24–25.

[82] Binius, *Concilia* 3.2. 422–23. For Colvener see Somerville, *Decreta* 10, n. 21, and Kéry, *Arras* 37 ff, especially n. 136. For Hénin-Liétard, see L.H. Cottineau, *Répértoire topo-bibliographique des abbayes et prieurés* 1 (Mâcon 1939) 1401.

[83] Binius wrote that the canons were taken *ex manuscripto... quem Lamberti Atrebatensis episcopi esse conjicio*.... It is unclear whether he meant that the book contained works of Lambert, was owned by him, or even was written by him.

[84] Labbe-Cossart 10. 615–18; Mansi, *Amplissima collectio* 20. 961–64.

with Lambert per se, or more generally with the church of Arras. The details can be found in the work of Kéry on the re-constitution of the episcopal see of Arras in 1093/94, and more recently in the study by Giordonengo on Lambert's register.[85] The books in question with the location of the Roman canons are as follows: Arras, Bibliothèque municipale, MSS 1051 (pp. 56–60), and 1062 (fols. 26–7), both are late seventeenth-century books from the abbey of St.-Vaast; Cambrai, Bibliothèque municipale, MS 841 (pp. 73–6), an eighteenth-century manuscript from Hénin-Liétard; Paris, BNF, lat. 12827 (fols. 120v-20v), a book copied c.1590, perhaps at Hénin-Liétard. To these witnesses, of course, must be added Colvener's lost source for the decrees, and also one other copy that is of special interest: a twelfth-century fragment that preserves the so-called 'vetus membrana' (VM) version of the canons of Clermont, found today in Paris, BNF, MS lat. 10402.

VM has been described and used by scholars at several points in recent decades.[86] The book contains pages from various manuscripts, and fols. 73–79 make up a single quire.[87] These pages may well come from Arras, for the fragment offers a rendition of the northern French tradition of the decrees of Clermont, and the presence of the legislation from the synod in 1099 affirms that link. Those texts are found at fols. 75v-76v, and the account is essentially the same as that in the early-modern manuscripts described above, with one change. The unnumbered provision that stands between cc. 17 and 18 in the Colvener–Mansi printing – *In eodem quoque concilio . . .*, condemning abbots who receive lay investiture of monasteries – is placed at the end, following a variant version of c. 18.

This 'Arras version' of the decrees can be paired with a transmission that exists in two manuscripts of the *Collection in Nine Books*, a canonical collection that probably was assembled in Thérouanne around the year 1100. The books in question are: Ghent, Universiteitsbiblioteeck, MS 235, dating c.1100, and Wolfenbüttel, Herzog-August-Bibliothek, MS Gud. lat. 212, written in the late twelfth century.[88] Sdralek's discussion of the manuscript at Wolfenbüttel indicated its general agreement with the text printed in Mansi, aside from a variation that is termed 'nicht inhaltlich' but which shortens what is presented in the Colvener–Mansi version as c. 18.[89] Cf. the chart on the following page.

The influence of the *Nine Books* is well known to historians of canon law, and it is thus not surprising that Waelkens and Van den Auweele discovered another exemplar of the compilation. Through the activity of canonists in northern France in the early twelfth century this work formed the basis for other collections in which the decrees

---

[85] See in the bibiliography; both works are well indexed and specific references will not be provided here.
[86] Among others see Somerville, *Decreta* 64ff., Detlev Jasper, *Das Papstwahldekret von 1059* (Beiträge zur Geschichte und Quellenkunde des Mittelalters 12; Sigmaringen 1986) 9–10 and passim (esp. 92), Somerville–Kuttner, *Pope Urban* 136, and Kéry, *Arras* 84, n. 4.
[87] Jasper, op. cit. (in the preceding note), 9.
[88] Van den Auweele and Waelkens, 'Collection' passim (e.g., 118, and 128) for Rome, and Sdralek, *Fragmente* 39–42. See also Kéry, *Collections* 262–63, Fowler-Magerl, *Clavis* 207–9, and most recently Oliver Münsch, 'Ein Streitschriftenfragment zur Simonie', DA 62 (2006) 619–29, esp. 620ff. for MS 212.
[89] Sdralek, *Fragmente* 41; Mansi, *Amplissima collectio* 20. 964. Cf. Beulertz, *Verbot* 34–5.

Mansi	Sdralek
Nullus primatum, archiepiscopum, & episcoporum, in ordinatione & consecratione episcoporum, vel abbatum, cappas, tapetia, bacinos, & manutergia, qualibet exactione requirat, vel suscipiat. (No primate, archbishop, and bishop, in the ordination and consecration of bishops or of abbots should require or receive by any exaction whatsoever, *cappas, tapetia, bacinos, & manutergia.*)[90]	Nullus archyepiscoporum vel episcoporum de consecratione episcopi vel abbatis neque cappam neque bacinos neque tapetia aut quodlibet munus exigere presumat.

from the Council of Rome were included. This occurred not en bloc, as in the *Nine Books*, but with canons disributed among the sections of these systematic works.[91] The compilations in question, all unedited and remaining to be analyzed in detail, are the *Collection in Ten Parts*, its abridgement known as the *Summa Decretorum Haimonis*, and the *Second Collection of Châlons sur Marne*.[92] Deriving from that same tradition also are canons from Rome included in a collection found in Paris, Bibliothèque Mazarine, MS 1285 (1012), fol. 55v (pencil enumeration): *Urbanus II in concilio Romano.*, where cc. 18–17 (in this order) are transcribed. A thorough search in that manuscript may reveal other decrees from the same synod, and additional manuscript witnesses may also turn up, either in lists of the decrees or with the legislation scattered here and there among books or parts.

Taking into account six witnesses for the Arras tradition[93], the two manuscripts of the *Nine Books*, seven copies of the *Ten Parts*, four copies of the *Summa Haimonis*, the 'exemplaria unica' of *Châlons II* and Mazarine MS 1285, all told more than twenty known manuscript witnesses survive for canons of the Council of Rome.[94] Their distribution was, therefore, more widespread than for the legislation of any council of Urban II since Clermont. Considering Urban's synods to which canons are ascribed without question, – Melfi, Benevento, Troia, Piacenza, Clermont, Tours, Nîmes, and Rome – the 'fortuna' of the decrees from Rome is most akin to that of Melfi.[95]

---

[90] For these exactions see J.F. Niermeyer, *Mediae Latinitatis lexicon minus* (Leiden 1964).

[91] This is analogous to what happened with canons from the so-called 'Northern French' rendition (from Arras) of the canons from Clermont: see Somerville, *Decreta* 46 ff. (and now cf. Giordanengo, *Arras* 186–93 [C.52]). For the *Nine Books* see Sdralek, *Fragmente* 6–39, Van den Auweele and Waelkens, 'Collection' passim, Kéry, *Collections* 262–63, and Fowler-Magerl, *Clavis* 207–9.

[92] For descriptions and manuscripts see Kéry, *Collections* 263–64, and 291–92, and cf. Fowler-Magerl, *Clavis* 209–14, and 238–29. Gossman's tabulation (in *Urban*) lists the canons of Rome found in *Ten Parts* (93–102), and *Châlons II* (79–88); no Rome canons are noted for *Châlons I* (77–78). He had no opportunity to examine the *Summa Haimonis* (ibid. 1), but canons from Rome occur therein, e.g., BNF, MS lat. 4286, fols. 15r, and 31v.

[93] That is the lost Binius–Colvener copy, the four early-modern copies, and the twelfth-century text in VM.

[94] For the manuscripts of *Ten Parts*, *Haimo*, and *Châlons II*, see the lists in Kéry, *Collections*. Ibid. 263, six manuscripts are noted for the *Ten Parts*, but to the list can be added the copy in Berkeley, Univ. of California Law School, Robbins MS 103 (see BMCL 13 [1983] xi, and 14 [1984] 95).

[95] For Melfi see Somerville–Kuttner, *Urban* 186 ff.; for Troia and Benevento see ibid. 302–5; for Piacenza see passim in this volume; for Clermont see Somerville, *Decreta* 46 ff.; for Tours and Nîmes see this chapter.

Disregarding for the moment the widespread distribution of texts from Melfi through the *Panormia* and Gratian's *Decretum*, both Melfi and Rome are represented by several full lists of nearly twenty canons, and groups of decrees from both assemblies are found in canon law collections. But the difference between the canonical fortuna of Melfi and that of Rome rests with the *Panormia* and Gratian. Through those two works decisions from Urban's synod in 1089 were widely circulated. The canons of Rome, however widespread they were in the early twelfth century, did not penetrate the *Panormia* or Gratian, and thus remained essentially a northen French phenomenon.

The following list of the incipits and explicits of the canon of Rome is taken from Mansi (20. 961–64).

1. Ea quae a sanctis—auctoritate firmamus. (Cf. Piacenza c. 1)
2. Quidquid igitur vel in—obtinere censemus. (Ibid. c. 2)
3. Si qui tamen a—vita commendat. (Ibid. c. 3)
4. Qui vero scienter se—esse decernimus. (Ibid. c. 4)
5. Quicumque sane cupiditate parentum—digni inveniantur. (Ibid. c. 5)
6. Illi vero qui per—sedis auctoritate. (Ibid. c. 6)
7. Si qui tamen ante emptionem—non patimur. (Ibid. c. 7)
8. Ordinationes quae a Guiberto—esse judicimus. (Ibid. c. 8)
9. Similiter autem & eas—nescisse damnatos. (Ibid. c. 9)
10. Qui vero ab episcopis—scientia commendat. (Ibid. c. 10)
11. Amodo vero quicumque a—amplius caritati. (Ibid. cc. 11–12)
12. Illud quoque praecipimus, ut—umquam exigatur. (Ibid. c. 13)-
13. Ut unica Domini nostri—periculum sustinebit. (Melfi, cc. 1c-2)
14. Nemo praeterea ad sacrum—uxorem habuerit. (Ibid. c. 3)
15. Nullus laicus decimas suas—est, offeratur. (Ibid. c. 5)
16. Nullus abbas, nullus ecclesiasticum—concessione praesumat.[96] (Ibid. c. 6)
17. Nullus abbas pretium exigere—occasione praesumat. (Ibid. c. 7)

In eodem quoque concilio—auctoritate interdixit.[97]

18. Adjecit etiam & constanter praecepit, ut nullus primatum—vel suscipiat.[98]

---

[96] See Berleurtz, *Verbot* 14.

[97] Ibid. Cf. 35, where the supposition that the presence of this text in Colvener's manuscript was 'einen isolieten historiographischen Zusatz der benutzten Handschrift' is contradicted by its presence in the other exemplars of the 'Arras version' of the Rome decrees that have been noted: see above. Sdralek's comments (*Fragmente* 41) about this 'Zusatz' imply its presence in the Wolfenbüttel manuscript, which is not the case. It is neither there nor in the Ghent copy of the *Nine Books*. (The author is grateful to Edward Reno III for this information.)

[98] See above for a comparison of the texts from Mansi and Sdralek.

Postscript

Urban II died on July 29, 1099, and the last entries in JL for his pontificate were dated in mid-May. Jerusalem was taken by the Crusaders on July 15, yet the pope who invariably was to be linked with the *iter Hierosolymitanum* never knew it.[1] Less well known than Urban's role in the First Crusade, but arguably of more lasting significance, was his legacy in Church law. The second recension of the *Decretum Gratiani* ascribes to him sixty canons including nearly the full textus receptus of the legislation from the Council of Piacenza.[2] Via Gratian those decrees were transmitted, copied, and glossed throughout the Middle Ages and into modern times within the living tradition of the Church's *Corpus iuris canonici*.[3] By contrast, Crusading in the late Middle Ages was dying 'a lingering death... losing its grip on the masses', as Jonathan Riley-Smith puts it.[4]

The goal of this volume has been to present and to investigate the evidence for Piacenza's history, including the synod's impact in the canonical tradition. The historical background of the assembly was given in Chapter 1, and a commentary on the decrees in Chapter 5. Nearly fifty twelfth-century manuscripts where lists of the canons survive were described and analyzed in Chapters 2 and 4, a tally that would be higher if all exemplars of the canonical collections where the provisions occur were included.[5] None of the lists of decrees was transcribed directly from any other known copy, and the surviving texts would thus represent only a fraction of what once existed. The *Gesta Romanae ecclesiae contra Hildebrandum* accused Urban of employing novel methods for distributing Piacenza's legislation.[6] Whatever truth is in that charge, and whatever those procedures might have been, the decrees circulated widely in a remarkably uniform transmission.

Among Urban II's synods Melfi, Clermont, and now Piacenza have been accorded modern monographic studies.[7] It seems unlikely that much new information

---

[1] That term does not occur in the surviving acts of Urban II, but appears in the 1123 Lateran Council of Calixtus II, c. 10, within a text that also mentions Urban: COD 192.

[2] See the tabulation in Gossman, *Urban* 135.

[3] Gratian's work, in origin not an authorized collection, was one of a series of major medieval compilations printed together in the sixteenth century and labeled the *Corpus iuris canonici*: see Sommar, *Correctores* 4, and the details presented by Katherine Christensen in the Introduction to Augustine Thompson, O.P., et al., *Gratian: The Treatise on Laws* (Studies in Medieval and Early-Modern Canon Law 2; Washington 1993) xviii–xix. The version of the *Corpus* promulgated in 1582 by Pope Gregory XIII, the 'Editio Romana', is termed by Sommar 'the official law of the Catholic Church'.

[4] Jonathan Riley-Smith, *The Crusades, a Short History* (New Haven 1987) 255.

[5] See Chapter 2, *Survival*, Introduction. Cf. ibid., at the beginnng of Lists of Canons.

[6] See in Chapter 2, *Enactment, Gesta*.

[7] Account also can be taken of the volumes of articles noted in Chapter 1, n. 25, commemorating the 900th anniversary in 1995 of Piacenza, and comparable works that were published on the 900th anniversary of the Council of Clermont.

about these gatherings will emerge, although, as discussed in Chapter 2, Appendix II, puzzles remain about canons attributed to Piacenza that are found outside of the textus receptus. Of Urban's three other councils from which significant groups of decrees survive–Troia, Benevento, and Rome–while more undoubtedly can be done for Benevento and Troia, the legislation from the Council of Rome in April, 1099, is most in need of study.[8] The 1099 synod was Urban's last, and it repeated among other texts most of Piacenza's canons, including those about orders and dispensation. This textual continuity is noteworthy and can be interpreted as demonstrating stability from 1095 onward for important elements of Pope Urban's program, at least as far as it is visible in these councils. But synods, of course, do not occur in a vacuum, and an assessment of the Piacenza–Rome continuity must be set in a larger context. The disorder in the records of Clermont's decrees and the question mark over legislation from the Lateran Council of 1097 urge caution about over-simplifying papal policy between 1095 and 1099.

---

[8] For Benevento and Troia, see Somerville–Kuttner, *Pope Urban*, Appendix II. Little material survives from the Councils of Tours and Nîmes in 1096. For those assemblies, and for the texts associated with the Lateran Council of 1097, see Chapter 6, the discussion of Pope Urban's synods at Tours, Nîmes, and the Lateran.

Bibliography

S. Anselmi Cantuariensis archiepiscopi opera omnia, ed. F.S. Schmitt, vols. 4–5 (Edinburgh 1949–51).

Bandini, A.M., *Catalogus codicum Latinorum Bibliothecae Mediceae Laurentianae*, 5 vols. (Florence 1774–78).

Barker-Benfield, B.C., *St. Augustine's Abbey, Canterbury*, 3 vols. (Corpus of British medieval library catalogues 13; London 2008).

Batlle: see Gassó.

Becker, Alfons, *Papst Urban II*, 2 vols. (MGH Schriften 19. 1–2; Stuttgart 1964, 1988).

—— 'Urbain II et l'Orient': see Palese–Locatelli, *Bari* 123–44.

—— 'Le voyage d'Urbain II en France', *Le concile de Clermont de 1095 et l'appel à la croisade* (Collection de l'École francaise de Rome 236; Rome 1997) 127–40.

Bernold of Constance, *Chronicon*, ed. G.H. Pertz (MGH Scriptores 5; Hannover 1844) 385–467; *Die Chroniken Bertholds von Reichenau und Bernolds von Konstanz 1054–1100*, ed. Ian S. Robinson (MGH Scriptores rerum Germanicarum, Nova series 14; Hannover 2003) 383–540.

—— *De excommunicatis vitandi, de reconciliatione lapsorum et de fontibus iuris ecclesiastici (Libellus X)*, ed. Doris Stöckly, unter Mitwirkung von Detlev Jasper (MGH Fontes iuris Germanici antiqui in usum scholarum separatim editi 15; Hannover 2000).

—— *De reordinatione vitanda et de salute parvulorum, qui ab excommunicatis baptizati sunt*, ed. F. Thaner, (MGH Lib. de lite 2; Hannover 1892) 150–56.

Beulertz, Stefan, *Das Verbot der Laieninvestitur im Investiturstreit* (MGH Studien und Texte 2; Hannover 1991).

Binius, Severinus, *Concilia generalia et provincialia* 3.2 (Cologne 1618).

Blumenthal, Uta-Renate, 'Conciliar Canons and Manuscripts: the Implications of Their Transmission in the Eleventh Century', in Peter Landau and Jörg Müller (eds.), *Proceedings of the Ninth International Congress of Medieval Canon Law* (Monumenta iuris canonici, Subsidia 10; Vatican City 1997) 357–79 (repr. ead., *Papal Reform and Canon Law in the 11th and 12th Centuries* [Variorum Collected Studies CS618; Aldershot 1998]).

—— *Gregor VII., Papst zwischen Canossa und Kirchenreform* (Darmstadt 2001).

—— 'De praua constitutione: a fragment of the council of 1078?', in Richard H. Helmholz et al. (eds.), *Grundlagen des Rechts. Festschrift für Peter Landau zum 65. Geburtstag* (Rechts- und Staatswissenschaftliche Veröffentlichungen der Görres-Gesellschaft, Neue Folge 91; Paderborn 2000) 141–54.

—— *The Early Councils of Pope Paschal II, 1100–1110* (Pontifical Institute of Mediaeval Studies, Texts and Studies 43; Toronto, 1978).

—— and Jasper, Detlev, '"Licet nova consuetudo"—Gregor VII. und die Liturgie', in Bruce C. Brasington and Katherine G. Cushing (eds.), *Bishops, Texts and the Use of Canon Law around 1100: Essays in Honour of Martin Brett* (Aldershot 2008) 45–68.

Borries-Schulten, Sigrid von and Spilling, Herrad, *Die Romanischen Handschriften der Württembergischen Landesbibliothek Stuttgart 1: Provenienz-Zwiefalten* (Katalog der

Illuminierten Handschriften der Württembergischen Landesbibliothek Stuttgart 2: Die Romanischen Handschriften; Stuttgart 1987).

Brackmann: see *Germania pontificia*.

Brett, Martin, 'The canons of the First Lateran Council in English manuscripts', in Stephan Kuttner and Kenneth Pennington (eds.), *Proceedings of the Sixth International Congress of Medieval Canon Law* (Monumenta iuris canonici, Subsidia 7; Vatican City 1985) 13–28.

—— 'Creeping up on the *Panormia*', in Richard H. Helmholz et al. (eds.), *Grundlagen des Rechts: Festschrift für Peter Landau zum 65. Geburtstag* (Rechts- und Staatswissenschaftliche Veröffentlichungen der Görres-Gesellschaft, Neue Folge 91; Paderborn 2000) 206–70.

—— see *Councils & Synods*.

Brooke: see *Councils & Synods*.

Caspar, Erich, *Das Register Gregors VII.* (MGH Epistolae selectae 2; Berlin 1920–23).

Cheney, Christopher, *Handbook of Dates for Students of English History* (Royal Historical Society Guides and Handbooks 4; London 1970).

Chronique de Saint-Maixent, ed. Jean Verdon (Les Classiques de l'Histoire de France au Moyen Age 33; Paris 1979).

Chroniques des comptes d'Anjou et des seigneurs d'Amboise, eds. Louis Halphen and René Poupardin (Paris 1913).

Classen, Peter, *Gerhoch von Reicherburg* (Wiesbaden 1960).

Il Concilio di Piacenza e le Crociate (Piacenza 1996).

Conciliorum oecumenicorum decreta, eds. G. Alberigo et al., 3rd edn. (Bologna 1973).

Cossart: see Labbe.

Councils & Synods with other Documents relating to the English Church 1.2, eds. D. Whitelock, M. Brett, and C.N.L. Brooke (Oxford 1981).

Cowdrey, H.E.J., *Pope Gregory VII, 1073–1085* (Oxford 1998).

Eadmer, *Historia novorum in Anglia*, ed. Martin Rule (Rolls Series 81; London 1884).

—— *The Life of St Anselm, Archbishop of Canterbury*, ed. and trans. Sir Richard Southern (Oxford 1979).

Elze: see Kuttner.

Fliche, Augustin, *La Réforme grégorienne et la Reconquête chrétienne (1057–1123)* (Histoire de l'Église 8; St.-Dizier 1950).

Fournier, Paul, 'Les collections canoniques attibuées à Yves de Chartres', BEC 57 (1896) 645–98; 58 (1897) 26–77, 293–326, 410–44, 624–76 (repr. in *Mélanges de droit canonique* 1. 505–678).

—— *Mélanges de droit canonique*, 2 vols., ed. Theo Kölzer (Aalen 1983).

—— and Le Bras, Gabriel, *Histoire des collections canoniques en Occident*, 2 vols. (Paris 1931–32).

Fowler-Magerl, Linda, *Clavis Canonum: Selected Canon Law Collections Before 1140* (MGH Hilfsmittel 21; Hannover 2005).

Friedberg, Emil: *Corpus iuris canonici*, 2 vols. (Leipzig 1879–81); *Decretum Gratiani*, in vol. 1, cited by *distinctio* and canon, i.e., D. 1, c. 2, for part 1, and *causa, questio*, and canon, i.e., C. 1, q. 2, c. 3, for part 2; *Decretales* of Gregory IX, in vol. 2, cited by X (= *Liber extravagantium*), book, title, and canon, i.e., X 1.2.3.

Gallia pontificia 3.1, ed. Beate Schilling (Göttingen 2006).

Gasparri, Laura, 'Osservazioni sul codice Vallicelliano C. 24', *Studi Gregoriani* 9 (1972) 467–513.

Gassó, Pius M. and Batlle, Columba M., *Pelagii I papae epistulae quae supersunt (556–651)* (Scripta et documenta 8; Montserrat 1956).

Gaudemet, Jean, 'Les sources du Décret de Gratien', *Revue de droit canonique* 48 (1998) 247–61.
Germania pontificia, eds. Albert Brackmann et al. (Berlin and Göttingen 1910–).
Gesta Romanae aecclesiae contra Hildebrandum, ed. Kuno Francke, (MGH Lib. de lite 2; Hannover 1892) 366–422 (VIII = *Decreta Turbani*, 408–16).
Gilchrist, John, ' "Simoniaca haeresis" and the Problem of Orders from Leo IX to Gratian', in S. Kuttner and J. Joseph Ryan (eds.), *Proceedings of the Second International Congress of Medieval Canon Law* (Monumenta iuris canonici, Subsidia 1; Vatican City 1965) 209–35 (repr. id., *Canon Law in the Age of Reform, 11th–12th Centuries* [Variorum Collected Studies Series CS406; Aldershot 1993]).
Giordanengo, Claire, *Le registre de Lambert évêque d'Arras (1093–1115)* (Sources d'histoire médiévale 34; Paris 2007).
Glass, Dorothy F., 'The Bishops of Piacenza, their Cathedral, and the Reform of the Church', in John S. Ott and Anna Trumbore Jones (eds.), *The Bishop Reformed* (Aldershot 2007) 219–36.
Goez, Elke, 'Der Thronerbe als Rivale: König Konrad, Kaiser Heinrichs IV. älterer Sohn', *Historisches Jahrbuch* 116 (1996) 1–49.
Gossman, Francis J., *Pope Urban II and Canon Law* (The Catholic University of America, Canon Law Studies 403; Washington 1960).
Gratian, *Decretum*: see Friedberg, *Corpus iuris canonici*.
Gregory VII: see Caspar.
Gregory IX, *Decretales*: see Friedberg, *Corpus iuris canonici*.
Gresser, Georg, *Die Synoden und Konzilien in der Zeit des Reformpapsttums in Deutschland und Italien von Leo IX. bis Calixt II., 1049–1123* (Paderborn 2006).
Hagenmeyer, Heinrich, *Chronologie de la première croisade, 1094–1100* (Paris 1902).
Hefele, Charles-Joseph and Leclercq, Henri, *Histoire des conciles* 5.1 (Paris 1912).
Heidrich, Ingrid, *Ravenna unter Erzbischof Wibert (1073–1100)* (Vorträge unter Forschungen, Sonderband 32; Sigmaringen 1984).
Hesso, *Relatio de concilio Remensi*, ed. W. Wattenbach, (MGH Lib. de lite 3; Hannover 1897) 21–8.
Hoffmann, Hartmut, *Gottesfriede und Treuga Dei* (MGH Schriften 20; Munich 1964).
Horst, Uwe, *Die Kanonessammlung Polycarpus des Gregor von S. Grisogono* (MGH Hilfsmittel 5; Munich 1980).
Italia pontificia, 10 vols., eds. Paul Fridolin Kehr et al. (Berlin & Zurich 1906–75).
Jaffé, Phillipp and Wattenbach, Wilhelm, *Regesta pontificum Romanorum ab condita ecclesia ad annum post Christum natum MCXCVIII*, 2nd edn. (Leipzig 1885–88)—entries to 590 by F. Kaltenbrunner, i.e., JK prefixes; to 882 by Paul Ewald, i.e., JE prefixes; and to 1198 by S. Loewenfeld, i.e., JL prefixes).
Jasper, Detlev, *Das Papstwahldekret von 1059* (Beiträge zur Geschichte und Quellenkunde des Mittelalters 12; Sigmaringen 1986).
——: see Bernold.
——: see Blumenthal.
Kehr: see *Italia pontificia*.
Kéry, Lotte, *Canonical Collections of the Early Middle Ages (ca.400–1140)* (Washington 1999).
——*Die Errichtung des Bistums Arras, 1093/1094* (Beihefte der Francia 33; Sigmaringen 1994).
Kölzer: See Fournier.
Kretzschmar, Robert, *Alger von Lüttichs 'Traktat De misericordia et iustitia'* (Quellen und Forschungen zum Recht im Mittelalter 2; Sigmaringen 1985).

Kuttner, Stephan, 'Some Roman Manuscripts of Canonical Collections', BMCL 1 (1971) 7–29 (repr. Id., *Medieval Councils, Decretals, and Collections of Canon Law* [Variorum Reprints CS 126; London 1980, 2nd edn. with 'New Retractationes' 1992]).

—— 'Urban II and the Doctrine of Interpretation: A Turning Point?', *Studia Gratiana* 15 (1972) 55–85 (repr. Id., *The History of Ideas and Doctrines of Canon Law in the Middle Ages* [Variorum Reprints CS, 113; London 1980, 2nd edn. with 'New Retractationes' 1992]).

—— and Elze, Reinhard, *A Catalogue of Canon and Roman Law Manuscripts in the Vatican Library* 1 (Vat. lat. 541–2299); 2 (Vat. lat. 2300–2746) (Studi e testi 328, 322; Vatican City 1986, 1987).

—— and Somerville, Robert, 'The So-called Canons of Nîmes (1096)', *Tijdschrift voor Rechtsgeschiedenis* 38 (1970) 175–89 (repr. in SK, *Medieval Councils, Decretals, and Collections of Canon Law*, as above, and in RS, *Papacy, Councils and Canon Law*, as below.

Kuttner: see Somerville.

Labbe, Philippe and Cossart, Gabriel, *Sacrosancta concilia*, 16 vols. (Paris 1671–72).

Landau, Peter, *Kanones und Dekretalen* (Bibliotheca eruditorum 2; Goldbach [bei Aschaffenburg] 1997).

Larrainzar, Carlos, 'El Borrador de la "Concordia" de Graciano: Sankt Gallen, Stiftsbibliothek MS 673 (= Sg)', *Ius Ecclesiae* 11 (1999) 593–666.

Laudage, Johannes, *Alexander III. und Friedrich Barbarossa* (Forschungen zur Kaiser- und Papstgeschichte des Mittelalters, Beihefte zu J.F. Böhmer, Regesta Imperii 16; Cologne 1997).

—— 'Ritual und Recht auf päpstlichen Reformkonzilien (1049–1123)', AHC 29 (1997) 287–334.

Le Bras, Gabriel et al., *L'âge classique, 1140–1378* (Histoire du Droit et des Institutions de l'Église en Occident 7; Paris 1965).

Le Bras: see Fournier.

Leclercq: see Hefele.

Libelli de lite (MGH), 3 vols. (Hannover 1891–97).

Locatelli: see Palese.

Mansi, Giovanni Domenico, *Sacrorum conciliorum nova et amplissima collectio*, 31 vols. (Florence and Venice 1759–98).

Migne: see *Patrologiae*.

Mews, Constant J., 'Monastic educational culture revisited: the witness of Zwiefalten and the Hirsau reform', in George Ferzoco and Carolyn Muessig (eds.), *Medieval Monastic Education* (London 2000) 182–97.

Mordek, Hubert, *Bibliotheca capitularium regum Francorum manuscripta* (MGH Hilfsmittel 15; Munich 1995).

Motta, Joseph, *Collectio canonum trium librorum* (Monumenta iuris canonici, Corpus collectionum 8; Vatican City 2005, 2008).

Ordericus Vitalis, *The Ecclesiastical History of Ordericus Vitalis* 5, ed. Marjorie Chibnall (Oxford 1975).

Palese, Salvatore and Locatelli, Giancarlo, *Il Concilio di Bari del 1098: Atti del Convegno Storico Internazionale e celebrazioni del IX Centenario del Concilio* (Per la storia della Chiesa di Bari, Studi e materiali 17; Bari 1999).

Patrologiae cursus completus, Series Latina, ed. J.-P. Migne, 221 vols. (Paris 1844ff.).

Pertz: see Bernold of Constance.

Pflugk-Harttung, Julius von, *Acta pontificum Romanorum inedita* 2 (Stuttgart 1884).

Picasso, Georgio, 'Il Concilio di Piacenza nella tradizione canonistica', *Il concilio di Piacenza* (repr. Id., *Sacri canones et monastica regula* [Bibliotheca erudita 27; Milan 2006]) 109–19.

Poggiali, Cristoforo, *Memorie storiche di Piacenza* 4 (Piacenza 1758 [with 'New Retractationes', 1992]).

Ponzini, Domenico, 'Situazione della chiesa Piacenza al tempo del Concilio di Piacenza', *Il concilio di Piacenza* 121–53.

Racine, Pierre, 'La civitas precommunale', *Il concilio di Piacenza* 3–18.

——'Le concile de Plaisance (1095) et la croisade', *Revue d'Alsace* 122 (1996) 19–28.

——'Santa Maria di Campagna alle origini delle Crociate', in Maurizio Giuffredi (ed.), *Santa Maria di Campagna: una chiesa bramantesca* (Reggio Emilia 1995) 15–25.

Recueil des Historiens des Croisades, Historiens occidentaux 5 (Paris 1895).

Reynolds, Roger E., *The Collectio canonum Casinensis duodecim seculi* (Monumenta liturgica Beneventana 3; Toronto 2001).

Riley-Smith, Jonathan, *The First Crusaders, 1095–1131* (Cambridge 1997).

Robinson, I.S., *Authority and Resistance in the Investiture Contest* (Manchester and New York 1978).

——'Bernold von Konstanz und der gregoriansiche Reformkreis um Bischof Gebhard III.', *Freiburger Diözesan- Archiv* 109 (1989) 155–88.

——*Henry IV of Germany, 1056–1106* (Cambridge 1999).

——*The Papacy 1073–1198* (Cambridge 1990).

——see Bernold of Constance.

Salmon, André, *Recueil de chroniques de Touraine* (Collection de documents sur l'histoire de Touraine 1; Tours 1854).

Saltet, Louis, *Les réordinations* (Paris 1907).

Santifaller, Leo, 'Saggio di un Elenco dei funzionari, impiegati e scrittori della Cancellaria Pontificia dall'inizio all'anno 1099', *Bullettino dell'Istituto Storico Italiano per il medio evo* 56/57 (1940) 1–865 (= entire volume).

Schneider, Herbert, *Die Konzilsordines des Früh- und Hochmittelalters* (MGH Ordines de Celebrando Concilio; Hannover 1996).

Sdralek, Max, *Wolfenbüttler Fragmente* (Kirchengeschichtliche Studien 1.2; Münster 1891).

Somerville, Robert, 'Canon Law, Inspired Law, and Papal Authority', in Ephraim Halivni (ed.), *Neti'ot LeDavid: Jubilee Volume for David Weiss Halivni* (Jerusalem 2005) 105–20.

——'Clermont 1095: Crusade and Canons', in Luis García-Guijarro Ramos (ed.), *La primera cruzada, novecientos años después: Il concilio de Clermont y los orígenes del movimiento cruzado* (Madrid 1997) 63–77.

——'The Council of Clermont (1095), and Latin Christian Society', *Archivum Historiae Pontificiae* 12 (1974) 55–90 (repr. Id., *Papacy, Councils and Canon Law*).

——'The Councils of Gregory VII', *Studi Gregoriani* 13 (1989) 35–53.

——'The Councils of Pope Calixtus II: Reims 1119', *Proceedings of the Fifth International Congress of Medieval Canon Law* (Salamanca 1976) (Monumenta iuris canonici, Subsidia 6; Vatican City 1980) 35–50 (repr. Id., *Papacy, Councils and Canon Law*).

——*The Councils of Urban II, vol. 1: Decreta Claromontensia* (AHC Supplementum 1; Amsterdam 1972) (chs. I–II, repr. Id., *Papacy, Councils and Canon Law*).

——'The Crusade in the Councils of Urban II beyond Clermont', in Luis García-Guijarro Ramos (ed.), *Acts of the Segundas Jornadas Internacionales sobre La Primera Cruzada (Huesca, September 1999)* (in press).

——'The French Councils of Pope Urban II: Some Basic Considerations', AHC 2 (1970) 56–65 (repr. Id., *Papacy, Councils and Canon Law*).

——*Papacy, Councils and Canon Law in the 11th–12th Centuries* (Variorum Reprints, CS 312; London 1990).
——'Pope Urban II, a Pseudo-Council of Chartres, and *Congregato* (C. 16, q. 7, c. 2 'palea')', in Thomas M. Izbicki and Christopher M. Bellitto (eds.), *Reform and Renewal in the Middle Ages and the Renaissance: Studies in Honor of Louis Pascoe, S.J.* (Studies in the History of Christian Thought 96; Leiden 2000) 18–34 (see errata insert for errors beyond the author's control).
——'The Presentation of the Canons of Piacenza (March, 1095): An Overview, Baronius to Mansi', in *Festschrift für Walter Brandmüller* (=AHC 27/28 [1995–96]) 193–207.
——(with the collaboration of Stephan Kuttner), *Pope Urban II, the Collectio Britannica, and the Council of Melfi (1089)* (Oxford 1996).
——and Zapp, Hartmut, 'An "Eighth Book" of the Collection in Seven Books', in Richard H. Helmholz et al. (eds.), *Grundlagen des Rechts: Festschrift für Peter Landau zum 65. Geburtstag* (Rechts- und Staatswissenschaftliche Veröffentlichungen der Görres-Gesellschaft, Neue Folge 91; Paderborn 2000) 163–77.
Sommar, Mary, *The Correctores Romani: Gratian's Decretum and the Counter-Reformation Humanists* (Pluralisierung & Autorität 19; Berlin 2009).
Southern, R.W., *Saint Anselm: A Portrait in a Landscape* (Cambridge 1990).
——see Eadmer.
Spilling: see Borries-Schulten.
Spinelli, Giovanni, 'Urbano II e il mondo monastico Italiano', *Benedictina* 47 (2000) 525–58.
Stöckly: see Bernold.
Stoller, Michael, 'Eight Anti-Gregorian Councils', AHC 17 (1985) 252–32.
Tangl, Georgine, *Teilnehmer an den allgemeinen Konzilien des Mittelalters* (Weimar 1922).
Taylor, Daniel S., 'A New Inventory of Manuscripts of the *Micrologus de ecclesiasticis observationibus* of Bernold of Constance', *Scriptorium* 52 (1998) 162–91.
Thaner: see Bernold.
Thomson: see William of Malmesbury.
Tyerman, Christopher, *God's War: A New History of the Crusades* (Cambridge MA 2006).
Van den Auweele, D., and Waelkens, L., 'La collection de Thérouanne en ix livres à l'abbaye de Saint-Pierre-au-Mont-Blandin: le codex Gandavensis 235', *Sacris erudiri* 24 (1980) 115–53.
Wattenbach: see Hesso.
Weiland, Ludwig, *Constitutiones et acta publica imperatorum et regum* 1 (MGH Legum sectio 4; Hannover 1893).
Whitelock: see *Councils & Synods*.
William of Malmesbury, *Gesta Pontificum Anglicorum* 1, eds. and trans. M. Winterbottom and R.M. Thomson (Oxford 2007).
Winroth, Anders, *The Making of Gratian's Decretum* (Cambridge Studies in Medieval Life and Thought, 4th Ser. 40; Cambridge 2000).
Winterbottom: see William of Malmesbury.
Zadoka-Rio, Élisabeth, 'Lieux d'inhumination et espace consacrés: Le voyage du Pape Urbain II en France (Août 1095–Août 1096)', in André Vauchez (ed.), *Lieux sacrés, lieux de culte, sanctuaires* (Collection de l'École françaises de Rome 271; Rome 2000) 197–213.
Zapp: see Somerville.
Ziese, Jürgen, *Wibert von Ravenna, der Gegenpapst Clemens III. (1084–1100)* (Päpste und Papsttum 30; Stuttgart 1982).
Zumhagen, Olaf, *Religiöse Konflikte und kommunale Entwicklung: Maitland, Cremona, Piacenza und Florenz zur Zeit der Pataria* (Städteforschung A/58; Cologne 2002).

Indices

Four indices are provided, i.e., an index of Church councils, an index of manuscripts, an index of papal texts [following Jaffé, *Regesta*, with an addition from Gratian], and a general index mainly of names but adding some concepts. Well known names, e.g., Ambrose of Milan, are not identified further. The edition and translation of the canons in Chapts.4 can serve as a guide to the synod's content, and an.index of Latin words from those texts, while perhaps useful, is not given. The following also can be noted. Monasteries listed in the general index are Benedictine houses unless otherwise indicated. In Chapt.3, "ff." is employed because certain names, e.g., 'Baronius', appear on almost every page of this historiographical chapter. Finally, at times in Chapts. 2 and 4, e.g., pp.77–79, the density of references to manuscripts by sigla precluded indexing each item by shelf mark; Readers are referred to the list of sigla and shelf marks found on pp.87–89.

Index of Church Councils

Bari, 1098: 4, 7, 8, 11, 116–18, 125–28
Benevento, 1087: 3 n.12
_____ 1091: 3, 8, 17, 27, 31–32, 49, 86, 103, 105, 109, 132, 135
_____ 1374: 32
Bordeaux, 1093: 63

Capua, 1087: 3 n.12
Clermont, 1095: 4, 8, 11, 15 n.81, 17, 23–24, 29, 31, 38, 48–49, 51 n.150, 52, 65, 72, 75, 81 nn.27 & 29, 84, 86, 103, 108, 112, 113 n.58, 114–22, 127–28, 132, 134–35
Constance, 1094: 28, 113

Guastalla, 1108: 41, 106 n.25

Lateran, 1076: 109
_____ 1078 [Lent]: 15 n.81, 34, 38 n.91, 42, 106 n.22, 112
_____ 1078 [autumn]: 39, 42, 53, 69, 112
_____ 1079: 21, 28
_____ 1080: 7 n.35, 39
_____ 1097: 3 n.12, 4, 116–17, 123–24, 127, 135
_____ 1110: 69–70
_____ 1112: 7 n.34, 34, 38
_____ 1123: 17, 31, 53, 74, 123, 134 n.1
_____ 1139: 53, 125
_____ 1179: 41, 81 n.29

Mantua, 1064: 112

Melfi, 1089: 3, 8, 15 n.81, 17, 21, 22 n.26, 27–28, 31, 39, 43, 52, 58, 65, 72–73, 74 n.9, 80, 83, 86, 102–3, 105, 114, 129–30, 132–34

Nîmes, 1096: 4, 49 n.141, 51 n.150, 115–17, 121–23, 127, 132, 135 n.8

Piacenza, 1132: 7
Pisa, 1135: 41

Quedlinburg, 1085: 113

Reims, 1119: 7, 20 n.18, 21, 41
_____ 1148: 41
Rome, August 1098 [Clementine adherents]: 125 n.56
Rome, 1099: 4, 29, 33 n.75, 37 n.89, 43, 45 n.117, 49 n.142, 52–53, 73, 77, 86, 111, 116–17, 125, 127–33, 135

Seligenstadt, 1023: 112

Toulouse, 1119: 31, 83
Tours, 1096: 4, 116–23, 127, 132, 135 n.8
Tribur, 895: 112
Troia, 1093: 3–4, 8, 17, 21–22, 27, 31–32, 49, 72, 86, 103, 105, 132, 135

Westminster, 1102: 22

Index of Manuscripts

Admont, Stiftsbibliothek 23[=Grat.1a]: 46–48
Arras, Bibliothèque municipale 1051: 131
_____ 1062: 131

Barcelona, Archivo de la Corona de Aragón, Ripoll 78[=Grat. 1b]: 48
Basel, Universitätsbibliothek A.V.15: 50 n.147
Berkeley, University of California, Law School, Robbins 106 [=*Ten Parts*]: 132 n.94
Brussels, Bibliothèque royale Albert Ier, lat. 495–505[=B]: 33, 76, 85. 111 n.44
_____lat. 11196–97[=Bg (*Gesta*)]: 50

Cambrai, Bibliothèque municipale 841: 131
Cambridge, Corpus Christi College 94: 53 n.154
_____Pembroke College 103: 151 n.150
Châlons-sur-Marne, Bibliothèque municipale 32: 112 n.47
Città del Vaticano, BAV, Archivio di S. Pietro C.118[=9L]: 46–47
_____ Barb. lat. 860 [=ΦVa]: 31–31, 60, 64, 66–67, 69, 71–72
_____ Reg. lat. 399 [=ΦVb]: 32
_____ Reg. lat. 987 [=ΦVp]: 31, 66–67, 72
_____ Reg. lat. 1026 [=ΦVr]: 31, 64, 66–67, 72
_____ Vat. lat. 478: 43–44
_____ Vat. lat. 629 [=Va]: 39, 66–67, 69, 71, 76, 83
_____ Vat. lat. 1208 [=V]: 22 n.27, 39, 63 n.14, 64, 66–67, 76, 80
_____ Vat. lat. 1346 [=7Lv]: 46–47
_____ Vat. lat. 1359: 51 n.150
_____ Vat. lat. 1360 [=Vp]: 45, 82
_____ Vat. lat. 1364 [=Vm]: 39, 65–67, 71, 76
_____ Vat. lat. 3031 [=3Lv]: 46–47
_____ Vat. lat. 6197: 39 n.93
_____ Vat. lat. 9866: 66 n.22.
Cologne, Historisches Archiv W.Kl. fol.199: 59
Cortona, Biblioteca comunale e dell'Accademia Etrusca 43: 46 n.127

Erlangen, Universitätsbibliotek 176: 119
Escorial, El, Real Biblioteca de San Lorenzo A.I.6 [=E]: 36–37, 76

Florence, Biblioteca Medicea Laurenziana, Calci 11 [9]: 37, n.89
_____Plut. xviii.14[=F]: 40, 76
_____
S. Croce 23, dext.5[=Fc]: 37, 76
_____ Biblioteca Nazionale Centrale, Conv. sopp.A.1[=Grat.1f]: 46–48
_____ Conv. sopp.G.1.836[=Fv]: 45, 82

Ghent, Universiteitsbibliotheck 235: 131, 133 n.97
Gottweig, Stiftsbibliothek 85[=G]: 41, 76

Hannover, Niedersächsische Landesbibliothek XI.671[=Hg (*Gesta*)]: 50

Klagenfurt, Studienbibliothek 10 [=Gerhoch]: 51

Lincoln, Cathedral Library 192[=Li]: 40–41, 76
London, BL, Add. 11440[=L]: 44, 81–82, 84–85
_____ Harley 3001[=Lh]: 26, 34, 76, 84
Lucca, Biblioteca Capitolare Feliniana 124 [=Lu]: 37, 68, 71, 76

Madrid. Biblioteca Nacional, lat. 7127[=Poly.m]: 46–47
Metz, Bibliothèque municipale 1212: 119
Milan, Biblioteca Ambrosiana A.46 inf. [=Mid]: 34, 76, 85
_____H.48 [=Mic]: 37–38, 76
_____M.79 [=Mip]: 38, 71, 76
Montecassino, Archivio dell'Abbazia 216: 22 n.27, 51 n.150
Munich, Bayerische Staatsbibliothek, clm 432 [=Bernold, *Chronicon*]: 50
_____ clm 4556: 36 n.84
_____ clm 5129[=Mub]: 35, 76, 78, 85
_____ clm 11316[=Mup]: 41, 76
_____ clm 22011[=Muw]: 41, 76

New Haven, Yale University, Beinecke Rare Book and Manuscript Library, Marston 158 [=Y]: 40, 76

Oxford, Bodleian Library, Can. Pat. lat. 39 [S.C. 19025][=O]: 34. 76
_____ Selden supra 90 [S.C. 3478][=Os]: 38, 76, 113–14

Paris, Bibliothèque de l'Arsenal 713: 151 n.150
_____BNF, Collection Baluze 7[=Pb]: 36, 40, 58, 76
_____ 380: 9 n.48
_____ lat.3187[=Pm]: 35, 76
_____ lat.3860: 122
_____ lat.3875[=Pc1]: 49
_____ lat.3876[=Pc2]: 49
_____ lat.3881[=ΦPa; =Poly.p]: 31, 46–47, 72, 85–86
_____ lat.4286[=*Summa Decretorum Haimonis*] 132 n.92
_____ lat.10402: 122 n.33, 131
_____ lat.10742: 51 n.150
_____ lat.11851[=*Annalista Saxo*]: 51
_____ lat.12827: 131
_____ lat.18083[=Pj]: 40, 58, 76
_____ nal 1761[=Grat.1p]: 46–48
_____ Bibliothèque Mazarine 1285 [1012]: 132
Pistoia, Archivio Capitolare del Duomo 135 [109][=3Lp]: 46–47
Prague, Národni Knihovna České Republiky VIII.H.7: 51 n.150

Rome, Biblioteca Vallicelliana C.24: 64–67, 69, 124–25

St.-Claude, Bibliothèque municipale 17 [3] [=C]: 36, 76
St. Gallen, Stiftsbibliothek 673[=G1s]: 48
Salamanca, Biblioteca Universitaria 2644 [=S]: 49
Strasbourg, Archives hospitalières 1291: 58–59
Stuttgart, Württembergische Landesbibliothek, Cod. theol. et phil. 2°210[=Stb]: 42, 76, 84–85
_____Cod. theol. et phil. 4°254[=Sta]: 35, 76, 84

Turin, Biblioteca Nazionale Universitaria D.IV.33[=T]: 44, 51 n.150, 81

Utrecht, Bibliotheek der Rijksuniversiteit 111: 58–59

Vienna, Österreichische Nationalbibliothek, lat.2153 [Iur. can. 38][=W]: 42, 69, 76
_____ lat. 2186 [Iur. can. 80][=7Lw]: 46–47
Vyssí Brod [Hohenfurt], Klásterni knihovna CXIX[=VB]: 42, 76, 85

Wolfenbüttel, Herzog-August-Bibliothek, Gud.212: 131, 133 n.97

Index of Papal Texts

JK 303: 106
JE +1366: 36, 40
JE +1996: 36
JL 4269: 38
JL 4431a: 104
JL 4558: 112 n.48
JL 5290: 37, 68, 112–13
JL 5383: 107 n.32
JL 5386: 107 n.32
JL 5393: 23 n.29, 124 n.49
JL 5409: 1, 44
JL 5456: 35
JL 5530: 4 n, 17, 5 n.23
JL 5531*: 4 n.18
JL 5532: 5 n.23
JL 5538: 10 n.58, 14
JL 5540: 8–10
JL 5541: 5, 7, 10 n.57
JL 5544: 5 n.22
JL 5546–47: 9, 10 n.54
JL 5548: 12
JL 5549: 10 n.56
JL 5551: 7
JL 5560: 11 n.64
JL 5561: 11 n.64, 68

JL 5600: 117 n.7
JL 5628: 120
JL 5636–5637: 117 nn.7–8, 121
JL 5653: 117 n.9
JL 5654: 117 n.7
JL 5670: 1 n.1, 43
JL 5694: 43–44, 71, 73, 110
JL 5716: 117 n.9
JL 5740: 106 n.24
JL 5760: 23 n.29, 107 n.32
JL 5761: 59
JL 5775: 123–24
JL 5779*: 127 n.66
JL 5788: 117 n.7
JL 5791: 118 n.10
JL 5800: 118 n.10
JL 5929: 127 n.62, 128 n.70
JL 5964: 117 n.9, 121
JL 6117–6118: 121
JL 6161: 121
JL 6436: 151 n.150
JL 6702: 121
JL 7093: 124 n.48
JL 8289: 45
Gratian C.19, q.3, c.2: 59

General Index

Adelbert, archbishop of Bourges: 10
Adhémar, bishop of Le Puy: 3
Admonitio synodalis: 42
Agustín, Antonio: 48, 64–65
Albert, cardinal-priest of S. Sabina: 9
Aldo, bishop of Piacenza: 6, 10
Alexander II: 112
Alexius I, Byzantine emperor: 11, 15–16, 25
Alfonso VI, king of Léon-Castile: 10
Amat, archbishop of Bordeaux: 10
Ambrose of Milan: 40, 42
anathema: 19
Angers: 118–19
Aniane, monastery: 31
Annalista Saxo: 18, 51, 68, 84–85, 102
Anselm, bishop of Lucca: 34–35, 39, 62
———— of Canterbury: 22, 126, 128–29
Apulia: 126
Aquileia: 45
archbishops, at Piacenza: 10
Arles: 121
Arnulf III, archbishop of Milan: 10, 12, 26
———— bishop of Cremona: 15 n.81
Arras: 130–32, 133 n.97
Augustine of Hippo: 40–41, 43, 106–107
Augustinian canons: 35, 41, 58–59

Baluze, Étienne: 9, 31, 36, 49 n.137, 122
Baronius, Cesare: 61ff.
Benedictines: 8, 35, 41–42
benefice: 105, 109, 114
Benevento: 32, 125
Beno, cardinal-priest of SS. Martino e Silvestro: 12, 18, 108
Berengar: abbot of St.-Laurent, Liège: 10, 13–14
———— bishop of Fréjus: 10
———— of Tours: 25–26, 28
Bernard, bishop of Bologna: 73
Bernard of Clairvaux: 38
Bernold of Constance: 1, 4, 8–9, 11–12, 15–16, 17–18, 20, 22–23, 24–29, 35, 42, 49–50, 102, 117–18, 122, 127
Bertrade of Montfort: 114, 118, 121
Beuerberg, house of Augustinian canons: 35, 85
Bible: 112
Binius, Severinus: 130, 132 n.93
bishops, invited to/attending the Council of Piacenza: 4, 10, 104
Bohemond: 11 n.62, 125 n.58
Bonizo of Sutri, bishop of Piacenza: 6, 37 n.88
Bonussenior, cardinal-priest of S. Maria in Trastevere: 9

Brecia: 37–38
Burchard of Worms: 36–37, 83, 112, 122
Burgos: 10

Calixtus II [Archbishop Guy of Vienne]: 3–4, 21, 32, 53, 74, 83, 116, 124–25
Cambrai: 10 n.54
Canterbury: 38, 53 n.154
cardinals, at the Council of Piacenza: 9–10
Celestines: 41
Cencius-Baluze canons of the Council of Clermont: see *Polycarpus-Cencius*
Chartres: 40
Chiusi: 39, 82
Chronicle of St.-Maxient: 63
Chronicon: see Bernold of Constance
Cistercians: 42, 77 n.19, 119
Cluny, monastery: 7, 39, 115
Collectio CCXCIV capitulorum: 51 n.150
Collectio Britannica: 107 n.32
Collectio Caesaraugustana: 24, 27 n.53, 48–49, 65, 73 n.6, 74 n.9, 77, 84
Collectio[canonum] Pragensis[I]: 51 n.150
Collectio Dionysio-Hadriana: 33
Collectio Novariensis: 37
Collection in Four Books: 35
Collection in Nine Books [Italy]: 45–47, 82–83
Collection in Nine Books [Thérouanne]: 33 n.75, 113 n.58, 131–32
Collection in Seven Books [Turin]: 44–47, 151 n.150, 81 n.29, 82–83, 111
Collection in Seventy-Four Titles: 42
Collection in Ten Parts: 153 n.154, 132
Collection in Three Books: 44–47, 51 n.50, 81 n.29, 82–83, 109, 111, 113–14
Collection in Twelve Parts: 36
Colvener, Georges: 130–31, 133 n.97
Compilatio tertia: 42
confession: 130
Conrad, king: 18 n.10, 26, 34–35, 72
Corpus iuris canonici: 134
'Correctores Romani': 64, 70 n.32, 124–25
Cossart: see Labbe-Cossart
council/synod, general/plenary: 1, 8, 117–18
Cremona: 5–6, 23, 34, 72
Crusade: 3, 15–16, 25, 28, 116–18, 120–22, 126–30
Cusanus, Nicholas: 50

d'Achery, Luc: 122
Daimbert, archbishop of Pisa: 10
d'Aquino, Antonio: 31–32, 64
Decretum, of Ivo of Chartres: 33

De ieiunio quatuor temporum: see Ember Days
Dereine, Charles: 58–59
Deusdedit, cardinal-priest of SS. Apostolorum in Eudoxia, and canon lawyer: 32
Diego Galmirez, bishop of Santiago de Compostela: 30
Diemo, archbishop of Salzburg: 10
Diemut, nun-scribe at the double monastery of Wessobrunn: 41
Dodo, bishop of Tarbes: 10
Donation of Constantine: 38, 123
Donizo of Canossa: (from the monastery of S. Apollonio): 11 n.62
Douai: 130
Durandus, William: 115

Eadmer of Canterbury: 126, 128–29
Easter, 1099: 127
ecumenical councils, Roman Edition: 31
Editio Romana, Gratian: 109–110
Ekkehard of Aura: 8
Ember Days: 28, 38, 68, 70, 112–13
Empire, medieval Western: 79, 107
Error generalis/specialis: 108
Eugene III: 53

fasting on Friday: 130
filioque: 126
Fleury: 122
Fliche, Augustin: 26–27
Fowler-Magerl, Linda: 59
Frothard, abbot of St.-Pons-de-Tomières: 10
Fulcher of Chartres: 123
Fulk, bishop of Beauvais: 10
____ IV, count of Anjou: 118, 121

Gebhard, abbot of Hirsau: 10
_____ bishop of Constance: 10, 24–26, 104, 106, 113
Gelasius I: 113
Gerhoch of Reichersberg: 17, 35, 51, 68, 84–85, 102
Gesta Romanae aecclesiae contra Hildebrandum: 17–24, 26, 29, 50, 52, 71. 73–74, 80, 86, 102, 108, 118, 134
Gezo, abbot of SS. Pietro e Marziano in Tortona: 37, 38 n.91
golden rose: 121
Gottfried, bishop of Maguelonne: 10, 124
Gratian [1 & 2]: 45–48, 51 n.150, 53, 59, 64, 72, 81 n.29, 82–84, 102, 105 n.18, 106 n.23, 109–15, 123–24, 128 n.73, 133–34
Greeks, at the Council of Bari: 126
_____ theology of at the Council of Rome: 129
Gregory I: 34, 36, 39–41, 113
_____ VII: 1–3, 21, 39, 43, 68, 73, 86, 110, 112, 114–15, 130

_____ cardinal-deacon of uncertain title church: 9
_____ cardinal-priest of S. Grisogono: 30
Grenoble: 4, 13
Gualcher, bishop of Cambrai: 10 n.54
Guidardi, Hugo, archbishop of Benevento: 32
Guy, archbishop of Vienne [Calixtus II]: 10, 13

Hautecombe, Cistercian monastery: 40
Heilsbronn: Cistercian monastery: 119
Hénin-Liétard, monastery: 130
Henry I, king of England: 128
_____ IV, German emperor: 1, 25, 106
Herman, cardinal-priest of SS. Quattro Coronati: 9
Hinschius, Paul: 66
Holste, Lukas: 39, 61ff.
Holy Spirit: 109
Hugh, abbot of Cluny: 10
_____ bishop/archbishop of Die/Lyons: 4–5, 15, 25
_____ bishop of Grenoble: 10, 12
_____ cardinal-deacon of uncertain title church: 9
_____ of St.-Victor: 58

indulgence: 130
Innocent I: 106
_____ II: 3, 53, 125
_____ III: 42
investiture: 65, 69, 105 n.16, 127–29
irritus –a –um: 105
Ivo, bishop of Chartres: 31, 41, 44–45, 63, 72, 107, 112

Jacobins: 40
Jerome: 59
John, cardinal-bishop of Porto: 9
____ cardinal-deacon of S. Maria in Cosmedin [John of Gaëta/Gelasius II]: 9

Labbe, Philippe-Cossart, Gabriel: 60ff., 72, 130
laity: 28
Lambert, bishop of Arras: 4–5, 9–10, 129–31
Languedoc: 3
Lateran Basilica: 123
Le Mans: 3
Lent: 113
Leo I: 113, 129
____ IX: 2–3, 21, 53, 116, 121
Letare Sunday: 121
Liber censuum: 72, 123
Liber pontificalis: 39
Liège: 13
Limoges: 3 n.12, 117
Lodi: 6
Loire: 120
Lucca: 30, 37

Magdeburg Centurions: 50
Manassas, bishop of Cambrai: 10
Mansi, Giovanni Domenico: 42, 60ff, 130–33
Mantua: 39
Marcoussis: see Celestines
Marmoutier, monastery: 120–21
Mathilda of Tuscany: 6, 11, 22 n.27
mercy: 105–106
meteors: 19 n.14
Milan: 6, 34
Montalcino: 39
Morimondo, Cistercian monastery: 38
Moses: 104

necessity/'necessity has no law': 106
Nicholas II: 104 n.14
Nicolaitans: 25–26, 28
Normans: 2
'Northern French' canons of the Council of Clermont: 132 n.91
Noyon: 15

Odilo, abbot of St.-Gilles: 10
Odo, cardinal-bishop of Ostia [Pope Urban II]: 15, 24, 113, 115
Ordericus Vitalis: 118, 120
ordination: 105–106, 110
ordo/ordines, for celebrating a council: 7
Orléans: 40
Orval, monastery: 33
Osca: 10
Otbert, bishop of Liège: 13–15
Otto, bishop of Imola: 10
____ bishop of Oléron: 10

Panormia: 33, 41, 44–45, 51 n.150, 133
Parisetti, Hieronymus: 124–25
Paschal II: 4, 14, 30, 41, 46 n.127, 52, 69–70, 113 n.58, 116, 126, 128 n.70
Pataria: 6
Paul the Deacon: 39
penance: 130
Pentecost: 113
Petau, Alexandre: 31
Peter, archbishop of Aix: 10
____ patriarch of Grado: 10
Pflugk-Hartung, Julius von: 69, 124–25
Philip, bishop of Luni: 10
____ king of France: 11, 25, 63, 118, 121
Piacenza, city: 5–6, 38
Pibo, bishop of Toul: 1, 43, 104, 106
Pisa: 4
Polling, house of Augustinian canons: 41
Polycarpus/Polycarpus Supplement: 6 n.32, 29–32, 45–47, 64, 66, 72–75, 81 n.29, 82–87, 103
Polycarpus-Cencius canons of Clermont [=Cencius-Baluze version of the canons of Clermont]: 119, 122–23

Pons, abbot of la Chaise-Dieu: 10
Ponte Mammolo: 30
Poppo, bishop of Metz: 14–15
Poussines, Pierre: 63–64.
Praxedis, empresses: 11, 25, 28
Procession of the Holy Spirit: 126
Pseudo-Isidorian Decretals: 39

Radbod, bishop of Noyon: 10, 15
Rainaud, archbishop of Reims: 4–5
____ bishop of Como: 112
Rangerius, bishop of Lucca: 37 n.89, 127–29
Rather of Verona/Liège: 33
Ravenna, ecclesiastical province: 5 n.27
Raymond, count of Toulouse: 8–9
Register, papal, Gregory VII: 21, 112
____ Urban II: 34 n.79, 72, 86
Reichenau, monastery: 12, 26
Reichersberg, house of Augustinian canons: 85
Reims: 34
Richard, abbot of St.-Victor, Marseille: 9, 11
____ II, archbishop of Bourges: 36
____ theologian of St.-Victor, Paris: 38
Rodulf, archbishop of Reggio in Calabria: 10
____ archbishop of Tours: 10
Roger, cardinal-deacon of uncertain title church: 9
Rome: 2–3
Ruinart, Thierry: 62 n.10
Rule of St. Augustine: 58

St.-Arbogast, house of Augustinian canons: 58
St. Augustine, monastery: 38, 53 n.154
St.-Bertin, monastery: 120
St.-Gilles, monastery: 8–9
St.-Maixent, monastery, and *Chronicon*: 130
St. Peter im Schwarzwald, monastery: 10
____ in Rome: 123, 127–33
St. Pölten, monastery: 42
St.-Vaast, monastery: 131
San Antimo, monastery: 39, 83
San Dionigi, monastery: 34
San Giacomo di Pontida, Cluniac priory: 12 n.65
SS. Maria di Campagnolo e Vittoria: 12 n.65
Salerno: 125
Sancio, bishop of Lescar: 10
Saragossa: 48
Saxony: 51
Sdralek, Max: 131–33
Second Collection of Châlons-sur-Marne: 132
Sermons, on the Mount/on the Plain: 104
Sermorens: 13
simony: 105, 109–110, 112
Spain: 37, 78 n.16
Summa Decretorum Haimonis: 132
synod: see council

Tedbald, abbot of San Stefano, Vercelli: 10

General Index

Terracina: 2
Teuzo, cardinal-deacon of SS. Giovani e Paolo: 9
Thérouanne: 113 n.58
Thoger, abbot of St. Georgen: 10
Thomasius, Michael: 124–25
Torres, Francesco: 69–70
Tours: 130
_____ St.-Martin: see Marmoutier
_____ St.-Mauritius: 121
'Turbanus': 19–21, 74

Udalrich II, abbot of Reichenau: 10, 26
Ulrich, bishop of Passau: 10

Vallombrosa, monastery: 45
'vetus membrana' [=VM=Paris, BNF, MS lat. 10402]: 131
Victor III: 2–3
Vienne: 13

Virgin Mary: 38 n.92, 115
Vyssí Brod, monastery: 42

Walter, Joseph: 58
Walter de Honnecourt: 119
Weiland, Ludwig: 17–18, 26, 29–37, 39, 41–42, 60ff., 71, 76, 86, 102–3, 114
Wessobrunn, double monastery: 41
Wibert, archbishop of Ravenna ['Pope Clement III']/Wibertine Schism: 1, 20, 25, 43, 49, 51–52, 73–74, 83, 104–106, 110–111, 123, 125, 127, 129
William, archbishop of Auch: 10
_____ bishop of Couseran: 10
_____ bishop of Orange: 10
_____ Rufus, king of England: 128:
Winrich, archbishop of Trier: 6, 10

Zwiefalten, double monastery: 26, 35, 42, 82